First published in 2020 by
UCL Press
University College London
Gower Street
London WC1E 6BT

Contents

List of figures

List of contributors

Haki Antonsson is Associate Professor in Medieval Scandinavian Studies in the UCL Department of Scandinavian Studies (SELCS). His main areas of research and teaching are the history and culture of Scandinavia between c.900 and 1300, the Christianisation of Scandinavia and the cult of saints and the associated Old Norse literature. Apart from numerous articles and book chapters, he is the author of *St Magnus of Orkney: A Scandinavian Martyr-Cult in Context and Damnation* (Brill 2007) and *Salvation in Old Norse Literature* (Boydell and Brewer 2018). He has also co-edited the anthology *Saints and their Lives on the Periphery: Veneration of Saints in Scandinavia and Eastern Europe c.1000–1200* (Brepols 2010, with I.H. Garipzanov).

Elettra Carbone is Lecturer in Norwegian Studies in the UCL Department of Scandinavian Studies (SELCS). Her main areas of research and teaching are nineteenth-century Norwegian and Nordic literatures, cultural mobility, sculpture and print culture. Apart from several articles, she is the author of *Nordic Italies: Representations of Italy in Nordic Literature from the 1830s to the 1910s* (Nuova Cultura 2016) and has co-edited volumes such as *The Norwegian Constitution and Independence of 1814* (Norvik 2015, with R. Hemstad), *Sculpture and the Nordic Region* (Routledge 2017, with S. Ayres) and *Love and Modernity* (Norvik 2013, with C. Thomson).

Richard Cole is Assistant Professor of Medieval History at Aarhus University. He was previously a Leverhulme Early Career Fellow at the UCL Department of Scandinavian Studies (SELCS). He has broad interests in medieval Scandinavian history and Old Norse philology. His articles have appeared in *Viking and Medieval Scandinavia, Saga-Book, Scandinavian Studies, Exemplaria* and *Harvard Theological Review*. Having previously focused on questions of racial and religious difference in Old Norse literature, he is currently working on a project to trace the emergence of bureaucratic mentalities in the Nordic Middle Ages.

Anne Grydehøj is Senior Teaching Fellow in Danish in the UCL Department of Scandinavian Studies (SELCS), where she teaches BA and MA students on a wide range of courses including language, comparative literature and modern literary theory. Her research within the field of crime fiction studies focuses on the problematics of citizenship and identity in contemporary European societies and cultures, which has led to a number of conference papers and articles. Her monograph on citizenship, gender and ethnicity in contemporary French and Scandinavian engaged crime fiction is forthcoming from the University of Wales Press.

Mary Hilson is Professor in History at the School of Culture and Society, Aarhus University, and was until 2015 Reader in Nordic History in the UCL Department of Scandinavian Studies (SELCS). Apart from several articles on the Nordic welfare states and consumer co-operation, she is the author of *The Nordic Model: Scandinavia since 1945* (Reaktion Books 2008), and has co-edited anthologies such as *A Global History of Consumer Co-operation since 1850: Movements and Businesses* (Brill 2017, with S. Neunsinger and G. Patmore) and *Labour, Unions and Politics under the North Star: The Nordic Countries 1600–2000* (Berghahn Books 2017, with S. Neunsinger and I. Vyff).

Mart Kuldkepp is Associate Professor in Scandinavian History and Politics in the UCL Department of Scandinavian Studies (SELCS). His main areas of research and teaching are European nationalisms, and twentieth-century Scandinavian and Baltic political history, with special interest in the contacts between the Scandinavian and the Baltic states until the end of the Cold War. He has published articles on several topics, including Sweden and WWI, the Scandinavian connection in early Estonian nationalism, and the supernatural in Old Norse literature. He is currently preparing a book on Swedish participation in the Baltic Wars of Independence (1918–1920).

Ellen Kythor was awarded her PhD in Scandinavian Studies in 2019 with the thesis 'An "Un-business-like Business": Publishing Danish Literature in Translation in the UK 1990–2015'. She was the recipient of the Impact PhD Studentship in Danish Translation, funded jointly by UCL and The Danish Arts Foundation and is the founder of the Association of Danish-English Literary Translators (DELT).

Annika Lindskog is Lecturer in Swedish in the UCL Department of Scandinavian Studies (SELCS). Her main areas of research and teaching are nineteenth-century music and landscapes, cultural memory, cultural history and language. She has published on a variety of topics and artistic expressions from Scandinavia and beyond, including on Linnaeus, Stenhammar, Sibelius, Frederick Delius, Brahms, landscape ideologies, collective identity formation, Swedish song and representations of north. She is also a classically trained singer, and coaches other singers and choirs in Swedish song.

Kristin Lorentsen is Lecturer in Norwegian for International Students at the University of Oslo. She was Teaching Fellow in Norwegian at the UCL Department of Scandinavian Studies (SELCS) 2017–19, where she taught Basic and Intermediate Norwegian. She has previously published an article on Bergsveinn Birgisson's hybrid nonfiction *Den svarte vikingen* as an identity-constitutive narrative, as well as her MA dissertation about mental health and identity in Gine Cornelia Pedersen's novel *NULL*.

Jakob Stougaard-Nielsen is Associate Professor in Scandinavian Literature in the UCL Department of Scandinavian Studies (SELCS). His main areas of research and teaching are in literary and cultural studies. He is the author of *Scandinavian Crime Fiction* (Bloomsbury 2017) and has co-edited the books *Translating the Literatures of Small European Nations* (Liverpool UP 2020, with Rajendra Chitnis et al.), *Nordic Publishing and Book History* (Scandinavica 2013, with Elettra Carbone) and *World Literature, World Culture: History, Theory, Analysis* (Aarhus UP 2008, with Karen-Margrethe Simonsen).

C. Claire Thomson is Associate Professor of Scandinavian Film in the UCL Department of Scandinavian Studies (SELCS). Her main areas of research and teaching are Nordic and Danish cinema, literature and cultural studies. Apart from numerous articles, she is the author of *Short Films from a Small Nation: Danish Informational Cinema 1935–1965* (Edinburgh UP 2018) and *Thomas Vinterberg's Festen* (U of Washington P 2013). A Director of Norvik Press and an editor of the Journals *Scandinavica* and *Kosmorama,* she has edited several anthologies including the co-edited volumes *Framed Horizons: Student Writing on Nordic Cinema* (Norvik 2012) and *A History of Danish Cinema,* forthcoming 2020 from Edinburgh UP.

Acknowledgements

First, we would like to thank most warmly UCL Press for the opportunity to put together this collection of studies and discussions, and for supporting their transition into a format that enables them to be widely disseminated and engaged with. Thank you also for your calm patience during what proved to be a longer process than we first promised. Second, we owe a Nordic mountain of gratitude to our esteemed colleagues at the Department of Scandinavian Studies, past and present, who have contributed to this volume. Thank you for your ideas, your visions, and for finding time to grapple with these chapters in the midst of a bustling and busy academic year. Third, a very heartfelt thank you to all our students on whom so much of this material has been unabashedly tested. Thank you all for your patience and endurance with our experiments, your good humour in the face of our – no doubt at times rather energetic – enthusiasms, and for all your feedback and engagement: without you this would have been a very different book. And lastly, thank you to colleagues at various other institutions around the world with whom we have continuous and ongoing dialogues about all sorts of matters Nordic. We hope you might find some of this interesting, and that you come back to us for more such dialogue when you've read it. At the time of preparing this book for publication, the Department of Scandinavian Studies at UCL passed its 100-year mark in 2017. We hope that this volume can contribute to taking us forward into new chapters of Scandinavian and Nordic studies, both here and further afield.

Editorial Introduction to Nordic Cultures

Annika Lindskog and Jakob Stougaard-Nielsen

> Scandinavia is [a] collection of countries we can't tell apart, whose flags are color variations of the same pattern. They've got interchangeable Lego royal families, and all their names end in '-son'. Scandinavia has long been held up as the paragon of a decent, evolved society [...]. In every survey of enviable smugness, Scandinavia comes first. (Gill 2012)

Beyond Scandinavia, it may be difficult to tell its small nations apart, as the article from *Vanity Fair* quoted above satirically suggests. Moreover, it is not always clear which nations we should include and what term we should use to name this northernmost region of Europe. Scandinavia and the Nordic countries are often used interchangeably. Within the region it is customary to think of Denmark (Danmark), Norway (Norge/Noreg) and Sweden (Sverige) as Scandinavia while the Nordic region, as defined by the Nordic Council of Ministers, also includes Finland (Suomi), Iceland (Ísland), the autonomous territories of the Faroe Islands (Føroyar) and Greenland (Kalaallit Nunaat) – tied to Denmark – and the Finnish Åland islands (Ahvenanmaa). While most of the Nordic nations do indeed fly flags that are colour-variations of a Nordic cross, and Denmark, Norway and Sweden are indeed constitutional monarchies, the peoples of the region tend to highlight their national peculiarities, their diverse languages and identities. One of the paradoxes of the region, according to historian Mary Hilson, is 'that its coherence has often seemed more self-evident to those outside the region than to those within it' (Hilson 2019).

This *Introduction to Nordic Cultures* is written from a perspective beyond the Nordic region with the ambition to draw out a wide range of shared experiences, histories, values, imageries and stories that have shaped the region's transnational identity. We have chosen to use the term Nordic (Norden) in our title, rather than Scandinavian, partly because this is gradually becoming the preferred term in multi-disciplinary research on the region, but also because it propels us to consider the diversity of the wider region, which stretches from the coasts of the Baltic in the South-East to the Arctic in the North-West, from nations with millennia of unbroken histories to more recent and still emerging independent nations, and a region which despite its contemporary well-defined national borders is one that has been fundamentally shaped by recurring migrations, shifting borders, international politics, trade and transnational cultural exchanges.

We have to go back to the Kalmar Union, which lasted from 1397 to 1523, to find an internal sense of a unified Nordic state proper. The Kalmar Union was a personal union of Denmark, Norway and Sweden that brought the three crowns initially under the control of Queen Margaret I. The union was dissolved when Sweden crowned Gustav Vasa and declared independence in 1523. This left Norway and its possessions, Iceland, Greenland and the Faroe Islands, under Danish control for the next four hundred years. In 1814, following Denmark's ill-fated alliance with Napoleon Bonaparte, Norway was ceded to Sweden under the terms of the Treaty of Kiel, while Denmark kept the North Atlantic provinces. This set Norway on its path towards full independence, which it finally achieved in 1905.

At the same time as the Nordic states gradually came into being as we know them today, with Finland, having been under Swedish and Russian rule, gaining independence in 1917, and Iceland ceding from Denmark in 1944, Nordic political collaborations tied the nations closer together by expanding transportation networks and enabling the flow of goods between the countries. Regional integration culminated in the 1950s with the Nordic Passport Union, which allowed citizens of the Nordic countries free movement across borders without the need for travel documentation. This decade also saw, in 1952, the formation of the Nordic Council, an inter-parliamentary body that still maintains, funds and furthers cooperation among the Nordic nations. While the Nordic countries have a strong sense of their own national histories and identities, and have chosen different paths – for instance in relation to EU and NATO membership – the region has a long common history of, at times forced, shared governance, infrastructures, cultures and languages.

For the most part belonging to three separate families, the languages of the region similarly represent great diversity while they also coexist even within nations and, in the case of Danish, Norwegian and Swedish, have some degree of mutual intelligibility. While Icelandic and

Faroese also belong to the North Germanic Indo-European languages, these are more distantly related and not immediately comprehensible to speakers of other Nordic languages. The Sami languages, spoken by peoples of Sápmi, a cross-border region of Finland, Norway, Sweden and Russia, belong to the Finno-Ugric language family together with Finnish. Many Sami are bilingual, and Finland has in addition a minority of Swedish-speaking Finns, as there are also many Danish speakers in Greenland where the official language, Kalaallisut, is an Inuit language more closely related to the indigenous languages of Canada.

The Nordic countries are easy to find on a map and share a long history of political, cultural and linguistic commonalities and competition. Yet, the closer we look, and dependent upon the historical and disciplinary perspective we take, this map of the Nordic region is prone to shifts and mutations, forming a vast patchwork of shared and contested geographies, histories and identities. It is this changing, patchworked and transnational regional identity to which this book will introduce the reader, at the same time as we recognise the importance of the common global 'brand' the Nordic has become in the wider world. To many observers outside the region, the Nordic transcends geography and has become an 'enviable' idea, even an imaginary social utopia, fashioned by foreign stereotypes and the image-making or nation branding of the Nordic countries themselves (see, for instance, the chapters by Hilson and Kythor).

From a perspective beyond the Nordic, the region is both a variegated geographical reality and an all-encompassing idea that at times tell us more about values and desires held outside of the region itself. Based mostly in London, the contributors to this volume have experienced such cultural appropriation of the Nordic up-front over the past decade.

One example of this was seen over the course of 2017, when London's Southbank Centre dedicated its programme of festivals to exploring Nordic art and culture under the title 'Nordic Matters'. This was the first time that the UK's largest arts centre had dedicated a year-long festival to one region of the world. 'Nordic Matters' became the culmination of a decade-long fascination in the UK with everything Nordic, at times referred to as the 'Nordic invasion', 'Scandimania', 'Hygge-mania' or 'Nordic cool'. While the British infatuation with the Nordic region has been noticeable in a veritable obsession with Nordic Noir, New Nordic Food and modern Scandinavian design, the festival, which had sixty thousand visitors on its opening weekend, featured a much wider range of Nordic cultural expressions including music, dance, theatre, visual arts, gastronomy, talks and debates. The public were invited to visit a Finnish rooftop sauna, a workshop on how to bake the perfect cinnamon bun, a Swedish baby rave party, building with Lego and an ABBA exhibition, but were also introduced to art installations such as 'Falling shawls' by Sami artist Outi Pieski, 'Euro' by the Danish artist group Superflex, and a wide range of music and literature events featuring writers from across the Nordic region such as Naja Marie Aidt, Per Olov Enquist, Linda Boström Knausgård, Kristín Ómarsdóttir, Kjell Askildsen, Hassan Blasim, Sofi Oksanen, Guðbergur Bergsson and Niviaq Korneliussen.

The unprecedented interest in the Nordic region extends far beyond its closest neighbours, as Nordic literature, television drama and gastronomy in particular attract global attention, while the Nordic welfare states consistently rank at the top of global indices measuring, for instance, well-being, prosperity, gender equality, good governance and freedom of the press. It is as a part of the world renowned for the exemplary success of its constituent cultures, as 'the paragon of a decent, evolved society', that the Nordic region 'matters' to Britain and the wider world today:

> The Nordic countries have long been at the forefront of social change. Their fresh approach to parenting and education puts young people's rights on the agenda. Their investment in sustainable energy sets inspiring benchmarks, and women in the Nordic countries are achieving a better quality of life by changing the structures of society.
>
> ('Nordic Matters')

While the Nordic countries do face social, cultural and political challenges common to nations across the globe, it is widely recognised that as a region, the Nordic countries have developed political, cultural and social solutions that enable them to tackle a range of social inequalities and adjust to global financial and environmental crises. Therefore, the Nordic countries matter despite their small size and limited international power. To understand how the Nordic region evolved into a fairly homogeneous transnational region, despite historical, cultural and linguistic differences, and came to prominence on the global stage, we must consider a wide range of the region's cultural expressions, histories and debates, which have shaped Nordic cultures and societies over centuries.

Introducing the Textbook

The locus of this textbook is an undergraduate core course at the Department of Scandinavian Studies at UCL. Aimed at our new students, the course was designed as an introduction to a wide range of topics and approaches to the histories and cultures of the Nordic region. This innovative course is co-taught by specialists in diverse disciplines and Nordic languages across the department, and from its first inception it took on the characteristic of a collection of instances which enable interdisciplinary and pan-Nordic inquiry. From specific points of focus, which offer insights into particular and local case studies, the course is designed to draw out practices, developments, trends and behaviours that enable more general discussions relevant to the wider Nordic region and beyond. As no general textbook existed for such a course (introductions within the field of Scandinavian studies have traditionally been focused on either a specific national context or single disciplines), we have spent many years developing appropriate materials and relevant perspectives in collaboration with our students and colleagues. The overall concern has been to introduce our students to central nodes in the region's long and diverse history, as well as to the diversity of its languages and cultures, centres and peripheries, and to the many disciplines of our field – from historiography, linguistics and cultural studies to literature, art history and film studies.

When this textbook took shape, the chapters commissioned either grew out of this course, or found new foci around which case studies were developed following the same approach. The scope turned out to be wider here than in the classroom, however, and all chapters now benefit from greater contextuality, more complex analyses and further-reaching relevance beyond their immediate themes.

Although the selection of topics did not set out to cover predetermined subjects or periods, the present chapters provide good coverage: they range historically from 800 AD to now, analyse a variety of texts, objects and images, consider both cultural trends and political processes, spread themselves over a very large proportion of the Nordic region geographically, and employ a range of disciplinary approaches.

The chapters have not been ordered chronologically, but are instead grouped into sections where we feel the topics covered have a particular relevance to each other. The chapters in the first part, Identities, are all specifically interested in what shapes and defines societies; they consider behaviour, processes and ideologies, as well as the means by which these are communicated and enacted. Haki Antonsson sets the scene, tracing the historical origins of what we today define as Scandinavia and its constituent parts through considerations of its social, political and cultural concerns, challenging a simplified historical trajectory and setting out a multi-layered complexity in the process. In the following chapter, Annika Lindskog considers Carl Linnaeus' 1732 expedition to the Lapland region and uses this specific eighteenth-century action by a single traveller into northern Scandinavia to explore cultural and political relationships with regions and resources – as well as land and landscape – in both historical and modern times. Antonsson and Lindskog then look at the construction of collective narratives in Iceland and Finland in the late nineteenth century, formed at intersections between political negotiations, nationally conceived self-definitions and cultural expressions, by considering 'Ísland' by Jónas Hallgrímsson and the Finnish epos *Kalevala*. The last part of the chapter turns its focus to cultural re-interpretations of these texts, and considers the role of music through Finland's most well-known composer, Jean Sibelius. Elettra Carbone and Jakob Stougaard-Nielsen then take us into the nineteenth century to consider how the arrival of modernity was experienced. As case studies, three literary texts from Denmark, Finland and Norway are considered for the ways in which they record the ambiguous feelings attached to personal and social change brought on by technical developments, urbanisation and new modes of travelling. Lastly, Mary Hilson examines the origins, related ideologies and potential future of a most seminal aspect – in both Scandinavian and international eyes – of Nordic society in modern political times: the welfare state.

In the second part, Texts, we again begin in medieval times, as Richard Cole introduces us to the multi-faceted expressions of the *Íslendingasögur* (the Sagas of Icelanders), using case studies to illuminate their particular literary techniques – including not least the 'gaps' they leave – and analyse the contemporaneous socio-cultural structures they relate to through close-reading of the tale of Bróka-Auðr from *Laxdæla saga*. Carbone's chapter on Ibsen's *A Doll's House* and its main character Nora, continues the discussion around the relationship between text and society, but pays attention also to how this text has responded to, and is continuing to respond to, new social contexts and structures within and beyond the Nordic region. Anne Grydehøj then focuses on a very recent textual trend in her chapter on Scandinavian crime fiction, or 'Nordic Noir', retaining the consideration of how these texts express fundamental aspects of the societies out of which they are born, and which they depict, but also taking time to consider the genre's extensive international appeal and success.

The last two chapters in this section widen the perspective from more traditional literary questions to consider modern voices of considerable integrity, but which here too emerge as deeply connected to the evolving societies with which they engage, not least (but in no way exclusively) from their multilingual perspectives. Kristin Lorentsen and Jakob Stougaard-Nielsen seek out texts from the traditionally perceived peripheries of the Nordic region, from Greenland and by Sami authors, which challenge their readers to consider how conflicts between traditional and modern conceptualisations of identity and society may help dismantle perpetual ideas of (geographical as well as ideological) centres and peripheries. Grydehøj similarly traces issues of identity, language and relationships between majority and minority cultures in her investigation of three texts by 'new' Scandinavians (from Sweden, Denmark and Norway respectively), and here too draws attention to perceptions of centres and marginality. In societies whose traditional homogeneity has made diversity a concept which needs to be learnt, these voices create texts which function simultaneously as socio-political essays and textual trail-blazers.

The chapters in the last section considers Images as a way to understand different conceptualisations of the Nordic. Stougaard-Nielsen starts by tracing the influence of one of the most powerful agents in Nordic self-perception in his chapter on nature, looking across symbolism and imagery in poetry and painting to the landscape itself in historical perspective, and to the ever-increasing concern for its, and our, future. Mart Kuldkepp continues the examination of identity and self-perception in times of fluctuations and population movements by focusing on the period of mass-emigration of Scandinavians in the nineteenth century, paying particular attention to how it caused various levels of scrutiny of ideas of home and belonging, both in the migrating groups and the remaining society or societies. C. Claire Thomson's chapter then homes in on another kind of Scandinavian identity projection and dissemination as it focuses on three mid-twentieth-century short informational films that display a domestic pride in a well-functioning healthcare system to home and international audiences alike. The chapter is in one sense of course closely related to Hilson's chapter in Part 1, but comes at it from a different disciplinary angle. This is only one example of how the chapters speak to each other across the volume, and continue an internal dialogue throughout. Ellen Kythor closes the volume with her examination of what we really think of 'Brand Scandinavia', considering 'brand commonality', perceived synonymity, 'othering', ideas of shared heritage, utopias, ethnic stereotypes and 'sexy Scandinavians'. As we started the volume with an interrogation of a common by-word for Nordic in Antonsson's chapter about the Vikings, it might seem as if we have come full circle as Kythor here puts specific Nordic exports like bacon, hygge and Carlsberg beer in a cultural and analytical context.

The organisation of the chapters may, then, suggest one way of connecting the individual discussions, but they are simultaneously related in many other ways. During the writing, several themes emerged – and not always how and where we expected them. As a result, the analyses throughout the volume highlight themes or core aspects of Nordic histories and cultures that have infused developments and determined individual and collective expressions across the region. Through the case-studies offered, we can observe continuous movements and fluctuations, and the ruptures and resources brought by various forms of migration. We can also trace questions around identities, self-perception and definitions, and how these are borne out in collective and individual actions. And lastly, concrete and ideological conceptions of locale and location, including tensions between centres and (perceived) peripheries, reveal themselves as determinants of the geographical and cultural entity that constitutes the Nordic region.

The volume is on one level, then, not just 'Nordic' – even if that is its focus – but also an example of an investigation which engages with the question of how societies form, transmute and re(-)form, how ideologies and preoccupations shape behaviours and structures within these societies, and how these might be stabilised and perpetuated, but also challenged and forced to change.

We have purposely 'forgotten' to write about a great many things. But we have not forgotten to try and 'de-bunk' myths of 'happy hygge' or idealised Vikings, and to challenge such easy readings of Nordic society. This volume aims for greater complexity, more nuanced analyses and more intricate understandings. There is much in the Nordic histories, cultures and societies that is not covered here, and for which we will – gladly – direct you to other writings (see for example the bibliographies at the end of the chapters). But we hope that what *is* here might provide a very good starting point for understanding where the Nordic region has come from, how it has got to where it is, and where it might be going.

Part I
Identities

1
Viking-Age Scandinavia: Identities, Communities and Kingdoms

Haki Antonsson

In the twelfth century the people of the north began writing about their own past. Saxo Grammaticus (*c.*1160–*c.*1220) in Denmark, Ari Þorgilsson (1067–1148) in Iceland and Theodoricus Monachus (writing in the late twelfth century) in Norway narrated how the Danes, Icelanders and Norwegians had cast away paganism and embraced Christianity. Further, these histories highlighted how the identity of these nations had been moulded by the development of political institutions. In Norway and Denmark this meant the monopolisation of royal power in the hands of specific dynasties. In kingless Iceland, however, the so-called *Althing* ('General Assembly') served Ari as the core of the country's history and identity. These historical works, which are some of the earliest Nordic compositions in the Latin alphabet, relate events that took place in the Viking Age (here defined as the period between *c.* 800 AD and 1050 AD). Even more importantly, they reveal what these authors thought about the history of their people and how they wished to portray this history to their contemporaries. Above all, they show that by the twelfth century the notion that Scandinavia was divided into separate nations, each with its own distinct history, had become an established idea.

Around 800 AD Scandinavia was both pagan and politically fragmented. There were certainly no Swedish or Norwegian kingdoms, while the nature of Danish kingship in this period is uncertain. By 1200 AD there were kings who claimed rulership over lands which broadly (but by no means entirely) correspond to our modern notion of Sweden, Norway and Denmark. Further, apart from the Sami in the north, every inhabitant of the region would expect to be baptised into the Christian religion. There was, however, nothing inevitable about the emergence of separate Scandinavian kingdoms and the conversion to Christianity. Complex cultural, political and geographic factors brought about these momentous changes.

This chapter does not aim to offer an overview of the state-formation or the Christianisation of Scandinavia. These two interrelated themes are well served by authoritative and easily accessible recent studies (see for example Winroth 2012 and 2014). Rather, the purpose of this chapter is to introduce salient ideas, problems and perspectives about Viking-Age Scandinavian society. In particular, the chapter highlights the importance of regional and local levels of religion, politics and identity and their relation to national identity. Following a brief introduction, the chapter will crystallise the chosen themes through the examination of four objects, each of which carries an inscription in the runic alphabet. These are the ninth-century Forsa ring from Hälsingland in Sweden, the two rune-stones of the famous Jelling monument(s) from tenth-century Jutland in Denmark, and the so-called Frösö stone which was crafted in eleventh-century Jämtland, a border region between Norway and Sweden.

'Scandinavia' in Early Sources

There are plentiful descriptions from various parts of Europe about marauding and invading people from the pagan north. Not surprisingly, Irish and Anglo-Saxon annals as well as Frankish chronicles depict Scandinavians in a decidedly negative way. The sources frequently present the belligerent people of the north as infernal agents of God, which, like plagues or swarms of locusts, were sent to punish the Christians for their sins and flawed religious observance. Such accounts comprise the earliest sustained writings about Scandinavia and its inhabitants.

For the centuries preceding the Viking Age, however, written references about Scandinavians are scarce. But the handful that do exist mention that the Scandinavians were prone to emigrate from their homeland. Around 550 AD Jordanes, writing in Constantinople (today's Istanbul), reported that in the past the island of 'Scandza' had served as 'a hive of races and a womb of nations' (since classical times the northernmost lands of Europe had been believed to form an island) (Jordanes 1908, 7). Jordanes recounts this near the beginning of his *The Origin and Deeds of the Goths*. The Goths constituted a tribe or people that was associated with the fifth-century collapse of the Roman Empire in Europe. Jordanes relates how in the distant past the Goths emigrated from their homeland and, following a long and circuitous route, became the most powerful enemies of the Roman Empire and eventually the founders of kingdoms in their own right. The term 'Goth' approximates to some familiar names in Scandinavia, most notably Västergötland in Sweden and the Baltic island of Gotland. Whatever the truthfulness of Jordanes' account about an emigration from Scandinavia – and scholars have long debated its veracity – this is the one thing writers thought worth reporting about the northern people.

In the early eighth century a Northumbrian monk by the name of Bede wrote one of the seminal texts of the Early Middle Ages (500–1000 AD). This is the *Ecclesiastical History of the English People*, a work that traces the origins of the 'English people' from the ruins of the Roman Empire to Bede's own time. Bede tells how, in the fifth century, people from modern Denmark and northern Germany arrived in Britain. Initially they arrived as mercenaries, assigned the task of fending off other 'barbarians', but soon the newcomers became the new masters and founders of new kingdoms (Bede 1969, 49–53). These Anglo-Saxon kingdoms were considered by Bede to be the constituent polities of the people he referred to as the English. Not long after Bede wrote his *Ecclesiastical History* an unknown author recorded the greatest of the Old English poems, *Beowulf*, which narrates the deeds of characters who lived in southern Scandinavia, the old homeland of the Anglo-Saxons. The epic poem follows the adventures of the main protagonist, Beowulf, a one-time king of the Geats (or the Götar) who, among other deeds, performs heroic feats at the court of the king of the Danes (see O'Donoghue 2008). In *Beowulf* we get a glimpse of the ancient and longstanding division of (what is now) Sweden (or rather the southern and central part of the country) into two peoples or tribes. These were the Götar who inhabited Götaland (modern-day southern Sweden, excluding Skåne) and the Svear who lived in south-central Sweden (Svealand).

Jordanes' *History of the Goths*, Bede's *Ecclesiastical History of the English People* and *Beowulf* are quite different kinds of texts. Nevertheless, all three relay the belief that the inhabitants of the north were divided into a number of tribes or peoples. These divisions do not correspond to our present-day division of the region's inhabitants into, among others, Danes, Norwegians and Swedes. Jordanes, for instance, mentions among others the 'Hallin', 'the people of Halland' (on Sweden's south-western coast), 'Raumariciae', 'people of the Raumar' (who likely gave their name to Romerike in south-eastern Norway) and 'Screrefennae', which may designate Finns/Sami of northern Scandinavia (see Brink 2008a). Bede mentions the 'Jutes' while, as already noted, Beowulf is a 'Geat' who accomplishes his heroic deeds among a people called the 'Danes'. Such testimonies, supported by later evidence, indicates that the peoples of Scandinavia formed a number of separate groupings among which the 'Danes' and 'Swedes' ('Svear') only represented two markers of communal identity among many. An early plausible reference to 'Norwegians' appears in an Old-English source from the end of the ninth century. There, a certain Othere, a merchant who visited the court of King Alfred of Wessex, testified that 'he lived the furthest north of all northmen [*Norðmonno*]' (Bately and Englert 2007, 125). As with the earlier mentioned references to Danes and Swedes, we cannot be altogether certain what Othere understood by the term *Norðmonno*.

As we examine the four objects and their inscriptions it is useful to keep in mind the two salient points of our discussion so far. One is the established idea – attested in the written records of the twelfth and thirteenth centuries – of the existence of distinct peoples called Danes, Swedes, Norwegians and Icelanders. The other is the existence of local and regional identities below these 'national levels', whose existence we can only glean from contemporary skaldic poetry, place-names, stray references in foreign written sources and, not least, runic inscriptions.

The Forsa Ring

Our first object – an iron ring, forty-three centimetres in diameter – has a peculiar story. For centuries the ring was a door-ring in the church at Forsa in Hälsingland, which is a province in eastern central Sweden. Considering the ring's connection with the local church one might be tempted to conclude that it was a Christian object. In one sense this is a correct assumption because the ring must have been a familiar sight to generations of church-goers. What then about the runes, which have been etched into the iron? There is nothing inherently pagan about runic inscriptions. Runes were carved throughout Scandinavia from at least the third century to the fifteenth century, at which point the region had been Christian for centuries. According to the experts, however, the runes on the Forsa ring are of a kind that date their making to the ninth or tenth century. Thus, it seems highly unlikely that the ring (see Figure 1.1) was crafted around the time the first church in Forsa was built in the eleventh century or the twelfth century. Our object was therefore crafted before the official conversion of the region to Christianity. What then was the ring's purpose?

To answer this question the runes must be read and interpreted. This is not an easy task, but with time scholars have come to agree on the most

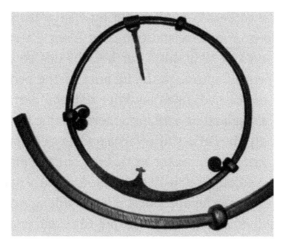

Figure 1.1 The ninth or tenth-century iron ring from Forsa church in Hälsingland, central Sweden. Source: Photo by Sven Rosborn. CC BY-SA 3.0.

plausible reading. The following is the most authoritative translation to date of the Forsa ring's Old-Norse runes. (Old Norse words feature in bold and [] signifies an inferred/reconstructed meaning within the text):

> One ox and two **aura** [in fine] [to?] **staf** [or] **aura staf** [in fine] for the restoration of a cult site [**vi**] in a valid state for the first time; two oxen and four **aura** for the second time; but for the third time four oxen and eight **aura**; and all property in suspension, if he doesn't make right. That, the people are entitled to demand, according to the law of the people that was decreed and ratified before. But they made [the ring, the statement or?], Anund from Tåsta, and Ofeg from Hjorsta. But Vibjörn carved.
>
> (Brink 2008b, 29)

Most surviving runic inscriptions from the Viking Age are etched in stone. More precisely, they adorn boulders that were usually erected in memory of a deceased family member, war-companion or friend. These runes frequently relate who commissioned and paid for the monument as well as the name of the carver. Similarly, the Forsa ring mentions three men who were involved in the making of the object: Anund, Ofeg and Vibjörn, the latter presented as the one who carved the runes. The Forsa ring, however, was manifestly not crafted and inscribed with a memorial purpose in mind. Its purpose was different.

The ring seems to express a law or a decree of some kind. The reading stipulates a fine for repeated unwanted activity or desecration of a holy site or location. As punishment for each transgression the fine doubles in value from one ox and two *aura* (*ørar* – a unit of measurement) to four oxen and eight *aura*. Further, the decree is authorised by 'the law of the people'. Although the identity of 'the people' referred to is not explicitly mentioned, one may infer that the decree refers to the inhabitants of Hälsingland or perhaps a more specific locality within this region. Accordingly, the Forsa ring offers a precious glimpse into the communal laws laid out by the people of this region. The earliest preserved written laws in Scandinavia date to the twelfth century and are therefore uncertain sources for the legal condition in the Viking Age. The origin of the Forsa ring and its inscription in the pre-Christian period is therefore highly significant.

From a still broader perspective, the Forsa ring highlights the importance of local authority in the Viking Age. In this period, power still lay mostly in localities where leading men, such as Anund from Tåsta and Ofeg from Hjorsta, decided on law and order. Numerous comparable local polities to the one revealed by the Forsa ring existed throughout Scandinavia. However, due to the nature of our sources – in particular the absence of Scandinavian writings in the Latin alphabet – the working of these local communities are obscured from our view. It is interesting to compare this relative obscurity with the plethora of written sources about the Viking-Age rulers, as narrated in the Norwegian, Danish and Icelandic histories of the twelfth and thirteenth centuries (see above).

In this respect, Iceland is a fascinating exception. There the origin, development and nature of the *Althing* became the focus of the earliest Icelandic historical work. This is the earlier mentioned Ari Þorgilsson's *Íslendingabók* (*Book of Icelanders*), which was composed sometime between 1122 and 1133 AD. This brief text recounts the history of the Icelanders from the settlement of their country in the second half of the ninth century to Ari's own time. The high point of the *Book of Icelanders* is the *Althing*'s adoption of Christianity into Iceland's laws in the year 999/1000. Ari describes a stand-off between pagans and Christians at the *Althing* over which custom and law should prevail in the country. The matter was resolved through the method of arbitration. The Law-Speaker, a respected person assigned the task of memorising and proclaiming the laws, deliberated on the matter and announced that henceforth it should be brought into law that all Icelanders should adhere to Christian laws (*Íslendingabók* 2006, 7–9).

Like Ari Þorgilsson's account of this momentous decision, the Forsa ring illustrates the absence of any barrier between the secular, political and religious spheres. The sacred site, its preservation and upkeep, is a communal responsibility. Those who damage or defile it are to be punished following the laws commonly held by the people of the region. That said, we do not know whether the cult site (*vé*) was a grove, a demarcated plot of land or, perhaps more unlikely, a temple of some kind. Neither, for that matter, can we establish whether it was dedicated to a specific pagan god (or gods).

Pre-Christian place names, which contain the names of the gods, reveal considerable regional variation in their popularity. For instance, in Sweden there is a preponderance of place names that reveal the veneration of Freyr, a god particularly associated with fertility and lordship, whereas in Denmark names associated with Óðinn (or Wotan) appear with greater frequency (for instance Odense – 'Odin's sanctuary'). By contrast, few if any place names in Iceland refer directly to Óðinn, while many contain the name Þórr (Thor). Each locality or region had its own unique form of relation with its deities as well as other local supernatural identities which, for the most part, have been lost from history. Which god or deity you looked favourably on depended on various factors, but it is likely that the most important factor was simply where you happened to be born (see Gunnell 2015).

Viking-Age Scandinavia consisted of many local communities of the kind suggested, however inadequately, by the Forsa ring. These communities served as the political, religious and social foci of Viking-Age Scandinavians. We should not, however, assume that these communities were necessarily, or even likely, isolated and autonomous units of self-government. In the Viking Age their power relative to neighbouring regions essentially depended on three factors. Agricultural prosperity was certainly one such factor, as is shown by the political prominence of regions such as Viken and Uppland in Norway and Sweden respectively. Second, strategic location was a significant factor in the importance of a given locality. Most pertinently, command over regional or even international trade led to the emergence of powerful local elites. Trøndelag in Norway and the southern borderland of the Danes are regions where this condition was met. Third, a threat or pressure from a powerful neighbour, such as the Frankish and later German empires of the ninth and tenth centuries, could concentrate political power in the hands of a smaller elite. All three criteria coalesce in the relatively compact Danish peninsula and its adjoining islands. Accordingly, it is not surprising that the first relatively powerful kingship in Scandinavia emerged, as we shall see, in Denmark.

The Frösö Stone

Turning to the chapter's second object, our attention is still on the local rather than the national level. The next region of interest is Jämtland, which today is central-eastern Sweden, but which in the Viking Age formed a semi-independent border region between Norway and Sweden. The object of interest is the so-called Frösö rune stone (Figure 1.2), which, on stylistic grounds, has been dated to the second half of the eleventh century. The name of this most northerly of rune stones reflects its present-day location. Until only some forty years ago (when it was moved because of building construction), it stood on Frösön, meaning Frey's island, in Storsjön, the region's largest lake. In this location, which is likely the original one, the rune stone overlooked the strait between the island and the mainland. When translated, the inscription on the stone, which is decorated with a cross and an image of a serpent-like creature, reads:

> Östman, Gudfast's son, had this stone raised and this bridge made, and he had Jämtland made Christian. Åsbjörn made the bridge. Tryn and Stein cut these runes.
>
> (Jansson 1962, 119)

Figure 1.2 Frösöstenen, the Frösö rune stone from Jämtland in Sweden, is the northernmost raised rune stone in Scandinavia, dated to the second half of the eleventh century. Photo by Lavallen.

As already mentioned, most rune stones were raised in memory of the dead. A common inscription on such stones relates how a son or a widow has raised a monument in memory of a father or a husband. The Frösö stone, however, is somewhat unusual (but by no means unique) in celebrating living individuals, in this case Östman (or Austmaðr), the son of Gudfast, and Åsbjörn. The inscription marks Östman's three achievements: that he 'Christianised' Jämtland, commissioned the stone and built a bridge. Considering the stone's location, we can assume that Åsbjörn's bridge once connected the island and the mainland. The combination of a rune stone and the building of a bridge is not unusual. In this way the patron advertised to a grateful traveller his or her dedication to the common good while also memorialising his or her name in perpetuity. In a Christian context the building of a bridge may also have carried religious connotations, namely symbolising the pilgrim's journey from this world to the next.

Östman's claim that he 'Christianised Jämtland' is certainly the most intriguing feature of the Frösö stone. Jämtland was, of course, not a kingdom or a principality; so we can be sure that Östman was not a king or prince. Rather, the region appears to have been governed through a representative assembly (or assemblies) of the kind we have already encountered. But who was Östman? The name of Östman's father, Gudfast (or Guðfastr), means 'the one loyal to God', suggesting that his family had been Christian for at least a couple of generations. Östman's claim to have turned Jämtland to Christianity identifies him as a figure of wealth and social standing. He had, after all, commissioned the Frösö stone, which involved the craftsmanship of Tryn and Sten as well as Åsbjörn's talent to construct the bridge. Perhaps Östman Gudfastson was a local magnate who thought his influence in the local assembly so crucial that he saw himself as effectively the person who had introduced Christianity to Jämtland.

Alternatively, Östman may have been a representative of the Swedish or Norwegian kings. By the thirteenth century, Jämtland formed a part of the Norwegian kingdom, and possibly the kings already had eyes on the region in the eleventh century. On the other hand, the Frösö stone bears stylistic similarities to rune stones raised in the same period in the region of the Svear, specifically around Lake Malar (Mälaren) not far from modern-day Uppsala and Stockholm. These kings of the Svear had seemingly ruled this region for centuries. Jämtland, however, was a region far away from the heartlands of Swedish royal power. The Frösö stone might, therefore, reveal a king's representative, Östman, boasting about delivering the one policy that preoccupied the Danish, Norwegian and Swedish kings of this period, namely introducing and furthering Christianity within their realms. If so, this would represent a growing authority of the kings over regional authorities. We must acknowledge the limits of our knowledge about the historical background to the Frösö stone. I have highlighted these alternative explanations to illustrate how our understanding of the Viking Age frequently depends on interpreting the limited sources at our disposal.

The Rune Stones of the Jelling Monument(s)

Our final example, which features two runic inscriptions, shifts our focus from the localised world of the Forsa ring and the Frösö stone to the supra-regional and religious aspirations of a Viking-Age king. The inscriptions in question feature on arguably the most impressive surviving Viking-Age monument, namely the Jelling monument (Figure 1.3) in Denmark's central Jutland (Jylland). It is more accurate to refer to the Jelling *monuments*, as the Jelling complex incorporates a number of components, including two large mounds which flank two rune stones of unequal size. The older and smaller mound was raised by King Gorm, presumably as a burial place for himself and his queen, whereas the second mound was erected by Harald Bluetooth who, with this act and the younger rune stone, transformed the complex into an imposing display of dynastic power and prestige.

A translation of the inscription on the smaller rune stone, which is not decorated, reads: 'King Gorm made this monument in memory of Thorvi (Thyre), his wife, Denmark's adornment' (Moltke 1985, 206). This is the earliest preserved reference to 'Denmark' from within Scandinavia. Unlike Östman Gudfastson, the sponsor of the Frösö stone, Gorm is a well-known historical figure. He was a Danish king who ruled between *c.* 936 and 958 AD. Compared to our previous two runic inscriptions, with the Jelling monuments we are manifestly confronted with a quite different political and social setting. While honouring the memory of his own wife, Gorm indirectly reminds the viewer of his rule over Denmark. The inscription is both personal and public and, as such, it illustrates how in this period no separation can or should be made between the two. The concept of the kingdom could not be differentiated from the personal and the dynastic.

The Jelling monuments express the evolving and strengthening idea that certain dynasties – in this case the Jelling dynasty – had claim to rulership over large territories and groupings of people. This notion is

Figure 1.3   Illustration of Christ on the larger and younger Jelling rune stone. Together with the older and smaller rune stone, Jelling church and two Viking-Age grave mounds they form the Jelling monuments, a UNESCO World Heritage site in Jutland, Denmark. Source: Photo by Roberto Fortuna, National Museum of Denmark. CC BY-SA 3.0.

explicitly conveyed on the younger Jelling rune stone which reads: 'King Harald commanded this monument to be made in memory of Gorm, his father, and in memory of Thorvi (Thyre), his mother – that Harald who won the whole of Denmark for himself, and Norway and made the Danes Christian' (Moltke 1985, 176). The other side of the stone depicts the crucified, yet triumphant, Christ. Harald's message is manifestly conceived as a kind of continuation of his father's message on the older Jelling rune stone.

Continental written sources show that by at least the early ninth century Danish kings were chosen from a restricted pool of one or two ruling dynasties. On the younger Jelling rune stone, however, Harald links this tradition with a powerful ideology, namely the Christian religion. In this, the inscription on the younger Jelling stone differs from Austmaðr Guðfastsson's boast on the Frösö stone that he turned the people of Jämtland to Christianity. Harald chose to connect the image of the crucified, yet conquering, Christ with his own claim to have converted the Danes to Christianity. The image is not of the suffering, bleeding Christ so familiar from crucifixes of the High and Later Middle Ages, but rather of Christ the chosen one who leads men to victory and everlasting life. The younger Jelling stone juxtaposes this with Harald's victorious assertion of his authority over the Danes and the Norwegians along with having converted the former to Christianity. The younger Jelling stone – indeed the whole Jelling complex – bears witness to the emerging ideology of a new kind of rulership, namely kings who claimed the submission of territories and peoples. Such marrying of royal authority and existing communal identity – in this case involving the Danes – played a significant role in forming today's familiar division of Scandinavia into three kingdoms and nations.

References

Bately, Janet and Anton Englert, eds. 2007. *Ohthere's Voyages: A Late 9th-Century Account of Voyages Along the Coasts of Norway and Denmark and Its Cultural Context*. Roskilde: Viking Ship Museum.

Bede. 1969. *Bede's Ecclesiastical History of the English People*, edited by Bertram Colgrave and R.A.B. Mynors. Oxford: Clarendon Press.

Brink, Stefan. 2008a. 'People and Land in Early Scandinavia'. In *Franks, Northmen, and Slavs: Identities and State Formation in Early Medieval Europe*, edited by Ildar Garipzanov, Patrick Geary and Przemysław Urbańczyk, 87–112. Turnhout: Brepols.

Brink, Stefan. 2008b. 'Law and Society: Polities and Legal Customs in Viking Scandinavia'. In *The Viking World*, edited by Stefan Brink and Neil Price, 23–31. London: Routledge.

Grønlie, Siân, trans. 2006. *Íslendingabók: Kristni saga = The Book of the Icelanders: The Story of the Conversion*. London: Viking Society for Northern Research.

Gunnell, Terry. 2015. 'Pantheon? What Pantheon? Concepts of a Family of Gods in Pre-Christian Scandinavian Religions', *Scripta Islandica: Isländska Sällskapets Årsbok* 66: 55–76.

Jansson, Sven B.F. 1962. *The Runes of Sweden*, translated by Peter G. Foote. Stockholm: Norstedt.

Jordanes. 1908. *The Origin and Deeds of the Goths*, translated by Charles C. Mierow. Princeton: Princeton University Press.

Moltke, Erik. 1985. *Runes and Their Origin: Denmark and Elsewhere*. Copenhagen: National Museum of Denmark.

O'Donoghue, Heather, ed. 2008. *Beowulf: The Fight at Finnsburh*, translated by Kevin Crossley-Holland. Oxford: Oxford University Press.

Winroth, Anders. 2012. *The Conversion of Scandinavia: Vikings, Merchants, and Missionaries in the Remaking of Northern Europe*. New Haven: Yale University Press.

Winroth, Anders. 2014. *The Age of the Vikings*. Princeton: Princeton University Press.

2

The North: Territory and Narrated Nature

Annika Lindskog

'What is north?', asks Peter Davidson in *The Idea of North* (2005). His book attempts not so much to give a definitive answer, but to probe into our ideas and perceptions of what – and where – 'north' is: how these are formed, what sustains them, and how we express and re-narrate them. It emerges that our conceptualisation of 'north' vacillates between obliqueness and specificity, between ephemeral notions and concrete matter: 'north' is an imagination, an abstraction, yet conditioned by physicalities, by geography, climate, activities, mood, space and conditions of habitation. Concepts of 'north' cannot therefore be pinned down or fixed – there is nothing definite about them, but they keep shape-shifting and they keep moving: as a concretisation of place, 'north' might be a map reference by which we orient ourselves, but as a compass point it also always points to somewhere else, a 'further north' from where we are located (7). Considering 'north' then requires awareness of how we relate to that north: are we in it, or looking at it? Is it near us, or something conceptualised as away from us? Is it something we experience physically, or something we observe and define from a distance?

Maintaining an awareness of such dualities, or tensions, in our perspective, and the understanding that *how* we look affects *what* we see, are highly relevant when we consider how we understand landscapes and geographies.[1] This chapter will focus on a journey made to northern Scandinavia in 1732 by a young, solitary student from Uppsala.[2] Carl Linnaeus (or Carl von Linné in the un-Latinised version) (1707–78) would later make a significant contribution to science as the 'father of taxonomy' – that is, through his categorisation and classification of plants and animals according to their sexual systems: his *Systema naturae*. Although this system has been superseded in modern times, it still forms an essential basis for our understanding and organising of the natural world. In 1732, Linnaeus was, however, only 25, and still very much a student. He had come from a provincial home in southern Sweden (Småland), where his father was a vicar and expected Linnaeus to follow him into theology.

Linnaeus epitomises, as we shall see, many attitudes and approaches which shape the eighteenth century, both in Scandinavia and beyond. Although it is said that the young Linnaeus was predisposed to a particular interest in plants and the natural world, his insistence on rejecting theological training and replacing it with scientific study in itself echoes the new attention given at that time to understanding the concrete mechanisms of the physical world, rather than only the spiritual. Linnaeus therefore entered university to study medicine, first at Lund and then at Uppsala. Here he landed amongst the foremost scholars and scientists in the country, and was taught and mentored by many of them, before he, partly by more diligent industry, overtook them and went on to become an internationally known ground-breaking scientist, teacher and collector in his own right.

This chapter will look at Linnaeus' engagement with the north in his 'Lapland journey' through his own documentation of the experience in the shape of a journal that he took with him, and in which he recorded what he experienced and encountered. Although most probably intended for publication at inception, Linnaeus never disseminated this journal further. It was only published long after his death – first in London in translation, followed by a number of different versions, mainly in Sweden in the twentieth century. Through this journal it is possible to trace a number of concerns and attitudes of the period. It is also, however, the beginning of a discourse around the region, its resources and its indigenous population: the Sami. This chapter will follow these narratives into twentieth-century Sweden, and through them consider how collective approaches to landscape and geographies are formed and enacted.

Iter Lapponicum: The Lapland Journey

When Linnaeus set out on his Lapland journey it was to 'reveal the Natural History of Lapland as regards rocks, soil, water, plants, trees, grass, mosses, quadrupeds, birds, fish and insects, as well as the diseases, health, diet, customs and daily life of the people' (Linnaeus 1995, 26).[3] Such was his fascination for everything at once. Linnaeus had been granted a stipend for the trip by Sweden's first scientific interest organisation, *Collegium*

Curiosum (then under its new name of *Kungliga Vetenskapssocieteten*). In its statutes, *Collegium Curiosum* stated that its aim was to promote the general study and exploration of the fatherland (see Zennström 1957, 22). Linnaeus' expedition, adventurous escapade of a curious young man eager to prove himself though it might on one level have been, was, then, not solely a private and individual whim, but embedded in scholarly and scientific structures in Uppsala, and undertaken with both national and royal approval. It is therefore an illuminating example of how specific and individual action and expression can both inform and exemplify large stratagems of its particular context, and Linnaeus' journey can be seen to represent a number of eighteenth-century concerns. Fjågesund (2014) writes of the late seventeenth century as witnessing 'a considerable growth in cultural as well as scientific self-confidence in the whole of northern Europe' (150), and *Nature* pointed out, in a special issue dedicated to Linnaeus in 2007, that although the classical world in which Linnaeus worked, and in which he 'believed in fixed species of knowable number created by God and observable by men' may seem to contrast with our present age of change, his classification 'was itself a response to a changing world – a world in which Europe's growing hegemony was bringing new species into the realm at headlong speed' ('The Legacy of Linnaeus'). Both the eighteenth-century scientific and political preoccupation with 'ordering the world for Europe' (Sörlin 2000), and the domestic politics of constitutionalised Sweden during its Age of Freedom, which engendered a lively and open debate on re-establishing Sweden as a great power through economic growth, are contemporary trends of which Linnaeus' journey is part.

Linnaeus rode out from Uppsala one May morning with larks trilling about him. His journal opens with the statement that he has been appointed to travel to 'Lappmark' in order to 'describe the 3 Kingdoms of Nature there' and has 'arranged [his] things accordingly'. There follows a list of what he has brought with him:

> My clothes were a small coat of linsey-woolsey cloth, unhemmed, with small cuffs and a collar of woollen plush. Neat trousers of leather, a wig with a pigtail. A green fustian cap with ear-flaps. Short boots on my feet. A little leather bag about 1 foot long, somewhat less in width, of white-tanned leather, with eyelets on one side to fasten it up and to hang it by. In this I put 1 shirt, 2 pairs of halfsleeves, 2 nightshirts, an inkhorn, pen-box, microscope, spyglass, a gauze hood to protect me from midges. This notebook. A bundle of paper stitched together in which to place plants – both

folio-sized. [...] Thus I departed from the town of Uppsala on the 12th May 1732, which was a Friday, at 11 o'clock am., when I was 25 years old all but half a (27).

This opening section demonstrates three significant approaches immediately: the detailed observation and listing, the lack of hierarchy or specific focus within these, and the presence and personality of the narrator.[4] These aspects will permeate not just the rest of the diary, but the character of the endeavour as a whole, as well as single actions within it. As the entry continues, it demonstrates another significant tendency in the following:

> Now all the earth was beginning to rejoice and smile, now beautiful Flora was coming to sleep with Phoebus:
> *The whole earth seethes and glows with the sweetness of Venus.*
> *Everything is full of force, everything in spring flower.*
> Now the winter rye stood half a foot high and the barley had newly shown a blade. The birch was beginning to burst forth and all the deciduous trees to show their leaves, apart from the alder and the aspen. [...] The lark sang for us the whole way, quivering in the air: *'Hear how it sings its tirilay, tirilay, tirilay'* (27, 29).

Apart from his general delight in his surroundings, and the importance he imbues it with –indicated by his efforts to note it down – the passage also demonstrates what is sometimes referred to as Linnaeus' 'nature lyricism'. The approach not only displays an engaged appreciation for the natural world clothed in lyrical garb, however, but also a certain open-mindedness: it is the articulation of the gaze of a curious traveller who is exploring and is expecting to discover, to see and to be enchanted, and to treasure what he discovers. We might further discern in this mixture of factual and scientific observations with poetical stylistics and embellishment another characteristic, not only of Linnaeus, but of the eighteenth-century Age of Enlightenment more generally. This is a characteristic which Rydén refers to as 'indistinctiveness' (2013; referencing Rothschild): a lack of absolute borders between areas, disciplines and topics, which makes it difficult to make 'a sharp distinction between culture and the material world for the eighteenth century as people of the period did not think in the same categories as we do'(12).

Nevertheless, the diary is here already also building up to what will become its main tension: that of viewing nature on the one hand as sensual, poetic and Divinely crafted, and on the other as a natural resource, as something 'cuirieust & nyttigt' ('rare & useful'), and of potential economic value.[5] Throughout the diary, Linnaeus periodically bursts into rapture over the splendour of (God's) Nature. As he detours to gaze at the Älvkarle falls, exclaiming at their grandeur, he first affords them poetic metaphors ('the mist from them was hanging in the air like smoke around a chimney above a large fire of woodchips'), before emphasising their natural provenance: '[they] owe nothing to the hand of man, being a creation of Nature' (32). At a later instance, the eighteenth-century view of nature as primarily a divine creation and gift to humankind is again underlined: while gazing at some 'innumerably small, newly-hatched' fish outside Luleå, translucent and with very large eyes, Linnaeus exclaims ('in wonder'): 'The whole world is filled with Thine Honour!' (101).

But at the same time, one of the main interests in 'Lapland', and the root-cause rationale for sending Linnaeus on this journey, was to establish what benefit the area could have for Sweden. To understand this approach, we need to understand the place that 'Lapland' occupied in contemporary consciousness. 'The science community celebrates most of [Linnaeus'] work,' wrote Marc Abrahams in *The Guardian* in 2007, 'but tends to overlook some of his writings about Lapland. Of course, the world in general tends to overlook writings, or most anything else, about Lapland.' Linnaeus too, when applying for funds, put forward the reasoning that since 'all of Europe' has now been fully 'searched', it is rather 'barbaric' (that is, uneducated, stupid) to not yet have accorded the same attention to Lapland: as 'ingen trakt i världen kunne gifva härligare observationer' (no region in the world might provide more wondrous observations) (Jacobsson, vol.II, 321, 319).

Although the general sentiment in both these observations is relevant – that of Lapland often being regarded as peripheral and picayunish in a variety of contexts – the indication that Lapland was entirely overlooked is not quite true. When Linnaeus set out on his five-month excursion, northern Scandinavia was neither unknown nor uninhabited, and it had already stimulated considerable interest. Fjågesund, in *Dream of the North* (2014), describes 'a rise of a northern culture', which 'with increasing self-confidence presented itself as distinctly different from the dominant Mediterranean and Catholic culture [and] had its roots as far back as the Middle Ages. [...] [This] also manifested itself in a growing interest in more specifically northern landscapes. One of these was Lapland' (139). Lapland also represented 'the Edge of Civilisation' – a half-way stage between civilisation and un-civilisation; ambiguous in terms of political and administrative control; very scantily described from a scientific point of view; ethnically and linguistically complex. It also had a largely nomadic Sami population who spoke a language no one understood, and with a religion and culture apparently as different as those of Africa; the region appeared as 'a world beyond the pale' (ibid.). It possessed exotic characteristics and represented a source of curiosity, and had already attracted some attention in Britain and Germany, in particular, in the late seventeenth and early eighteenth centuries.

Neither was Linnaeus quite the first Swede to explore Lapland. Northern Sweden was already partially 'settled' by the central state and the church, and earlier accounts and maps existed. None however matched the comprehensiveness, detail and engagement that Linnaeus' would possess. Scheffer's popular and widely distributed *Lapponica* (originally published in Latin in 1673, translated into English the next year and published in a second edition in 1704 with an additional report of King Carl XI's journey to Torneå in 1694) was a collection of texts sent to him by others: he himself had never been there. Linnaeus' mentor, Olof Rudbeck the younger, did go, and in 1695 travelled along the northern coast and the Torne River up to Torneträsk, then back along the Lule River to Kvikkjokk, then finally back down along the Finnish east coast (a route almost identical to the one Linnaeus would follow). Rudbeck's specific area of investigation was astronomy and in particular the midnight sun, but he also carried a sketch book and made diary notes. Many of these were, however, destroyed by the great fire of Uppsala in 1702, so no complete account of this expedition was ever published.[6] These (and other) ventures show that Linnaeus' interest in Lapland was far from random, but instead part of a contemporary pattern. 'The regions of the far north were the subject of a scientific exoticism', writes Sörlin (2000), 'that in certain respects is reminiscent of scientific curiosity about distant continents', and the leading Swedish naturalists at the time 'unanimously agreed that the north was a splendid and unique scientific resource' (58).

This highly pragmatic approach to Lapland is evident in how Linnaeus not only records what he comes across, but also evaluates it and appreciates its potential profitability. He finds, for example, some red soil in Hälsingland which 'might be suitable as red dye' (38), in Umeå in Västerbotten he makes a detailed list of the crops that are being cultivated (57), and when he receives some iron ore in Luleå Lappmark, he notes in detail where the mine is located and what the yield is (103). That he is travelling to 'write up' the region is also evident in his recurrent use of superlatives to underline how rich in resources the area is: 'it is my belief', he notes in Hälsingland again, 'that every type of granite in the world could be found here' (40), and in Lycksele he writes of 'the finest timber I have ever seen' (70).

This natural plenitude also doubles as a strategic cultural value, however, which is perhaps most evident when Linnaeus finally reaches the mountains (*fjällen*). As he travels on from Jokkmokk, he glimpses them first from afar: 'Just as when white wisps of cloud rise above the horizon, their peaks rose towards the sky […] There was nothing but hill upon hill. In short, I beheld the mountains.' In the evening he also sees the midnight sun for the first time and records it as 'to my mind, it is far from being the least of nature's miracles. *What traveller from afar would not want to see it?*' (110; my emphasis). What comes to the fore here is the extent to which Lapland could also be seen to provide a rhetoric of the exotic, something that might equal the discoveries (and colonisation) other nations were proclaiming on distant continents. Such a landscape needed to be 'special' enough to attract the awe of others, and Linnaeus strengthens this particular narrative around the landscape when he finally reaches the foot of the mountains:

> When I reached its slopes I seemed to be led up into *a new world*, and, as I ascended [the slope], I might as well have been in *Africa or Asia*, for the soil, the situation, and all the plants were *unfamiliar* to me. I had now arrived in the mountains. […] All of the *rare* plants I had seen before and rejoiced in existed here as if in miniature; what is more, there was such an *abundance* of them that I was terrified that there were *more than I could possibly deal with* (114; my emphasis. See Figure 2.1).

To aid the narration of these far northern geographies as exotic and adventurous, Linnaeus also creates an image of himself as the intrepid discoverer. The fact that he is not quite the first traveller into this region seeps through, inadvertently or otherwise: he is spurred to go in search of the abovementioned falls at Älvkarleby 'having heard so much about them' (31), he mentions a river he needs to cross in Leksand with a reference to what Rudbeck had told him about it (32), in Ångermanland he notes that he must be near his fellow-student Artedi's home village (54), and even on his encounter with the mountains he writes that they are 'exactly as depicted in form and colour on the frontispiece of Rudbeck's [d.y.] *Lapponia Illustrata* (published 1701, 110).

Yet the rhetoric with which Linnaeus' presents his explorations continuously underlines his own efforts, his singular role, and the hardship, toil and danger he has to withstand. Thus, in search of a cave in Ångermanland, he manages only 'with great difficulty' to persuade some local men to guide him and relates how trying to reach it 'could have been

Figure 2.1 Drawing from Linnaeus' diary to illustrate 'The Mountains' (Fjällen). With kind permission from The Linnean Society, London.

the end of our lives' (50). On the way to Lycksele Lappmark, the hardship intensifies and the risks he is taking are more pronounced: 'The road became more horrible and I rode in mortal danger [...] [we were] far from civilised inhabitations [...] travelling on by-ways where the devil himself could not have located me [...] [it] put me in mortal peril [...] many people had sought to persuade me that the journey to Lycksele was impossible in the summer' (58–60). This part of the journey does seem to end in rather spectacular hardship, as Linnaeus reports grinding to a halt in the middle of nowhere, soaked, fatigued and starving, declaring: 'I wish I had never undertaken this journey [...] I had reached the Styx.' He then meets what he calls 'a Fury', a local woman whose remote dwelling and difference in appearance gives her a mythical aspect, and who asks him what 'harsh circumstances of fate' have driven him 'where no one has ventured hitherto' and where she has 'never before seen strangers' – the inclusion of her question in the text even providing external corroboration of Linnaeus' self-characterisation as adventurer extraordinaire (76).

Linnaeus' account here clearly underlines his role as an intrepid and solitary explorer, and in so doing further strengthens the characterisation of the region as unconquered, virgin land ready to be 'discovered', claimed and globally promoted, concurring with and exemplifying eighteenth-century colonial tendencies and preoccupations. The diary thus expresses a duality of approach to the region and its landscape, as well as persistent tensions that are particularly evident when it comes to issues of value and utilisation. Linnaeus' long and unsorted list of 'everything' at the outset of the journey is echoed consistently in his uncategorised reactions to each new place and aspect he encounters, and his report manages to be at once intensely focused in gaze yet unstructured in purpose. The same lack of structure and unresolved tensions are evident in Linnaeus' reports on the Sami.

Oh, Happy Lapp!

Iter Lapponicum counts as one of the most important early anthropological sources on Sami life and culture. It is invaluable for the wealth of detail Linnaeus includes about their habits, tools, food, the reindeer industry and general conditions. It is also, as Graves (1995) points out, unusual for its time and of particular value because it deals with facts, practicalities and everyday life, and does not dwell on 'superstition, myth and rumour', which had until then been common (16). Here too Linnaeus is curious about everything without selection, and often observes relatively objectively. Many observations are, however, also tinged with awe: he marvels at how the Sami use their natural resources to make very comfortable bedding, at how skilled they are at recognising their own reindeer when they are so numerous and all so similar ('It was quite amazing to me that they could recognise these animals when they were swarming about like ants on an anthill'; 119), and at the ingenuity with which they transport their boats around rapids (on their heads) – to name but a few examples.

But he also sets great store by their natural surroundings and how they interact with them, and gradually, a view emerges through the text which attributes much of the 'happiness' of the Sami to how they live within the landscape. Deep into the mountains he attempts, for example, to respond to a question from Dr Rosén about why the Sami are 'so fleet of foot', and recounts first aspects of their physiology, then their training, footwear and diet. But as he considers further the reasons for the physical qualities of the Sami in general, he highlights 'the absolute purity of the air', 'the absolute purity of the water', their adaptation to climate and conditions of the landscape, and their 'tranquillity of mind' (124–7). Throughout his notes, Linnaeus repeatedly highlights the Sami's intimacy with their geographical surroundings, and relates it to what he sees as particularly desirable aspects of the Sami life.

This imagery of the 'happy Lapp', whose source of happiness is a substantial concord with the landscape in which they live, was one that Linnaeus would propagate on his return to Uppsala and make use of to support various arguments in his future career. But this portrayal is one-dimensional and leaves out other aspects of Sami existence – including many hardships created primarily through interference from the central state. As Koerner argues, this 'Linnean fiction' of the 'happy Lapp', is an 'especially strained variant of primitivism'. In the eighteenth century, Koerner points out, the Sami:

> suffered from small-pox, measles and alcoholism; as nomads crossing state-borders, they laboured under double or triple taxation; they were conscripted into Lapland's mines; they were driven from their hunting grounds, fishing creeks and grazing lands; and the Lutheran churches burdened them with tithes, catechism exams, and compulsory church attendance.
>
> (Koerner 1999, 73–4)

Linnaeus records some of these aspects in the journal as well, questioning the way farmers with no fishing rights can take over Sami lakes (and thereby cause the local Sami to starve) without any authorities intervening (71), or why a church could not be built in an area where enforced attendance at a church much further away necessitated three or four days' travel in each direction, often at a time when the seasons made travel particularly perilous (79). He even notes down some of the Sami responses to these issues, including at one point a lengthy quote about why complaining to the authorities to pursue those who trespass on their fishing rights is fruitless (81). These records, then, also bear witness to a sensitivity to the realities of the Sami, and even a recognition of some of the political structures responsible for them, though they may not necessarily have transferred to Linnaeus' later narratives around them.

When Linnaeus returned to Uppsala, he did not, as already mentioned, publish his journal. He did, however, disseminate his experience, and his view of that experience, in other ways: for example through a report to the Society, and through *Flora Lapponica* (1737), published in Amsterdam where Linnaeus built up his early career. The frontispiece of *Flora Lapponica* (see Figure 2.2) consists of a drawing of a mountainous landscape, with some deer, a tent and a sole figure holding a drum. It is clearly a representation of the author and a part of the process of asserting his authority over the landscape, yet it is hugely misleading: the deer do not look like reindeer, the mountains are dramatically peaked like the Alps, not flatly rounded like their northern Scandinavian cousins, the pine trees grow impressively tall in an area which is mostly above the so-called tree line, and the neatness and calm of the setting belies the daily toil and struggle in a challenging terrain and climate. Linnaeus himself poses as a natural inhabitant in this setting, yet his dress, the tent and the drum he is holding are loans from the host culture, all of them more or less inaccurately employed or in fact illegal for him to possess (see Koerner, 65–6).

In a well-known portrait painting (see Figure 2.3) Linnaeus later commissioned to impress a wealthy patron, his appropriation of Sami culture is repeated, as he here too wears a Sami costume and holds a Sami drum. Again, though, his connection with this culture, and the authority he claims through these presentations, is compromised. Fara rails against Linnaeus' 'attempts at masquerading' in Sami costume:

Any Sami could have told Linnaeus how ridiculous he looked. His beret, a present from a Swedish tax collector, was suitable for

Figure 2.2 Frontispiece for *Flora Lapponica*, published 1737. With kind permission from The Linnean Society, London.

women in summer. His winter fur jacket, which he had bought in Uppsala, came from a different region, and his reindeer leather boots were made not to wear but to export for rich, gullible southerners. His shaman drum – another gift – was an illegal possession. To complete the look, Linnaeus dangled assorted tourist souvenirs from his belt.

(Fara 2003, 27)

Linnaeus' actions with and away from the Sami reveal the constant double-sidedness of his approaches to Lapland and its indigenous inhabitants: a tension between what must be acknowledged as genuine interest, respect and compassion on the one hand, and on the other an imperialistic, colonial desire to 'other', and to claim ownership of that 'other' – culturally as well as in territorial terms.

Mapping Territory – Narrating Nature

All Linnaeus' collections were sold off by his widow after his death – which is why the majority of them have since the early nineteenth century been housed and looked after by The Linnean Society in London – and the Linnean voice was not very distinctly heard throughout the nineteenth century. The turn of the century and the early twentieth century, however, witnessed renewed interest in his work. At the beginning of the twentieth century, Swedish prosperity and identity were under pressure from several sides: late industrialisation meant heavy reliance on unmodernised agriculture, large numbers of the population fled the resulting poverty by emigration (see for example chapter 12 in this volume), and it was also about to lose Norway and thus its last vestige of any ideas of 'great' or colonial power. Land and landscape came to feature prominently in shoring up the wobbling state both practically and ideologically (from this period stem for example many organisations concerned with nature and heritage preservation, tourist and outdoor societies promoting active engagement with the landscape, as well as the very Scandinavian 'allemansrätten' – the right to roam), and the 'north' was yet again approached as a particular resource of value. Here was to be found the natural capital on which Sweden would eventually build its increased wealth, the extraction of which would propel her firmly into industrialisation: vast amounts of timber, hydropower and iron-ore. As Sörlin has comprehensively laid out in 'Framtidslandet' (1988, 'The

Figure 2.3 'Carolus Linnaeus e Lapponia Redux Aetat'. Life-size portrait of Linnaeus in Sami costume by Martin Hoffman, 1737. With kind permission from The Linnean Society, London.

land of the Future'), the north of Sweden now became Sweden's 'Alaska', much as it had for Linnaeus been its 'Africa or Asia'.

Even a new school book in geography, commissioned from the seminal Swedish author (and later Nobel Prize winner) Selma Lagerlöf, published 1905–6, in which a small boy is able to fly the length and breadth of the country with some wild geese, exploring different regions and hearing the local stories, puts 'the north' in a special category. As the geese near the northernmost parts of the country, the boy, Nils, recalls a story an old man once told him about Lapland. It features another set of birds who considered moving to the region and sent four of their number in advance to survey it. As the area was so vast, however, they split up to cover different parts with the result that when they returned to report, they could not agree on what was out there, and the flock leaders had to intervene:

> Do not quarrel. We understand from what you say that up there are to be found both a large mountain region and a large lake district and a vast forest area and a vast agrarian area and a large archipelago. That is more than we had expected. It is more than most kingdoms can pride themselves on having within their borders.
>
> (Lagerlöf 1981, 468)

Lagerlöf's textbook, *Nils Holgerssons underbara äventyr* (The Wonderful Adventures of Nils Holgersson), provides a narrative for Sweden through the boy's visit to each part: every province has its story, and out of them emerges a country as translator Peter Graves puts it (Graves, 2013, 360). Nils himself is a latter-day – and somewhat younger – Linnaeus in his role as explorer of the country: it is through his seeing that we see, through his listening that we hear, and it is through his interaction with the areas he traverses that we learn about them. Nils also acts as an agent of change in the contexts he encounters, and like Linnaeus, represents not a passive travelling gaze, but a creator of a new narrative about the places with which he interacts. Both Nils and Linnaeus demonstrate how physical immersion in territorial geographies can be used to command authority over such narratives, and how these in turn can be used to mould physical territories into ideologies of ownership and dominance.

Landscapes are 'contested terrain', says Sörlin (1999), as they 'provide the raw material for images and projections of territorial entities, be they by empires, nations, regions or localities', while also being 'culturally reproduced and mediated' (103). Both Linnaeus' Lapland journey and the later twentieth-century rhetoric as exemplified in *Nils Holgersson*, illustrate a deep interconnectedness between nature and localities on the one hand, and patriotism and growing prosperity, both cultural and material, on the other.[7] Linnaeus' ambiguous – and ambitious – view of his 'north', is echoed in the gradual appropriations of the same north in the twentieth century and into modern times, with similar and still unresolved tensions repeating themselves in terms of the approach to nature, the relationship between urban centres of cultural and political power and peripheries of those same powers, and conflicts around land, territory, ownership and cultural dominance. The texts that engage with this relationship essentially represent different ways landscapes can be encoded and decoded, imbued with value, and employed to form wider attitudes and opinions.

During the eighteenth century the view of nature was shaped against the background of various religious, moral and political attitudes, and during the earlier half of the century, when Linnaeus travelled, a moral and Christian approach would maintain that it was the duty of man to cultivate and make use of the divinely provided nature. Linnaeus' account is clearly rooted in this approach, but also demonstrates, as we have seen, a vacillation between various points of interest, and a lack of a considered and balanced focus – and with that also a receptiveness to a variety of influences – evident in each gaze, and each narrative construction he presents. In *Iter Lapponicum* we discover some shaky science ('a woman was greatly pained by three frogs, since she had drunk some water containing spawn in the spring'; 67), as well as some of the ongoing debates Linnaeus engaged with (e.g. arguing with Scheffer on whether reindeer ruminate or not; 118). We find some of Linnaeus' frank opinions on the people he meets ('I was astonished that such great arrogance and ambition, such great foolishness and vulgarity [...] should be found in men of the cloth' [Jokkmokk, 108]), and repeatedly observe his ability to alter his own assumptions when he encounters something new. We learn about northern Scandinavia: about the mosquito-like 'knorts' Linnaeus encounters in the Västerbotten summer that are so small that he does not even try to describe them (94), about the abundance of birch around Umeå (still today a symbol of the town [92]); about the loveliness of the countryside on Midsummer's Day (102), and about Sami children who make antlers of birch twigs and play at being rutting reindeer (Norway, 148). We follow Linnaeus when there is too much of interest for him to note down in any coherent order, and when he, finally, cannot find anything newsworthy ('Nothing particular showed up today'; Piteå on 15 June [93]). We encounter his close involvement and his humour when he takes a step back and comments detachedly, and glimpse his future trajectory when his own ambition shows itself ('If, in the case of every animal, I knew how many teeth it had and how they were arranged [...] I think I should be able to construct the most natural system of all for quadrupeds'; 88).

Linnaeus' journey and the record he made of it in the journal are both part of and have taken part in shaping continuing narratives around Lapland and the north. We must be sensitive to the role 'played by images and imagination in shaping the ways that geographical information and understanding are constituted', writes Cosgrove (2008, 8). A symbolic or iconographic approach to landscape 'recognises that there is a politics to representation' and that '[l]andscape representations are situated: the view comes from somewhere' (Seymor 2000, 193).

Linnaeus' engagement with Lapland reverberated against his own context and helped shape both eighteenth-century and future approaches to the region in various ways. Reading it today, we can learn much not only about Lapland, the young scientist and the society that was his context. It can also teach us that our landscapes and our geographies simultaneously contain their own absolute integrity yet can be subjected to our domination of them. The 'north' then, remains in tension – between its constituent parts and our imagination of it; between the concrete matter of scientific determination, and poetic, emotional and spiritual responses; between its own vast independent existence, and our claims to ownership and control. Linnaeus exemplifies the negotiation required between observing and inhabiting, the different perspectives inherent in proximity and distance, and the constant complexity with which we engage with our landscapes, our territories and our geographies.

Notes

1. The concept of tensions in landscapes is mostly indebted to John Wylie, as he sets it out in *Landscape* (2006).
2. The route took him up to northern Sweden, into the Norwegian mountains, and returning via the Finnish east coast.
3. All page numbers refer to Graves' 1995 translation.
4. The diary is written in a constantly changing mixture of vernacular (Swedish) and Latin, with a few dialectal Småland words or spellings thrown in, in a 'stream of consciousness' style structured only by the diarised chronology. Linnaeus also inserted some drawings – some of these are beautifully detailed and lucid, others less so. Virtually all later publications and translations bar Graves attempt to 'tidy up' these issues, and Linnaeus' text appears in them more or less restructured, trimmed, ordered and/or redrawn. In Grave's translation Latin source text is indicated by italics.
5. 'Frihetstiden inträder med dess brinnande intresse för handle och näringar, för "oeconomie" och [...] för allt som kan inbegripas i uttrycket "curieust & nyttigt".' *Svenska Linne-sällskapets årsskrift (SLÅ)*, 1931, 41–7.
6. It should be noted, however, that Linnaeus both lived with and was taught by Rudbeck, and is likely to have been more informed by his investigations than he makes evident.
7. See e.g. Lindskog 2011, for further exploration of these issues in the context of the Swedish north.

References

Abrahams, Marc. 2007. 'Notes from Lapland: Linnaeus and the Lost Secrets of Lapland', *The Guardian*, 19 June. Accessed 5 October 2019. https://www.theguardian.com/education/2007/jun/19/highereducation.research1.

Cosgrove, Denis. 2008. *Geography and Vision: Seeing, Imagining and Representing the World*. London: I.B. Tauris.

Davidson, Peter. 2005. *The Idea of North*. London: Reaktion Books.

Fara, Patricia. 2003. *Sex, Botany and Empire: The Story of Carl Linnaeus and Joseph Banks*. Cambridge: Icon Books.

Fjågesund, Peter. 2014. *The Dream of the North: A Cultural History to 1920*. Amsterdam: Rodopi.

Koerner, Lisbet. 1999. *Linnaeus: Nature and Nation*. Cambridge, MA: Harvard University Press.

Lagerlöf, Selma. 1981. *Nils Holgerssons underbara resa genom Sverige*. Stockholm: Bonniers Juniorförlag.

Lagerlöf, Selma. 2013. *Nils Holgersson's Wonderful Journey through Sweden*, translated by Peter Graves. London: Norvik Press.

Lindskog, Annika. 2011. 'Natures and Cultures: The Landscape in Peterson-Berger's *Symfonia lapponica*', *STM-Online* 14. Accessed 5 October 2019. http://musikforskning.se/stmonline/vol_14/lindskog/index.php?menu=3.

Linnaeus, Carl. 1995. *The Lapland Journey*, edited and translated by Peter Graves. Edinburgh: Lockharton Press.

Linnaeus, Carl. 2003–5. *Iter Lapponicum = Lappländska resan 1732*, edited by Roger Jacobsson and Sigurd Fries. Umeå: Kungliga Skytteanska samfundet.

Nature Editorial. 2007. 'The Legacy of Linnaeus: Taxonomy in an Age of Transformation', *Nature* 446 (7133): 231–32. Accessed 5 October 2019. https://doi.org/10.1038/446231b.

Rydén, Göran, ed. 2016. *Sweden in the Eighteenth-Century World: Provincial Cosmopolitans*. London: Routledge.

Seymour, Susanne. 2000. 'Historical Geographies of Landscape'. In *Modern Historical Geographies*, edited by Brian Graham and Catherine Nash, 193–217. Harlow: Longman.

Sörlin, Sverker. 1988. *Framtidslandet: Debatten om Norrland och naturresurserna under det industriella genombrottet*. Stockholm: Carlsson.

Sörlin, Sverker. 1999. 'The Articulation of Territory: Landscape and the Constitution of Regional and National Identity', *Norsk Geografisk Tidsskrift* 53 (2/3): 103–11.

Sörlin, Sverker. 2000. 'Ordering the World for Europe: Science as Intelligence and Information as Seen from the Northern Periphery', *Osiris* 15: 51–69.

Wylie, John. 2007. *Landscape*. London: Routledge.

Zennström, Per-Olov. 1957. *Linné: Sveriges upptäckare, naturens namngivare*. Stockholm: Arbetarkultur.

3

Narrating Nations: Iceland and Finland in Texts

Haki Antonsson and Annika Lindskog

In the first half of the nineteenth century, the Finns and the Icelanders were politically and culturally in a similar situation. Both peoples found themselves under foreign rule in a period of great national ferment throughout Europe. Broadly speaking, this early phase of nationalism emphasised the historical, linguistic and cultural distinctiveness of nations. In Finland and Iceland, this period saw scholars, intellectuals and artists engaged with what they believed constituted the essence of their respective people. This involved the discovery, preservation and promotion of what were considered the essential attributes and characteristics of the respective nations.

An important part of nationalism is the belief that each nation possesses unique qualities that distinguish it from other nations. These qualities can involve a number of cultural, historical and geographical features. They can for example be rooted in an idea that a given nation has inhabited a particular region for a long time, perhaps even from time immemorial (see chapter 11 in this volume). Another powerful source of national identity is language. Language is the key repository for, and controller of, a common cultural heritage. It has the potential to connect any present with a meaningful past. Such a connection is, for example, established through the reading of vernacular literature from the Middle Ages.

Nineteenth-century Germany, for instance, saw a growing interest in medieval texts, such as the *Niebelungenlied* and the Norse *Poetic Edda,* which were considered elements of a common Germanic heritage. The same period also saw systematic collecting of folktales, e.g. the brothers Grimm in Germany and the Norwegians Asbjørnsen and Moe – at least in part fuelled by the idea that these artless tales, stretching back into the mists of time, contained the essence or soul of the imagined nation.[1]

In this period a growing number of Finns and Icelanders began to consider the past as the key to the essence and identity of their respective nations. What was particular to these cultures was the fact that they had for centuries been dominated by foreign powers. The guiding idea was that the Finns and the Icelanders constitute proper nations whose distinctive cultures could compare with the more established nations of Europe. In the nineteenth century, however, this did not necessarily signify a political ambition of national independence.

Although the past was the critical source of national identity and cultural heritage for both the Icelanders and the Finns, there were also profound differences between them. This chapter explores these similarities and differences by discussing two texts which were published respectively in Finland and Iceland in the same year, 1835. These texts represent different types of narratives and we shall look at how they both articulated and influenced national ideologies in their respective contexts.

Before examining the texts themselves, a brief historical contextualisation is essential. Since the Middle Ages the history of Finland had been closely connected with Swedish history or, rather, the fortunes of the Swedish Crown. In the early thirteenth century, the relatively newly formed kingdom of Sweden had extended its authority to (what is now) south-western Finland. Religion was one justification for this expansion. The Finns, a term which is here used as an overall term for the region's inhabitants, were not Christians, and in the thirteenth century the Crusades – signifying the expansion of Catholic Christendom – were at their high-water mark. The Swedish Crown brought the southern and western parts of Finland under its authority within the context of a broader crusading movement in the Baltic. Parallel to this development was the establishment of the Catholic Church, which arguably more than anything established a link between Finland and the rest of Europe. There followed an influx of Swedish settlers to Finland, and these lands became an integral part of the Swedish kingdom with their chief administrative and urban centre in Turku (Swedish Åbo). Within the Swedish realm Finland simply became the 'Eastern land' (Östland). Until the early nineteenth century, power in Finland was essentially wielded by aristocrats beholden to the Swedish king. In 1808–9, Sweden lost a war against the mighty Russian Empire and consequently the Swedish king had to relinquish the 'eastern third' of his realms, which essentially constitutes modern day Finland. Thus was established the 'Grand Duchy' of Finland, which, although in theory having autonomous status within the Russian Empire, was directly ruled by the representatives of the Tsar.

The 1808–9 war between Sweden and Russia was part of a Europe-wide (indeed global) conflict, which is traditionally referred to as the Napoleonic Wars. The Danish Crown's relinquishing of Norway to Sweden in 1814 was another consequence of this. Although in theory forming a separate kingdom, Norway had effectively been under Danish rule since the end of the Kalmar Union in the sixteenth century. Denmark's loss of Norway brought to the surface a historical conundrum, namely the status of Iceland.

In the ninth and tenth centuries, Iceland had been settled by mainly Norse people, many of whom (perhaps the majority) had emigrated from Norway. Until 1262–4 the country was governed by a curious constitutional arrangement, which is now sometimes referred to as the Icelandic Commonwealth, although the Icelanders of the time had no specific term for their own polity. The principal feature of the Icelandic Commonwealth was the absence of any kind of executive power, such as a prince or a king. The constitutional arrangement laid down that the country should be divided into forty or so chieftaincies (*goðorð*). For each *goðorð* a single person (invariably a male) represented the people of his region or locality at the annual *Althing* (General Assembly). In the late twelfth century, cracks began to appear in this political arrangement, and by the 1220s the main power-brokers in Iceland began to war amongst themselves, which resulted in the Icelanders eventually declaring in 1262–4 their fealty to the Norwegian king.

In 1380, the Kingdoms of Norway and Denmark entered a dynastic union and in 1397 both joined Sweden in the Kalmar Union. The union of the three kingdoms lasted (with some interruptions) until 1523 when Sweden left. In the remaining alliance between Denmark and Norway, Denmark was by far the stronger partner, and in the seventeenth and eighteenth centuries Norway was essentially one part of a Danish empire which now also included Iceland. The events of 1814, when Denmark was effectively stripped of Norway, left the Icelanders in a special position. In 1262–4 the Icelanders had sworn personal loyalty to the Norwegian Crown but this historical thread had now been severed. In a practical sense this may not have been of great importance. Iceland had for all intents and purposes been a colony of Denmark for centuries, although its official status within the kingdom was always somewhat uncertain.

Thus in the early nineteenth century, Finland and Iceland both experienced historical ruptures of a kind. The rupture was certainly greater in the case of the Finns – as their centuries-long political and cultural links were more forcefully altered – but in both cases the developments served to enhance awareness of the countries' historical trajectories.

However, the conditions for forging a common cultural identity in Finland and Iceland differed considerably. One of the most significant differences related directly to language and its ability to document past histories. Icelandic (and Old Norse, its medieval ancestor) had been a literary language since the twelfth century. An early part of the Commonwealth period (*c*.930–1015) is the setting for the *Íslendingasögur* ('The Sagas of Icelanders'), and Ari Þorgilsson's *Íslendingabók* ('The Book of Icelanders'), composed between 1122 and 1133. This is one of the earliest Nordic histories, which relates the history of the Icelandic people from the settlement of their country in the late ninth century to Ari's own time. Such texts, together with the many medieval sagas, form an almost obsessive recording of Iceland's history in the Commonwealth period (see chapter 6 in this volume).

In contrast, hardly any literary texts in the Finnish language survive from the medieval period. (Old) Swedish and Latin were the dominant languages of administration and learning in the Swedish kingdom, and so it remained until the formation of the Grand Duchy of Finland in 1809. Finnish had, however, emerged as a literary language in the wake of the sixteenth-century Reformation, as it was a tenet of the Protestant faith that all Christians should have direct access to God's word, and this meant that Scripture had to be made available in vernacular translations. The first translation of the New Testament into Finnish, by the bishop of Turku, Mikael Agricola (*c*.1510–57), was published in 1548. In many countries the translation of the Bible profoundly influenced the preservation and development of the vernacular language, and this was especially so in Finland due to the limited tradition of Finnish as a language of learning.

As established earlier, an essential process in forging national identity can be found in linking the present to a national historical past through the vernacular language and literature. The very different linguistic and literary traditions in Iceland and Finland, would, as we shall see, lead to different approaches and different rhetoric.

Jónas Hallgrímsson's 'Ísland'

This Icelandic text is a short poem composed by one individual, commonly considered Iceland's 'national poet', in a seeming burst of inspiration as befits the usual image of the Romantic poet. Jónas Hallgrímsson (1807–45) was educated at the University of Copenhagen, like most members of Iceland's intellectual and political elite of the nineteenth century. There he was influenced by the prevailing intellectual current of Romanticism, which upheld the importance of the nation and its character (see chapter 11 in this volume). In 1835, Hallgrímsson, along with four like-minded Icelanders based in Copenhagen, founded the first journal in Icelandic, *Fjölnir* (named after a legendary Norse king), whose aim was to educate and inform the Icelanders back home about the state of their own nation and intellectual developments further afield. In the inaugural edition of *Fjölnir*, Jónas Hallgrímsson published a short poem entitled simply 'Ísland' ('Iceland'). It begins with a simple exclamation: 'Ísland! Farsældar frón og hafsælda hrímhvíta móðir!' ('Iceland! fortunate isle. Our beautiful, white-crested mother!'). The metaphor is of Iceland as a female figure, indeed as a mother, who attends to the needs of her children. A similar notion appeared in France following the 1789 revolution, where the figure of Marianne came to be seen as the embodiment of the nation. The French and the Icelandic cases are, however, notably different. Marianne is the embodiment of abstract virtues which distinguish the French Republic, namely 'liberty' and 'reason'. In Hallgrímsson's poem we find Iceland's nature – the very island – personified as a living, vital and positive force.

Immediately in the next line, however, the poem asks an urgent question: 'Where are your fortune and fame, freedom and virtue of old?'[2] The sense here is of a better time – a 'Golden Age' – on which the Icelanders of Hallgrímson's time look back in wonder and admiration. The implication is that somewhere along the line the Icelanders have lost their way and a national decline has set in. Thus, at the beginning of 'Iceland' Hallgrímsson establishes a clear contrast between the inadequate state of contemporary Iceland and the Iceland of the forefathers:

> All things on earth are transient: the days of your greatness and glory flicker like flames in the night, far in the depths of the past.

Although Icelanders of his own time can glimpse the 'Golden Age', they can only do so briefly and transiently. In the next lines the poet becomes more specific about the nature of this vanished 'Golden Age':

> Comely and fair was the country, crested with snow-covered glaciers,
> azure and empty the sky, ocean resplendently bright.
> Here came our famous forebears, the freedom-worshipping heroes,
> over the sea from the east, eager to settle the land.
> Raising their families on farms in the flowering laps of the valleys,
> hearty and happy they lived, hugely content with their lot.

This idyll is the Iceland of the Commonwealth period and, in particular, the 'Saga Age', which corresponds to the time-frame in which the Sagas of the Icelanders are set (roughly the tenth and eleventh centuries). We sense a current of energy here as the first settlers establish a thriving, independent society, which allows them to carve out a meaningful life. The intended contrast with the poor Iceland of the first half of the nineteenth century – beholden to Denmark in so many ways – is obvious. But note also how Hallgrímsson highlights Iceland's landscape. This is not simply a decorative feature, but will emerge as a leading theme in the poem.

The poem then moves from the general landscape to a specific location and to a place-bound activity. This is the Icelandic *Althing*, which was reputedly established in 930 and served as the judicial and legal centre of the Icelandic Commonwealth until its termination in 1262–64. The place is *Þingvellir* (literally 'the field of the Assembly'), which is some 50 km away from Reykjavik, Iceland's present-day capital:

> Up on the outcrops of lava where Axe River plummets forever
> into the Almanna Gorge, Althing convened every year.
> There lay old Þorgeir, thoughtfully charting our change of religion.
> There strode Gissur and Geir, Gunnar and Héðinn and Njáll.

The poet here evokes two familiar scenes or images from the 'Saga Age' that are associated with *Þingvellir*. One is the Conversion to Christianity in the year 999 or 1000 – when the Icelanders came to a peaceful settlement at the Althing to adopt Christianity – while the other refers to the heroes of *Njáls saga*, the longest and most celebrated of the Sagas of the Icelanders. But note also the continuing 'landscape theme'. The river running through the site of the ancient assembly is a constant in Iceland's history. Unlike the fate of men and institutions – like Gunnar, Njáll and the *Althing* itself – it is eternal. We recall the poem's beginning which referred to Iceland with its mountains, glaciers and rivers as 'our bountiful mother'. The Iceland of the poem is the mother of the poet's Icelandic contemporaries but, as it is eternal, the country's nature is also the mother of the earliest settlers and the heroes who bestrode the heroic age of the sagas. In this way, the past and the present are connected not just through words or a literary tradition, but also through Iceland's indelible landscape. The poem goes on to contrast the heroes of old with the Icelanders of its own time:

> Heroes rode through the regions, and under the crags on the coastline
> floated their fabulous ships, ferrying wealth from abroad.

O it is bitter to stand here stalled and penned in the present!
Men full of sloth and asleep simply drop out of the race!
How have we treated our treasure during these six hundred
summers?
Have we trod promising paths, progress and virtue our goal?

The heroes and Jónas Hallgrímsson's contemporaries are linked by a bond of ancestry, which is enhanced by reading about the past, about the proud, industrious and independent Icelanders of the 'Saga Age', a period in which Iceland was independent of foreign rule. The poet holds these heroic ancestors as exemplars, as models, for the Icelanders of the present who can and should steer the right course. In this way, Jónas Hallgrímsson's 'Iceland' is not directly a call for political independence, but rather a reminder of Iceland's glorious past, and a rhetorical articulation of how this past can inform the national consciousness and a continuing national narrative.

The Finnish text, also published in 1835, and which similarly illuminates important aspects in the early formation of cultural and national identity, is by contrast of enormous length consisting of some 23,000 verses divided into fifty sections, and is not attributable to any one author.

Kalevala

Between 1828 and 1834, Elias L. Lönnrot (1802–84), a graduate of Turku University and a governmental administrator, conducted five field trips in eastern Finland, especially in Karelia which, then as now, was divided between Finland and Russia. Lönnrot's aim was to record, collect and publish the traditional oral poetry of the Finnish people. His method was simple but effective. He sought out individuals in eastern Finland, especially the remote and rural Karelia, who he suspected of possessing knowledge of traditional poetry and lore.

The result of this and numerous other such visits came out in 1835 with the first edition of the *Kalevala* (known as *Old Kalevala*), which contained thirty-two poems (or 'runes') and over twelve thousand verses. The beginning of *Kalevala* reminds us that it is above all an ancestral oral tale passed on and performed by countless generations:

I have a good mind
take into my head
to start off singing

begin reciting
reeling off a tale of kin
and singing a tale of kind.
The words unfreeze in my mouth
and the phrases are tumbling
upon my tongue they
scramble
along my teeth they
scatter.[3]

The geo-historical conditions of the Eastern Karelian villages of Viena, from which Lönnrot collected some of the most significant parts of *Kalevala*, are a significant reason why the tradition of singing poems endured so long there. Perhaps the most important factor is that literacy, including a school and library system, came late to the region, and in the meantime, the oral tradition remained the most effective means of transmitting cultural heritage and knowledge from one generation to the next. The villages were remote and separate, on the periphery of both Russia and Finland, and the oral tradition was the mainstay of daily life: bedtime stories, lullabies, and fishing and hunting incantations were among the ceremonies and celebrations that were perpetuated and valorised by skilled practitioners of the oral tradition.[4] In this, the oral tradition that makes up *Kalevala* adheres to a number of the criteria of 'national' culture that were referred to at the beginning of this chapter: its connection to tradition, to a historical and individual past, to specific places and inherited land, and to the everyday life of the people who make up the 'nation'.

In 1849, after further collecting expeditions, Lönnrot published a new edition of *Kalevala,* which had now grown to fifty poems. This later edition became the standard version of *Kalevala* and the one which with time became part of the canon of world literature. Although Lönnrot was not the first to collect the traditional poems of Finland, the thoroughness and the grand conception of his second *Kalevala* struck an immediate chord as it aligned with a general movement for the discovery and promotion of Finnish culture. Lönnrot's achievement lay not only in his collection and transcription of the poems, but also in his arrangement of this fragmentary material into a coherent cycle which had a clear beginning and an end.

In contrast to the Finnish case, in the nineteenth century, national sentiment among Icelanders – especially among the educated class – emerged from a number of sources. An especially important one was the existence of medieval literature and history, which showed Iceland's special identity and distinction among European nations. In Finland, however, the past, and especially the medieval past, could hardly be separated from Swedish history and domination.

In this context, the setting of *Kalevala* is important: its stories take place in a remote, partly mythical, past, before the earliest recorded accounts of the Finnish people commence with the establishment of Swedish presence in the Middle Ages. With the Swedes came Christianity, and *Kalevala* is set in a pre-Christian world where, in the poem's first song or 'rune', the earth emerges from the shell of a broken duck's egg. The poem introduces Väinämöinen, the first human (though he is of godly ancestry), who is arguably *Kalevala*'s central hero as the poem follows his many quests and adventures. Indeed, *Kalevala* concludes with Väinämöinen leaving the land but vowing to return in the fullness of time. Other characters include the tragic Kullervo, who we shall return to shortly, and Louhi, the evil mistress or queen of the northernmost land of Pohjola. Although *Kalevala* is full of magical objects, supernatural feats and larger than life, indeed semi-mythological characters, its central subjects are decidedly human in nature. It explores the nature of hatred, love, lust, greed and friendship, and it often does so through the most ancient of literary motifs: the quest, either successful or frustrated, for a person or object of desire.

Kalevala became an essential part of the nineteenth-century movement that sought to formulate and promote a Finnish cultural identity and which, in particular, upheld the importance of the native language as an essential element of Finnish nationhood.

Figure 3.1   Kullervon-sotaanlähtö. Postage stamp depicting the Kalevala-inspired painting 'Kullervo Goes to War' by A. Gallen-Kallela, 1935.

Kalevala provided a specifically 'Finnish' past, which depicted a period prior to the era of foreign domination. Perhaps still more importantly, *Kalevala* offered a whole mythological world seen to be unique to the Finnish nation. In the course of the nineteenth and early twentieth century, an increasing number of Finland's most influential poets, painters and composers drew inspiration from *Kalevala* – and the one of most specifically national significance was arguably Jean Sibelius.

Jean Sibelius (1865–1957) was born into a country that was not yet independent, as discussed earlier in this chapter, but whose development into a sovereign state would occur during his lifetime. As this chapter highlights, political sovereignty cannot by itself form a nation of substance, but requires parallel cultural narratives to foster a national, collective self-description. The two texts hitherto discussed form a substantial part of such narratives. This last part of the chapter will consider how such texts can, through their use and dissemination, develop, strengthen and shape these narratives further. This is where Sibelius comes in.

Born into one of Finland's many Swedish-speaking families, Sibelius went to a Finnish(-speaking) school and would later dedicate himself to improving his Finnish – partly after falling in love with Finnish-speaking Aino Järnefelt (whom he later married and whose family were ardent Fennomans), but partly also in response to an increased focus on the Finnish language as the core of an aspiring 'true' Finnish cultural identity. In line with common practices at the time, after studying at the Helsinki Music School (now the Sibelius Academy), Sibelius spent 1889–91 in Berlin and Vienna, seeking the further training that institutions in Scandinavia could at this time not provide. His breakthrough as a composer came with a work begun while he was still in Vienna.

The *Kullervo Symphony* (Op.7) premiered in Helsinki in 1892. Scored for soprano, baritone, male voice choir and orchestra, it centres on the *Kalevala* character Kullervo, tracing his narrative, and setting texts directly from *Kalevala* for two of its five movements. Kullervo is a tragic character: mistreated as a child and forced to flee when his family is attacked, on his return he inadvertently seduces his own sister, whom he did not know had survived. He sets off to seek revenge for his family, but is too remorseful to bear his actions and eventually commits suicide. The troubled subject matter is echoed in the music: the first movement (*Introduction*) opens with 'ominous humming strings' over which clarinets and horns play 'a kind of destiny theme'; its second movement (*Kullervo's Youth*) sees a soothing 'lullaby motif' turn violent; the third movement's act of incest (*Kullervo and His Sister*) is relentlessly narrated by a male voice choir (using harmonisation to intensify the pressure of certain narrative points); the fourth movement (*Kullervo goes to war*) is '*alla marcia*'; and in the fifth movement (*Kullervo's Death*) 'the circle seems to close when the fateful main theme returns', the sound of the choir 'is now something close to raw screaming', and then 'one last hasty crescendo, during which the hero throws himself on his sword' closes the piece (all quotes from sibelius.fi: 'Kullervo').

According to James Hepokoski in *New Grove (II),*[5] it is possible to identify certain major characteristics of the musical setting of *Kullervo*. There is, for example, a preponderance of melancholically tinged melodies and a recurring characteristic 5/4 rhythmical pattern, particularly in the third movement (the most common number of beats in a bar in modern Western music is three or four – working with five beats in a bar elongates it and gives it a distinctly different, slightly uneven rhythm, since it has to be subdivided into un-equal parts). These two points in particular may be seen to underline its cultural connection: the melancholic mood is often considered particularly (if not exclusively) 'Finnish', and the use of the 5/4 measure can be linked both to the traditional folk styles and the syllabic rhythm of the Finnish language. We can also identify reiterative accompaniment patterns, which are stylistically reminiscent of folk or rune singing and further link the symphony with the heritage culture from which Kalevala emerged. In a thematic analysis, we might note a preponderance of long so-called pedal points (that is, one single note sustained in the bass over a number of bars), over which an 'epic recycling' of brief melodic ideas occurs, as well as what Grove calls, 'brooding' thick and minor-mood textures, 'redolent of stern historical burdens and inescapable tragedy' (Hepokoski, 2001, 322–3). With such interpretations Hepokoski relates these musical features to themes and ideas both in the immediate narrative and also in their cultural and historical context. Lastly, and equally significantly though more abstract in its interpretative possibilities, we might also consider the originality of the composition: this was not 'conservatory correctness', and Sibelius bypasses significant traditional features to achieve a unique tonal expression.

For a Finnish society that had for centuries been controlled and dominated by external powers, such unmistakably 'independent' utterances, based on what was understood, as established earlier, to be a singularly Finnish cultural heritage, were of significant value. Although critical reception of the *Kullervo Symphony* was in part sceptical precisely due to its 'unusualness', it still inspired enough enthusiasm and awe to result not only in Sibelius' 'overnight' breakthrough, but in his acknowledgement as the national composer of Finland. Although the *Kullervo Symphony* seems now to be understood more as an end of a particular period in

Sibelius' compositional development rather than a beginning, and it was not performed again in Sibelius' lifetime after 1893, the understanding that it established Sibelius as a composer able to articulate national concerns and aspirations illustrates the power of cultural acts to reinterpret, re-narrate and thus develop collective histories and national definitions. *Kullervo* here becomes a reference to the idea of national independence, and its inspiration and innovation is attributed to its cultural context. There was considerable press coverage of the premiere, and Huttunen suggests it was one of the most important national events before 1917, as it became its own national myth – mentioned time after time as the birth of a new, truly Finnish music (Huttunen, 2004, 13).

As Finland struggled for its independence under increased attempts at 'russification' from the Russian authorities in the late 1890s – stripping Finland of aspects of its political authority, limiting free speech, closing newspapers etc. – music became 'an increasingly intense form of cultural-political practice', with live performance events becoming 'vital points of focus for national expression' (Huttunen, 10). Sibelius composed several patriotic pieces of a semi-popular character in this period, among them the nowadays very well-known symphonic poem *Finlandia* – written to accompany a number of *tableaux vivantes* depicting Finnish history for an event in 1899, the event itself a covert protest against increasing censorship from the Russian Empire. Such pieces, and especially *Finlandia*, with its current iconic status and representative power of expressing something particularly 'Finnish', are examples of how music, as well as other art forms, can be closely engaged in and intertwined with cultural and political developments, as well as with constructions of cultural and national selves.

'Sibelius for Baltic people, but also all Nordic people, is a hero', said Estonian conductor Paavo Järvi in a radio interview in August 2018, before conducting Sibelius' Fifth Symphony at the BBC Proms in London with the Estonian Festival Orchestra:

> The great man of music, the person who has made all of us believe that we also *can* do something, on a world level so to speak. And there's a reason why every second person in Finland is a composer, and a famous one – it is because of him, he is a role model. In a country that is small, like Finland, these role models have an *enormous* importance. (Järvi, BBC3, 2018)

Järvi's comment highlights the interrelationship that exists between the countries of the region – something that will be continuously evident throughout this volume (and Finland and Estonia are, according to Järvi, 'the same culture, [just] a different tribe, [they] are the same people, coming from the same place' [ibid.]). But it also illuminates Sibelius' power as a figurehead for cultural and national ideas of the entire region, and suggests a powerful legacy, most decidedly still prevalent today.

Finland declared independence from Russia in 1917, while Iceland became a sovereign country a year later (although the ties with the Danish Crown were not fully severed until 1944). The literary texts examined in this chapter – Jónas Hallgrímsson's 'Iceland' and the *Kalevala* – appeared in the early phase of nationalism in Finland and Iceland. At this stage the focus was less on political independence from foreign rule and more on the shaping of a national culture for the countries concerned. The prevailing view was that the nation had to reach a level of self-awareness of its own identity before progressing to the stage of national sovereignty. And this identity was, above all, found in the language of the people – the vernacular language – and their unique past. '[The] *Kullervo* [*Symphony*] is at the same time a masterpiece and a baggy monster of a work, bursting at the seams', writes sibelius.fi. But *Kullervo*'s original expression, rooted in the mythical ancestry of *Kalevala*, as well as its setting of the Finnish language to music in a way which celebrated its individuality, beauty and strength, enacted a multitude of desires, struggles and preoccupations in the national collective. *Kullervo* and Sibelius thus also illustrate how cultural expression and agency can further enhance development of these ideas, and how the significance of inheritance and ancestry live on through their dissemination, use and appropriation.

Notes

1. See for example Tim Blanning, *The Romantic Revolution* (2010), in particular chapter 3: 'Language, History, Myth' (108–75). Blanning also considers the significance of connecting land and landscape with the national past; an aspect highlighted also in other discussions in this volume.
2. From here on the translation is that of Dick Ringler (edited and translated), *Jónas Hallgrímsson: Selected Poetry and Prose. See* http://digicoll.library.wisc.edu/Jonas/Island/Island.html.
3. Bosley, 1999, 53.
4. See 'The Vieni Karelian Folklore Villages' at *Juminkeko: Kalevalan ja karjalaisen kulttuurin informaatiokeskus,* www.juminkeko.fi.
5. The Grove Dictionary of Music and Musicians has since 1878 and in consecutive editions been a central reference work on classical music; since 2004 Grove Music Online (Oxford University Press).

References

Blanning, Tim. 2011. *The Romantic Revolution*. London: Phoenix.

Hallgrímsson, Jónas. 1996–98. *Selected Poetry and Prose*, edited and translated by Dick Ringler. Madison: University of Wisconsin–Madison. Accessed 7 October 2019. http://digicoll.library.wisc.edu/Jonas/.

Hepokoski, James. 2001. 'Sibelius, Jean'. In *The New Grove Dictionary of Music and Musicians, Volume* 23, edited by Stanley Sadie and John Tyrrell, 319–47. 2nd ed. London: Macmillan.

Huttunen, Matti. 2004. 'The National Composer and the Idea of Finnishness: Sibelius and the Formation of Finnish Musical Style'. In *The Cambridge Companion to Sibelius*, edited by Daniel M. Grimley, 7–21. Cambridge: Cambridge University Press.

Karlsson, Gunnar. 2000. *Iceland's 1100 Years: The History of a Marginal Society*. London: Hurst and Company.

Kirby, David. 2006. *A Concise History of Finland*. Cambridge: Cambridge University Press.

Lönnrot, Elias. 1999. *The Kalevala: An Epic Poem after Oral Tradition*, translated by Keith Bosley. Oxford: Oxford University Press.

Proms Interval: Sibelius' Fifth Symphony (Prom 42: Estonian Festival Orchestra, Paavo Järvi, in Pärt, Grieg, and Sibelius), 13 August 2018, BBC Radio 3.

'The music: Kullervo'. http://www.sibelius.fi/english/musiikki/ork_kullervo.htm

4
Modern Experiences

Elettra Carbone and Jakob Stougaard-Nielsen

From the second half of the nineteenth century, the Nordic countries, which had until then remained largely agrarian economies, experienced great economic growth. The successful industrialisation and urbanisation of the region was triggered and supported by a number of interconnected factors, such as the increase of export demand (particularly from Great Britain), the rise of capital imports, and the increase in consumption linked to population growth and the early industrialisation directed to the domestic market (Ljungberg and Schön 2013, 101–5). Each Nordic country followed a different path towards industrialisation, all of which converged, however, on the same 'road to prosperity' that ultimately led them to become 'Small Successful European Economies' whose openness to international trade offset the disadvantage of scale (Mokyr 2006, 9–10). Denmark was the leading Nordic economy in terms of income, urbanisation, modernisation of agriculture and the creation of new urban occupations; Norway benefitted from the export growth stimulated by trade with Great Britain and invested heavily in its urbanisation, but the initial period of expansion was followed by stagnation as the country had too narrow a base for its growth; Sweden and Finland remained fundamentally rural economies and developed later both in terms of modernisation of agriculture and urbanisation (Ljungberg and Schön 2013, 102–19).

Improvements in transportation played a key role in the region's economic success; the construction of railway networks made possible the 'exploitation and exportation of natural resources' and 'supplied settlements with the food and energy needed to sustain growth', stimulating urbanisation and shaping 'the long term economic landscape of the entire region' (Enflo, Alvarez-Palau and Marti-Henneberg 2018, 52).

This chapter explores the impact of modernisation on the Nordic region. We shall consider how technological change, industrialisation and urbanisation impacted the experience of (and anxiety about) an emerging, turbulent modern world in three case studies from Denmark, Norway and Finland. The focus will be on the tension between mobilities and immobilities, and we examine how, as Hannam, Sheller and Urry claim, there are 'places and technologies that enhance the mobility of some peoples and places even as they also heighten the immobility of others' (2006, 3). The three case studies selected for this analysis aim to demonstrate how 'mobility' – both in the form of travel and in the form of power – can be understood to be 'a resource to which not everyone has an equal relationship' (Hannam, Sheller and Urry 2006, 3), and how the arrival of modernity in the Nordic countries is represented as a combination of new technological and socio-cultural mobilities and immobilities.

Known primarily for his popular fairy tales for children, Hans Christian Andersen (1805–75) was also one of the first Danes to experience train travel, and he recorded his resulting 'railway fever' in the travelogue *En Digters Bazar* (*A Poet's Bazaar*, 1842), which complements a series of his later tales that both celebrate and worry about the technological revolutions of his time – including the transatlantic telegraphic cable, the introduction of gas street lighting and travel by air. The view of modernisation represented in Juhani Aho's (1861–1921) comic novel *Rautatie* (*The Railroad*, 1884), on the other hand, is less enthusiastic than Andersen's. Here Aho engages with the impact that modern times had on rural Finland by representing an old couple's disappointing encounter with the railway. Lastly, the anxiety brought by modernisation and industrialisation is also the topic of 'Ved Akerselva' ('By Akerselva', 1910), a short story by the Norwegian author Kristofer Uppdal (1878–1961), included in his collection *Ved Akerselva og andre forteljingar* (*By Akerselva and Other Stories*). Industrialisation divided Kristiania, Norway's capital, in two areas: the poor East End (*østkant*), the industrial part of the city, and the wealthier West End (*vestkant*). This socio-economic divide is at the centre of Uppdal's text, which represents the results of the capital's economic stagnation after its dramatic industrialisation and urbanisation: since there were no jobs, immigrants who came to the capital from the countryside in search of employment ended up living at the edge of society, struggling for survival with no hope of joining in with the progress of modernity.

Embracing Modernity

Within the Nordic region, Denmark was a forerunner in the construction of a railway network, opening the first railway line between Kiel and Altona (part of the Duchy of Holstein) in 1844, and the second between Copenhagen and Roskilde in 1847. Yet in his travelogue, *A Poet's Bazaar*, the always restless Hans Christian Andersen recorded his first experience of travelling by train while on his journey through Central Europe, Italy and Greece to Constantinople (today's Istanbul) in 1840–1. This was a time when travelling over land by stagecoach on rough roads was an uncomfortable, exhausting and tedious affair. It was, therefore, with great anticipation that Andersen entered a new world of travel on 10 November 1840, when he took the train from Magdeburg to Leipzig in Germany.

The novelty of railway travel in the early 1840s is tangible in the opening lines of the chapter 'The Railway' in *A Poet's Bazaar*: 'Since many of my readers have never seen a railway, I shall try first of all to give an impression of one' (Andersen 1985, 39). Andersen not only goes on to provide an intimate and detailed record of the novelties of train travel for his readers at home, but also describes the psychological and somatic effect of his experience as a virtual 'railway fever' (*Jernbane-Feber*). This 'fever' resulted from the disorienting and exhilarating modern experience of speed, a concomitant new way of relating to space and time, the thrill of the commotion and jostling of passengers, the howling of machines and steam, and the danger and the magical wizardry of the engines, carriages and crisscrossing tracks. Exhilarated by the whole experience, he writes: 'And what a tremendous effect this invention has on the spirit! One feels so powerful, just like a magician of olden days. We harness the magic horse to our carriage and space disappears. We fly like clouds before the storm, as birds of passage fly' (Andersen 1985, 42). One might have expected the Romantic storyteller of fairy tales to have longed nostalgically for past modes of travel, but Andersen celebrates the poetic potential and comforts of the new railway:

> I have heard many say that the coming of the railway would be the end of the poetry and romance of travel [...] I am of the completely opposite opinion. It is in the cramped, overfilled stage-coaches and diligences that poetry vanishes. In them one becomes dull, and in the best of weather one is plagued by dust and heat and in the winter by bad roads.
>
> (Andersen 1985, 42)

Throughout his literary career, which would become one of the most successful in the Nordic countries and the wider world, Andersen continuously explored encounters between the old and the new world emerging all around him. He sought to record his experience of the modern world and the complex experience of finding himself in the midst of great social and technological change. Paradoxically, he did this using the traditional form of the fairy tale: 'Our time is the time of the fairy tale', as he wrote in one of his later tales 'Dryaden' ('The Wood Nymph', 1868). Perhaps because his own life's journey presented itself as a modern fairy tale of mobility – at the age of only 15 he left his poor childhood home in semi-rural Odense by stagecoach to search for fame and fortune in the elite circles of cosmopolitan Copenhagen – physical and social mobility would become central to the settings and themes of many of his stories.

Andersen depicted the modern experience with a complex set of concerns: in his stories the modern urban world dramatises the conflict between old traditions and social hierarchies and the new, producing both pleasure and pain, anticipation and anxiety. Depictions of the changing social reality and technological advances instrumental to the formation of the modern city can be found throughout Andersen's work: in his 1852 tale 'Om Aartusinder' ('Thousands of Years from Now') he imagines transatlantic air travel on wings of steam forming virtual caravans of air ships that bring young American travellers to Europe; the new technology of electrified telecommunication, 'the electromagnetic thread under the world sea', is used as a character in 'Den Store Søslange' ('The Great Sea Serpent', 1871); and the impact of gas lighting on the city of Copenhagen is recorded in the tale 'Gudfaders Billedbog' ('Godfather's Picture Book', 1868). While such tales mostly present Andersen's wonder at the new world emerging all around him, other tales represent a desire for the new, infused with a sense of danger, with violence and destruction, and the loss of simpler times. In 'The Wood Nymph', for instance, masses of tourists arrive by train at the Paris World Exposition in 1867, 'the wonder of the world', where they trample down the young nymph, the 'child of the forest', whose life is withering away in the polluted Parisian air.

Perhaps most memorably, Andersen captures the marvels and dangers of modern urban life in 'Vanddraaben' ('A Drop of Water', 1847). In this short tale a drop of ditch-water appears to contain 'a whole town of savages' when viewed through a troll's magnifying glass, reflecting the chaos and violence of the modern city – probably intended to refer to London, the largest, busiest and most polluted metropolis in nineteenth-century Europe, which Andersen had visited in 1847. Through his many travels, Andersen encountered the attractions and horrors of urban life in the century's largest metropolitan areas such as London, Paris and Naples, and he would refer to these experiences directly in his tales to instil wonder in his Danish readers in the comparatively provincial capital of Copenhagen.

However, the population of Denmark also grew dramatically in the urban areas in the first half of the nineteenth century. In the 1840s, the movement from the country to the city took on proportions of a mass migration, stimulated by the early industrialisation. Until the 1850s, Copenhagen's city limits were still defined by the area inside the old fortifications, the ramparts, bastions and city gates, and as a result of this restriction the city became increasingly overpopulated. With its lack of a proper sewage system, the presence of a great number of household animals such as horses used for transportation, and an insufficient and polluted water supply, Copenhagen experienced terrible epidemics, such as the major outbreak of cholera in 1853. Cholera is a waterborne disease that had already ravaged London in 1831, and such epidemics highlighted the need for proper hygiene and sanitation, as well as the mortal dangers of life in the overcrowded city. While Andersen's drop of water may have appeared as merely a wondrous story in 1847, by the time of the epidemic in 1853, the terrifying reality of the overcrowded city depicted in the tale would seem an eerie premonition of the dangers of rapid urbanisation.

Fearing Modernity

The Finnish writer Juhani Aho shared Andersen's fascination with technology and how it forced its way through people's ordinary lives (Nummi 2012, 7). Several of his early works — such as his short story 'Helsinkiin' ('Helsinki', 1889) and his novellas *Yksin*, (*Alone*, 1890) and *Maailman murjoma* (*Ill-used by life*, 1894) — included references to new means of transport, showing how they shortened distances but also how, by connecting 'the remote, stagnant village idyll and the fast-paced city', they could bring change (Laitinen 1998, 92–3). Aho's first novel, *The Railroad* (see Figure 4.1), deals with this tension, presenting a comical representation of how the arrival of the railway in Finland was perceived by some people living in the remote countryside as 'a threat to their peace of mind' (Laitinen 1998, 93).

Today *The Railroad* is one of Finland's bestsellers; after a slow start, it became particularly popular thanks to the illustrations of the artist Eero Järnefelt (1863–1937), which appeared in the reprint edition of

Juhani Aho

THE RAILROAD

Translated by Owen Witesman

Figure 4.1 Cover of the English translation of Aho's *The Railroad* (*Rautatie*, 1884), featuring Matti and Liisa waiting for the train at Lapinlahti station, one of Eero Järnefelt's (1863–1937) original illustrations. © Norvik Press Ltd.

1892. By the time the book was published in 1884, twenty-two years had passed since the opening of Finland's first railway line between Helsinki and Hämeenlinna. The project was initiated by Tsar Alexander II (1818–81) and his government in an attempt to connect the capital to the rest of the country and, eventually, to the rest of the Russian Empire of which the Grand Duchy of Finland was then a part. Several more lines had since opened, but the one Aho writes about, namely the Savo railway extending to Lapinlahti, was yet to be built and would only be completed by the beginning of the twentieth century.

As the novel's subtitle states, *The Railroad* is quite simply 'the tale of an old man and an old woman who had never seen it before' (Aho 2012, 3). The main characters are Maatti and Liisa, an old childless couple living in a remote part of the countryside and earning their income in the form of subsistence, not money, through their labour as tenants of the parsonage. Having spent a whole spring and winter fantasising about the new railway built through the nearby village of Lapinlahti, they finally decide to walk to the station to see it for themselves. In his introduction to the English translation of the novel, Jyrki Nummi argues that Maatti and Liisa are '"genuine" rural Finns' (Nummi 2012, 12). They live their ordinary 'small-scale' lives most of the time isolated from the rest of the world, busying themselves with the same activities every day (weaving, milking the cow, chopping wood). Their existence depends on nature as they use traps to catch hares to eat, follow the natural rhythm of day and night (they do not own a watch and cannot tell the time) and even pay their rent to the pastor in grain. The arrival of the railway in their closest village, and their own visit to the station, break the monotony of their lives; however it also threatens their peace of mind and the status quo of their rural idyll (Nummi 2012, 15–6).

Throughout the novel Matti and Liisa are torn between curiosity and anxiety about the arrival of the railway, a reaction that is common in nineteenth-century representations of trains. The train becomes, in fact, a symbol of 'modern anxiety and potential freedom' (Fraser and Spalding 2012, x). While the rest of the village seems to have embraced the potential brought by this new means of transport, Matti and Liisa first attempt to join in this collective enthusiasm but ultimately refuse to let modernity become part of their lives. This becomes particularly clear if we observe their use of language. Matti and Liisa's resistance to change is mirrored by their struggle to adopt the new terminology and discourse of the railway.

As the Russian philosopher and literary critic Mikhail Bakhtin (1895–1975) states in his essay 'Discourse in the Novel' (1934–5), there are generally no neutral words, as language is steeped in all the contexts in which it has been used (Bakhtin 1981, 293). Language is always someone else's until it has been appropriated by the speaker who populates it with her own intentions (Bakhtin 1981, 293–4). When Matti first finds out about the railway from the foreman of the parsonage, who is about to take up the position of station man, and the pastor, he can only repeat what they say. Since he has neither seen nor heard of a railway or a train before, he has no vocabulary of his own to describe them (Aho 2012, 27, 30–1). Unable to picture the trains and the tracks, on his way home from his visit to the parsonage he is tormented by the haunting juxtaposition of the images the foreman and pastor used to describe trains (horse-drawn carriages, steam boats and rooms on wheels):

> Each time he imagined it, it looked different. Now and then he would be on the verge of figuring it out, but then it would change again. First it was as if there were before his eyes a four-wheeled wagon with wheels both large and small, always wanting to look like the ones on the dead pastor's old carriage. And in front of the carriage there seemed to be two horses, with the pastor sitting with his wife under the hood, and opposite them, the young gentleman and ladies; in the coachman's seat sat the driver, hands outstretched, and, next to the driver, Matti, as a small boy, a little afraid and holding on tight.
>
> (Aho 2012, 38–9)

Even when he finally visits the station at Lapinlahti with Liisa, still unable to use the 'modern' words he has by now heard so many times, he continues to refer to the train as 'the machine' or 'wild beast', and to the iron rails as 'logs' (Aho 2012, 100, 115). Although they cannot appropriate the language of the railway, Matti and Liisa cannot stop thinking about this modern contraption. In the first part of the novel Matti plays out a delicate balancing act between gaining more information about the railway from those who have seen it, such as Ville the waterman, and hiding his ignorance of it. When he tells Liisa about the railway, he attempts to repeat what he has heard but only manages to mix up all the information he has gathered. His statement that the railway can reach America, dismissed by the pastor during their earlier conversation, incurs Liisa's derision. While Matti attempts to come to terms with the railway, Liisa initially refuses to admit that such a thing could actually exist. It is only after her visit to the pastor and his wife that she comes back full of curiosity about the railway. As Matti cannot stand the idea that Liisa may now know more about it than him, he dismisses everything she says as lies, just as she had done with him. However, as the narrator points out: 'both of them thought of the railroad, even though they did not speak of it. They dreamed of it often and heard each other speaking of it in their sleep' (Aho 2012, 75).

As Ralph Roth and Marie-Noëlle Polino observe in their study of the relationship between the city and the railway in Europe, an interesting aspect of the rise of public transport from the nineteenth century onwards is that 'one can witness a diverse cross section of humanity travelling together side-by-side in these train compartments' (Roth and Polino 2003, xviii). People belonging to different social strata and geographical areas are enclosed together for the duration of their journey. During their eventual train ride, Matti and Liisa meet a 'man of the world', 'a journeyman' and, like anything else that does not belong to their ordinary universe, he represents a threat to their peaceful existence: the encounter has 'catastrophic' consequences for them as he gets Matti drunk, causing them to miss their stop and have to pay for an additional ticket. By the end of their disappointing experience, they attempt to re-establish their railway-free existence by trying to forget and avoid any conversation about it. In order to be carefree, it seems, Matti and Liisa's existences need to be railway-free. Aho presents this as a comical attempt to ignore modernity; yet while Matti and Liisa may manage to go back to their ordinary lives by the end of the novel, the world around them continues to change.

Surviving Modernity

There are no trains in Uppdal's 'By Akerselva', where unemployed factory and construction workers coming to the city from the countryside live in upturned boats and where economic growth and expansion seem to have reached a saturation point in Kristiania. The collection *By Akerselva and Other Stories*, of which this short story is one of twelve interconnected texts, appeared in 1910 and was Uppdal's first book of prose fiction. Similarly to Aho's *The Railroad*, the texts in the collection explore how 'the prosperity and stability of the village are replaced by uncertainty and the new power of industry' (Ostrauskaite 2004, 309). The stories are episodes from the life of Kal Østad, a man who, having moved from the countryside to the capital of Norway, has become one of the many victims of economic stagnation. In this first prose collection, Uppdal develops what would become his longstanding interest in the working classes (Mishler 1993, 221).

Throughout the story we get regular reminders that the city is divided, both socially and geographically: the 'world of shadows', the 'big city' and the 'fine houses' (Uppdal 1982, 92, 95, 96). The narrator of the story belongs to the 'world of shadows'; he is one of the modern 'trolls' living under overturned boats, afraid of the sunlight and of 'gaily dressed people' (Uppdal 1982, 97). There is no sense of camaraderie among the 'black shadows' who, having arrived in the capital in hope of work and a better future, are left, like the narrator, increasingly 'ragged and scruffy' (Uppdal 1982, 95). As the story opens, the narrator is kicked in the face by 'a newcomer', i.e. a new immigrant to the city, who has stolen his boat. Unable to offer these newcomers work, the city only seems to corrupt them with 'beer and wine and whisky and girls', or lure them to commit suicide: '[T]he river laughed and teased me: "Why don't you lie down in my embrace! You'll find no better embrace, you'll find no better rest. Come to me, you poor creature who cannot cope with this life"' (Uppdal 1982, 93, 97). The narrator describes the capital's dramatic saturation by referring to the constant flow of new construction workers hoping to pick up a few kroner, while other workers, like Little Kalle leave again in search of new opportunities. The story sketches out how immigration, one of the city's most important drives towards industrialisation in the first part of the century, transformed into one of its most complex problems.

The initial flow of capital and human resources towards Kristiania was, in fact, one of the most important factors that triggered the industrial expansion of the city and its consequent urban and socio-demographical transformations during the nineteenth century. In particular, the building activities in the capital not only needed continuous investment, but also created new employment opportunities. The latter attracted a great number of immigrants who caused unprecedented demographical growth: between 1815 and 1900, the number of inhabitants living in the capital jumped from 14,000 to 228,000 (Myhre 1995, 25, 78–94). However, by the time 'By Akerselva' was written, economic growth had slowed down and the demand for housing had reached its peak. In 1899 alone, Kristiania had a surplus of 14,000 immigrants, and building companies, despite their efforts, were not able to plan and carry out the construction of new blocks quickly enough to satisfy the demand (see Figure 4.2). The situation was so critical that local authorities even reached the point of offering a travel loan to immigrants who were homeless and wished to leave the capital (Baltzersen 1977, 149–50; Myhre 1994, 372–4). The poor immigrants to the city, namely the 'black shadows' Uppdal represents in his story, are affected by poverty, alcoholism and prostitution.

These three problems were all highlighted in the research by Eilert Sundt (1817–75), a Norwegian social scientist who in 1850 received a public grant to assess the living conditions of industrial workers in Norway (Baltzersen 1977, 77; Myhre 1994, 388–91).

It is not surprising that the narrator in Uppdal's story talks about his need to be intoxicated to numb physical and emotional pain, as excessive consumption of alcohol among the working class was related to social and psychological factors (Roberts 1992, 107–8). It is also not surprising that Sølvi, the girl from the narrator's village, who he meets at the end of the story, has ended up a prostitute. Explaining the reason behind her current situation, Sølvi states: 'I was working at a factory and earning five or six kroner a week, and I couldn't manage on that, so I began to walk the streets in the evenings' (Uppdal 1982, 100). Sølvi's condition was far from unusual: many women between 14 and 40 years of age were pushed to make the same choice for the same reason, especially since, besides earning only one third or half of men's wages for the work they did manage to find, they were often the first to be laid off in situations of crisis (Schiøtz 1977, 75–84, 158, 178 and Schiøtz 1979, 79).

Figure 4.2   The river Akerselva seen from Hausmann bridge (Hausmannsbro) looking towards Christian Krohgs gate. Photograph taken by the Norwegian photographer Martinius Skøien (1849–1916) between 1880 and 1910. Source: National Library of Norway.

While the modern 'trolls' live their static existence under boats at the edge of society, the big city and those who are still part of its activities continue to pulsate. As a new day begins, the narrator observes the city waking up as factory chimneys start to puff out smoke, houses wake up and trams start whirring along. In the heart of the big city there are still people who can earn their living and participate in Kristiania's new modern experiences: 'there were young and old people who came out with a flask of coffee in their hands and a lunch pack under their arms, dock workers in leather breeches and blue sweaters and with a clay pipe sticking out from a stubby face, and the girls for the factories' (Uppdal 1982, 95). While the East End (*østkanten*) established itself as the poor, industrial part of the city, the city centre became the core of the capital's activities. Industrial buildings – initially mostly located along the river

Figure 4.3 The painting 'Struggle for Survival' ('Kampen for tilværelsen', 1889) by the Norwegian naturalist painter and author Christian Krohg (1852–1925). Source: National Gallery of Norway.

Akerselva in order to make use of the available hydropower – spread further and further towards the city centre when steam engines and later electricity came into use, as here they could be closer to their distribution network, i.e. the harbour and the city's two railway stations, the West Station (Vestbanen, 1854) and the East Station (Østbanen, 1878) (Baltzersen 1977, 73–9). This in turn pushed the wealthier middle class westwards in the attempt to escape not only from the hustle and bustle of the industrial activities but also as far away as possible from the danger of the epidemics that regularly broke out in the overcrowded accommodation of industrial workers in the East End (Baltzersen 1977, 137; Moe 1972, 12; Myhre 1994, 92). *Vestkanten* is what Uppdal's narrator refers to as the 'fine houses' (Uppdal 1982, 96). This is where the 'black shadows' beg for food and are able to get 'bread crusts and other waste food' (Uppdal 1982, 96). In a conversation with other 'wretched tramps', the narrator discusses this common practice, immortalised in the painting *Struggle for Survival* (*Kampen for tilværelsen*, 1889) by the Norwegian naturalist painter and author Christian Krohg (1852–1925; see Figure 4.3). In fact, the whole of Uppdal's story is a representation of 'the cruel struggle for survival' (Uppdal 1982, 92), fuelled by the hope of social mobility, a hope that, despite the story's emphasis on immobility, is renewed at the end when the narrator and Sølvi decide to join forces in an attempt to make something of their lives.

Mobilities and Immobilities of Modernity

In the case studies dealt with in this chapter modernity equals mobility in the form of 'obligatory as well as voluntary forms of travel', and all the texts offer examples of how 'moving between places physically or virtually can be a source of status and power' (Hannam, Sheller and Urry 2006, 10). Hans Christian Andersen's own social and physical movement from a rural province to cosmopolitan Copenhagen and from there into the wider world was reflected in his lifelong fascination with modern transportation and communication technologies and the liberating yet still angst-provoking experiences of rapid modernisation and urbanisation.

For Matti and Liisa, travel is not necessary in the sense that they have to move beyond their idyllic rural home, but it becomes necessary as a social obligation. The railway takes over their minds as, through their visits to the parsonage, they realise that it has become an integral part of the community to which they belong. When they visit Lapinlahti station they initially have no intention of boarding the train, but they are given tickets and are physically pushed into a carriage by Ville, the former waterman who now repairs railway tracks. Their disappointing experience will, however, discourage them from joining in the enthusiasm others seem to display towards this new means of transport which has created a tangible connection between rural Finland and the rest of the world.

Matti and Liisa are not the only ones to be disillusioned by their experience of modernity. For the narrator in 'By Akerselva' and all the 'black shadows' who, like him, chose to travel to Kristiania in search of upward social mobility, there is nothing but disappointment, anger and downward mobility. For now, their existence has become immobile as they are stuck under upturned boats while the rest of the capital continues to take part in the modern life of the city. Only by joining forces, as the narrator and Sølvi do at the end of the story, will the 'black shadows', 'By Akerselva' suggests, change the downward spiral of their existences.

References

Aho, Juhani. 2012. *The Railroad*, translated by Owen Witesman. London: Norvik Press.

Andersen, Hans Christian. 1949. *The Complete Andersen*, translated by Jean Hersholt. New York: Heritage Press.

Andersen, Hans Christian. 1985. *A Visit to Germany, Italy and Malta, 1840–1841*, translated by Grace Thornton. London: Peter Owen.

Bakhtin, M.M. 1981a. 'Discourse in the Novel'. In *The Dialogic Imagination: Four Essays*, edited by Michael Holquist; translated by Caryl Emerson and Michael Holquist, 259–422. Austin: University of Texas Press.

Bakhtin, M.M. 1981b. *The Dialogic Imagination: Four Essays*, edited by Michael Holquist; translated by Caryl Emerson and Michael Holquist. Austin: University of Texas Press.

Baltzersen, Bjørn. 1977. *Ei bok om Oslo: Planlegging og byutvikling før 1950*. Oslo: Arkitekthøgskolen i Oslo.

Enflo, Kerstin, Eduard Alvarez-Palau and Jordi Marti-Henneberg. 2018. 'Transportation and Regional Inequality: The Impact of Railways in the Nordic Countries, 1860–1960', *Journal of Historical Geography* 62: 51–70.

Fraser, Benjamin and Steven D. Spalding. 2012a. 'Introduction: Riding the Rails: Cultures of Trains'. In *Trains, Culture, and Mobility: Riding the Rails*, edited by Benjamin Fraser and Steven D. Spalding, ix–xii. Lanham, MD: Lexington Books.

Fraser, Benjamin and Steven D. Spalding, eds. 2012b. *Trains, Culture, and Mobility: Riding the Rails*. Lanham, MD: Lexington Books.

Hannam, Kevin, Mimi Sheller and John Urry. 2006. 'Editorial: Mobilities, Immobilities and Moorings', *Mobilities* 1 (1): 1–22.

Hanson, Katherine and Judith Messick. 2001. 'Afterword'. In *Lucie*, by Amalie Skram; translated by Katherine Hanson and Judith Messick, 148–67. Norwich: Norvik Press.

Kjeldstadli, Knut and Jan Eivind Myhre. 1995. *Oslo – Spenningenes by: Oslohistorie*. Oslo: Pax Forlag.

Laitinen, Kai. 1998. 'The Rise of Finnish-Language Literature, 1860–1916'. In *A History of Finland's Literature*, edited by George C. Schoolfield, 64–144. Lincoln: University of Nebraska Press.

Ljungberg, Jonas and Lennart Schön. 2013. 'Domestic Markets and International Integration: Paths to Industrialisation in the Nordic Countries', *Scandinavian Economic History Review* 61 (2): 101–21.

Mishler, William. 1993. 'Norwegian Literature, 1910–1950'. In *A History of Norwegian Literature*, edited by Harald S. Naess, 200–76. Lincoln: University of Nebraska Press.

Mokyr, J. 2006. 'Successful Small Open Economies and the Importance of Good Institutions'. In *The Road to Prosperity: An Economic History of Finland*, edited by Jari Ojala, Jari Eloranta and Jukka Jalava, 3–17. Helsinki: Suomalaisen Kirjallisuuden Seura.

Myhre, Jan Eivind. 1994. *Oslo bys historie, bind 3: Hovedstaden Christiania fra 1814 til 1900*. Oslo: J.W. Cappelens Forlag AS.

Myhre, Jan Eivind and Jan Sigurd Østberg, eds. 1979. *Mennesker i Kristiania: Sosialhistorisk søkelys på 1800-tallet*. Oslo: Universitetsforlaget.

Naess, Harald S., ed. 1993. *A History of Norwegian Literature*. Lincoln: University of Nebraska Press.

Nevanlinna, Anja Kervanto. 2003. 'Following the Tracks – Railways in the City Centre of Helsinki: Bygone Past or Unwritten Urban History?'. In *The City and the Railway in Europe*, edited by Ralf Roth and Marie-Noëlle Polino, 203–20. Aldershot: Ashgate.

Nummi, Jyrki. 2012. 'Introduction: The Vanishing Idyll in Juhani Aho's *The Railroad*'. In *The Railroad*, by Juhani Aho; translated by Owen Witesman, 7–17. London: Norvik Press.

Ojala, Jari, Jari Eloranta and Jukka Jalava, eds. 2006. *The Road to Prosperity: An Economic History of Finland*. Helsinki: Suomalaisen Kirjallisuuden Seura.

Ostrauskaite, Milda. 2004. 'Kristofer Uppdal (1878–1961)'. In *Twentieth-Century Norwegian Writers* (Dictionary of Literary Biography 297), edited by Tanya Thresher, 307–13. Detroit: Gale.

Roberts, James S. 1992. 'Drink and Industrial Discipline in Nineteenth-Century Germany'. In *The Industrial Revolution and Work in Nineteenth-Century Europe*, edited by Lenard R. Berlanstein, 102–24. London: Routledge.

Roth, Ralf and Marie-Noëlle Polino. 2003a. 'Introduction: The City and the Railway in Europe'. In *The City and the Railway in Europe*, edited by Ralf Roth and Marie-Noëlle Polino, xvii–xxxvi. Aldershot: Ashgate.

Roth, Ralf and Marie-Noëlle Polino, eds. 2003b. *The City and the Railway in Europe*. Aldershot: Ashgate.

Schiøtz, Aina. 1977. *Prostitusjonen i Kristiania ca 1870–1890: En sosialhistorisk undersøkelse*. Oslo: Universitetet i Oslo.

Schiøtz, Aina. 1979. 'Prostitusjon og samfunn i 1870- og 1880-åras i Kristiania'. In *Mennesker i Kristiania: Sosialhistorisk søkelys på 1800-tallet*, edited by Jan Eivind Myhre and Jan Sigurd Østberg, 71–89. Oslo: Universitetsforlaget.

Schoolfield, George C., ed. 1998. *A History of Finland's Literature*. Lincoln: University of Nebraska Press.

Thresher, Tanya, ed. 2004. *Twentieth-Century Norwegian Writers* (Dictionary of Literary Biography 297). Detroit: Gale.

Uppdal, Kristofer. 1982. 'By Akerselva', translated by Janet Garton. In *Slaves of Love and Other Norwegian Short Stories*, edited by James McFarlane, 91–100. Oxford: Oxford University Press.

5
The Nordic Welfare Model

Mary Hilson

The five Nordic countries are often imagined as a unit, especially by the outside world. As the final chapter in this volume discusses, external stereotypes of the Nordic region have been crucial in shaping the internal self-images found in the Nordic countries. Moreover, these external stereotypes have often – though never exclusively – been positive, or even utopian. From the 1930s, foreign observers praised the Nordic region as a stable and democratic 'middle way' between the extremes of capitalism and communism, while from the 1980s and especially since the turn of the millennium it has become common to refer to the Scandinavian or Nordic model (Jalava and Stråth 2017). The exact meanings of the term Nordic model are disputed. Most scholars would probably agree, however, that it refers to the similarities in social and political development in the Nordic countries, including, among other things, the stability of parliamentary democracy; the preference for consensual solutions to social conflicts, especially in the labour market; and the universal, tax-funded welfare state (Hilson 2008).

This chapter focuses on the welfare state as perhaps the best-known feature of the so-called Nordic or Scandinavian model. The organisation of the chapter is inspired by the large Nordic research network on the Nordic welfare states, NordWel, which operated in 2007–14 under the title 'The Nordic Welfare State: Historical Foundations and Future Challenges' (NordWel 2018). In the first section, I briefly examine some of the attempts to classify different welfare regimes, and ask to what extent it is justifiable to speak of a distinctive Nordic welfare model. In the second part of the chapter, I consider the historical foundations of the Nordic welfare states and the main influences on their formation. Finally, I examine briefly some of the future challenges for the Nordic welfare states.

Welfare Models

The welfare state is not a Nordic invention. All societies have had to make some provision to take care of individuals who for reasons such as youth, old age, illness or accident are temporarily or permanently prevented from looking after themselves. Different societies have also developed more or less elaborate schemes by which individuals can either make provision for themselves (insurance against future ill luck) or others (for example religious codes on almsgiving). In the Nordic countries, like elsewhere in Europe, until the end of the nineteenth century welfare was provided through a combination of informal networks of family and neighbourhood, private philanthropy and locally administered Poor Laws (Christiansen and Markkola 2006, 15).

This changed from the late nineteenth century, as states began to take a greater interest in the welfare of their citizens. Their interest was triggered by several factors. First, the much greater scale of poverty and hardship engendered by urbanisation and industrial capitalism placed older poor relief schemes under great pressure. It also triggered fears of the consequences of ignoring such problems, whether this was of social unrest and potential revolution, or of the decline in the health and vigour of populations required to undertake productive work and to fight for their states. Second, democratic reforms and the mass mobilisation of new political parties representing the working classes created new political demands for welfare reforms, though it was often other parties that actually passed the necessary legislation. It should be noted, moreover, that although many of the European welfare states trace their earliest roots to the legislation on old-age pensions and other forms of social insurance passed during the two decades or so before the First World War, these provisions remained very limited. They were often means-tested and were intended to provide only the very basic minimum of assistance.

It is thus not until the mid-twentieth century that we can really begin to speak of welfare *states* as such, with the emergence of systems where the state became a major or even the main provider of welfare. Such arrangements were usually seen as part of broader socio-economic policy, a 'virtuous circle' where a healthy and well-educated workforce would contribute to increases in productivity, which would in turn stimulate economic growth and lead to greater welfare (Kettunen 2011). Here, the Nordic countries seem to stand out among other European countries for the comprehensiveness of their welfare systems and the extent to which welfare was provided by public institutions financed out of general taxation. But although the nation state came to be the natural frame for the provision of welfare, its development was a transnational phenomenon. National debates on welfare legislation were informed by the transnational exchange of ideas, and especially the experiences of advanced industrial countries such as Germany and Britain. Notable examples include the social insurance legislation introduced by Bismarck in Germany during the 1880s, and the proposals for social security made in William Beveridge's 1942 report in the UK, which was widely discussed in Sweden and Norway (Åmark 2005; Kettunen 2011). Transnational exchange was also important within the Nordic region.

Although shaped by transnational events and debates that were broadly similar, national welfare states did not develop identically, but were also shaped by what scholars refer to as 'path dependencies', which is the legacy of nationally specific historical developments, as well as by specific political choices (Petersen and Åmark 2006). An extensive body of scholarship in the comparative social sciences has shown how welfare states differ, for example according to whether they provide only a basic safety net distributed through means-testing, or universal services available to all citizens regardless of need. In turn this is linked to how welfare is financed – whether through general taxation, compulsory social insurance or private philanthropy – and the extent to which the state has a role as the main provider of welfare services such as healthcare and education, or whether it shares these responsibilities with other institutions. Many such typologies are possible, but probably the most influential is that developed by sociologist Gøsta Esping-Andersen (1990). According to Esping-Andersen, welfare states differed from each other in the extent to which they 'decommodified' social relations; in other words, the extent to which individuals were forced to rely on the market to meet their material needs (through selling their labour and buying goods and services), or were entitled to receive benefits and transfers as citizens. In turn, this meant that the welfare states were important in the ordering of social relations, with different types of welfare systems producing more, or less, equal societies.

Comparative analysis of data from 18 welfare states led Esping-Andersen to develop his famous 'three worlds' of welfare capitalism. In the liberal model, associated with the Anglo-Saxon countries, there was minimum provision of means-tested benefits, and social security systems thus tended to reproduce social stratification. In the corporatist or conservative model, associated with Central European welfare states, rights to welfare were linked to the status of individuals within the labour market through compulsory insurance schemes, and thus tended to reproduce existing social hierarchies. Finally, in the social-democratic welfare model, associated with the Nordic countries, social relations were highly decommodified; moreover, because benefits were universal, this reliance on the state rather than the market for welfare services also extended to the middle classes, so these states tended to undermine social hierarchies and produce more equal societies (Esping-Andersen 1990).

It must be noted that all attempts to classify welfare states deal in ideal types, and no welfare state can be expected to conform perfectly to the typology. Thus, even if the Nordic welfare states are considered ideal types in their provision of public sector, universal, tax-financed welfare, none of these characteristics is met entirely. The family continued to have a strong role in all of the Nordic welfare states, for example in the care of very young children or elderly parents. Nor were all benefits and services provided universally (Edling 2006). Klas Åmark's comparative history of the welfare state in Norway and Sweden found that welfare benefits tended to be directed towards male wage-earners in permanent full-time employment; other groups such as women and self-employed small farmers were much less well provided for (Åmark 2005). Esping-Andersen has been criticised for overlooking important aspects of the welfare state in his typology, not least the impact of welfare policies on gender relations (Emmenegger et al. 2015). The classification can also be criticised for emphasising social insurance and cash benefits as the main ways in which the welfare state functions, ignoring the goods and services that are provided in kind. The UK's National Health Service (NHS) is after all an example of the universal welfare state, delivering free healthcare to all citizens according to need.

Moreover, the development of the Nordic welfare states was uneven. Denmark and Sweden must be regarded as Nordic pioneers in the adoption of welfare reforms, especially neutral Sweden because of the exceptionally strong position of its economy after the Second World War. Norway, Finland and especially Iceland were less prosperous and remained largely agrarian societies until well into the post-war period, so that the major expansion of the welfare state did not take place until the 1970s. For this reason, welfare state historians have coined the phrase 'one model – five exceptions' to describe the Nordic welfare states (Christiansen and Markkola 2006). Nonetheless, there is a broad consensus that the Nordic welfare states do cluster as a group with certain shared characteristics (Hilson 2008). The idea of a 'Nordic model' of welfare may be understood in two ways. On the one hand, it functions as a heuristic device to shape comparative analyses of the welfare state and its development in the Nordic region. On the other, it has often served as a vision and a source of identity, shaping the exchange of policy ideas and the development of welfare legislation across the region.

Historical Roots of the Nordic Welfare States

What then is distinctive about the Nordic welfare states as they have developed in the twentieth century, in contrast to welfare regimes in other parts of Europe and beyond? The constraints of space mean that it is not possible to offer a comprehensive survey of the development of social policy in five countries, so instead the chapter explores two inter-related themes: first, the role of social democracy and other ideological influences; second, the importance of the state.

Is the Nordic model a social democratic model? The Swedish Social Democratic Party (SAP) claimed that it was, when in 2011 their appli-cation for copyright of the term was approved by the Swedish Patents Agency (Marklund 2013, 280). The designation carries two slightly dif-ferent meanings. On the one hand, it reflects the notion that social dem-ocratic parties were the principal architects of the welfare state, through their influence on legislation and policy while in government. On the other hand, in Esping-Andersen's (1990) typology the designation social democratic refers more broadly to the impact of welfare policies on the Nordic societies, above all the historically relatively high levels of social equality. There are various ways to calculate inequality and relative pov-erty, for example based on the share of income or wealth concentrated in the highest or lowest income groups, but on most measurements the Nordic countries continue to be characterised as relatively equal societies (World Inequality Database 2018). In 2016 inequality in the five Nordic countries remained lower than that in the UK, the US and the OECD aver-age, measured by the Gini index (OECD 2018). With the exception of Iceland, however, inequality had also increased during the decade since 2007, especially in Sweden (OECD 2016). According to Jørgen Goul Andersen, rising inequality in the Danish case could be attributed to changing policies and especially reforms that had made the tax system less progressive and redistributive (Goul Andersen 2018).

Historian Francis Sejersted (2011) referred to a 'social democratic order' in Norway and Sweden in the decades from the 1930s to the 1960s. The Nordic social democratic parties abandoned the Marxist-inspired commitment to class struggle relatively early and embraced instead a vision of modernity that included, among other things, the belief that individual freedom rested on material security; tolerance of capitalist enterprise as a means to provide that security, especially in the export sector; trust in technocratic solutions to economic and other problems; and the coupling of social democracy with national integration (Sejersted 2011).

In Sweden, the social democratic vision of the welfare state was encapsulated in the concept of the *folkhem* or people's home, as a metaphor for the new society. The term was first used by SAP leader Per Albin Hansson (Prime Minister 1932–46) in a speech to the *riksdag* (the Swedish parliament) in 1928, though it was actually borrowed from right-wing political discourses in the early twentieth century (Dahlqvist 2002). The *folkhem* expressed the vision of a welfare state that took care of its citizens from the cradle to the grave, and where individuals could expect to be treated equally regardless of social status, and kindly without the stigma that had been attached to earlier recipients of welfare benefits. The *folkhem* was to be built not just metaphorically, however, but also literally in bricks and mortar, through the state's investment in housing and social institutions that were designed to reflect expert opinion with regard to hygiene and rationality (Saarikangas 1997). The culmination of this thinking came with the Swedish government's famous 'Miljonprogram' that saw the construction of 1 million flats between 1965 and 1975 in new suburban developments (Östberg and Andersson 2013, 36–40).

Many of the leading politicians associated with welfare reforms in the Nordic countries were indeed Social Democrats: Per Albin Hansson, Gunnar and Alva Myrdal in Sweden; K.K Steincke and Thorvald Stauning in Denmark; Einar Gerhardsen and Johan Nygaardsvold in Norway. For some of them, like Sweden's Gustav Möller, their visions of a humane welfare system were shaped by their own formative experiences of poverty and hardship (Tilton 1991). But the Nordic welfare states were not exclusively the products of strong social democratic parties. First, the model does not hold true for Finland and Iceland, where communist parties had a much larger share of the working-class vote, and where different political models thus prevailed (Jonsson 2001; Kettunen 2001). In Iceland the dominant party of government was the centre-right Independence Party, while in Finland governments formed of broad political coalitions were more common. Second, even in Denmark, Norway and Sweden, social democratic parties were often obliged to form agreements with or govern in coalition with bourgeois parties. Indeed, it was only after the negotiation of red-green – so-called because they were negotiated between social democratic (red) and farmers' (green) parties – political compromises in the 1930s that they were able to gain parliamentary majorities. The passing of welfare legislation always rested on a process of compromise, for example in 1958 when the Swedish supplementary pension reform was agreed in the *riksdag* (Hilson 2008, 43–4).

Lutheranism and the Nordic Welfare State

A 'historical turn' in welfare state scholarship has drawn attention to other ideological influences on the development of the Nordic welfare states, and especially to the ideas that shaped the trajectories of the Nordic welfare states before the influence of social democracy. For example, Peter Baldwin (1989) has emphasised the role of agrarian liberal parties in securing welfare reforms during the 1890s and 1900s in Denmark and Sweden, and in doing so establishing the principle of (partial) universalism, which was to endure in later legislation.

Scholars have also debated the influence of religious cultures on the development of welfare states, noting of course that the Nordic countries are distinguished for being largely mono-confessional and dominated by Lutheran Protestantism (Markkola and Naumann 2014).[1] The Reformation created new understandings of poverty and established the principle that poor relief was a matter for collective responsibility. The evolution of poor relief systems after the Reformation was of course a long and complex process, but historians of Denmark in particular have paid increased attention to the influence of a specifically Lutheran morality through the early modern poor laws into the first universal welfare reforms of the late nineteenth century (Koefoed 2017; Petersen 2016, 2018).

An important legacy of the Reformation was the close relationship established between the state and the reformed Protestant church (Knudsen 2000). Responsibility for the poor laws rested with the state, but relief was administered through the local parish structures, with pastors inevitably playing an important role in this process (Markkola 2011; Koefoed 2017). It cannot be assumed that there was an unbroken continuity between the Reformation in the sixteenth century and the emergence of the modern welfare states in the twentieth. But it is often suggested that the general perception of the state as a largely benign institution, and a broad tolerance of its interventions in citizens' lives, is a peculiar characteristic of the Nordic societies that owes something to the Lutheran influence (Sørensen and Stråth 1997). Moreover, the Lutheran church has also been cited as an important influence on the curbing of corruption in the Nordic states (Frisk Jensen 2018), the legacy of which has been relatively high levels of trust in the effectiveness of public institutions. Some social scientists have also argued more broadly for the importance of social capital and trust at the micro level in explaining support for the universal welfare state in Scandinavian societies (Svendsen and Svendsen 2016), though this is of course extremely difficult to measure accurately in a comparative context. During the twentieth century, representatives of the state Lutheran Churches were often uneasy about or even openly critical of the welfare state, which they feared would undermine traditional moralities and family ties (Markkola 2014).

Critiques of the Welfare State

From the 1960s, new criticisms of the welfare state started to emerge. On the political left, a new generation of activists radicalised by the upheavals of 1968 criticised welfare policy for falling short in its aims to improve equality and undermine class differences, while those on the right argued that the welfare state stifled individual choice and entrepreneurship, 'crowding out' resources from the private sector (Einhorn and Logue 2003, 305–24). The immediate consequences of this were seen in the emergence of new political parties campaigning against high taxes and bureaucracy in the early 1970s (Arter 2006, 89), which foreshadowed the rising influence of neoliberalism in the 1990s and after.

Inspired partly by Michel Foucault's theorisation of the operation of power (Gould 2001), from the 1970s feminist scholars turned their critical attention to the welfare state, examining its role in the creation and consolidation of social norms (Hirdman 1989; Åmark 2004). The welfare state had undoubtedly helped improve the lives of women as well as men, but it needed to go further in reforming gender relations, in particular through interventions in family life such as support for parental leave and collective childcare. Such questions had been discussed earlier – for example by Swedish Social Democrat Alva Myrdal during the 1930s – but it was only from the 1970s that there was a substantial increase in support for the so-called 'dual breadwinner' model, that is families where both parents undertake paid work outside the home following the birth of children. There were also differences between the Nordic welfare states, with gender differences remaining stronger far later in Norway for example (Sainsbury 2001). It has often been noted that the Nordic labour markets remained highly gender segregated, so that in many cases women moved from unpaid care work in the home to paid care work outside it, in welfare state institutions such as nurseries and care homes for the elderly (Lewis and Åström 1992).

During the 1990s another historical aspect of the welfare state attracted public attention, namely the practice of compulsory eugenic sterilisation. Eugenics originated in nineteenth-century evolutionary science and was widely debated across Europe and North America during the late nineteenth and early twentieth centuries. Eugenics, or 'race hygiene', referred to the study of the influence of hereditary factors on the population and interventions to prevent the transmission of what were regarded as undesirable hereditary disorders between generations, with the aim of improving the quality of the population as a whole (Koch 2010, 34–9). There were two waves of eugenic thought: 'mainline eugenics' from the late nineteenth century was based on the idea of racial difference; 'reform eugenics' during the 1930s was informed by new thinking about genetics (Roll-Hansen 2005).

In the Nordic countries, discussions of the 'social question' in the early twentieth century were connected to fears about population decline due to falling birth rates. What was unusual about the Nordic countries in an international context was that these ideas resulted in legislation allowing the compulsory sterilisation of individuals for whom reproduction was deemed undesirable, such as those with hereditary mental or physical disorders (Broberg and Roll-Hansen 2005). These groups were also prevented from marrying. Estimates of the numbers affected by these policies vary, but sterilisations were carried out on tens of thousands of individuals across the region between the 1930s and the 1960s (Roll-Hansen 2005, 263). Although Nordic eugenics legislation was not specifically based on the pseudo-scientific racial theories associated with Nazi Germany, certain minority groups such as travellers were nonetheless targeted, because they were perceived to deviate from desirable norms of behaviour for 'productive' members of society (Spektorowski and Mizrachi 2004; Broberg and Tydén 2005, 124–30). It should also be noted that women were significantly over-represented in the numbers sterilised (Runcis 1998, 277). Eugenic sterilisation was abandoned in all the Nordic countries during the 1970s, but the issue became headline news in Sweden in the summer of 1997, leading to public enquiries and the adoption of compensation schemes for the victims of eugenic sterilisation (Broberg and Tydén 1998).

The Future of the Nordic Welfare States

The early 1990s was a difficult period for the welfare state; one might even say a crisis. Several developments combined simultaneously. The fall of the Soviet Union placed neoliberalism in the ascendancy: across the world politicians referred to the need to roll back the state, tackle welfare dependency and introduce market reforms into public institutions. In Sweden and Finland, the effects of this paradigmatic shift were exacerbated by a very severe recession during the early 1990s, and in 1991 a new bourgeois government took office in Sweden on a platform of welfare retrenchment (Timonen 2003). This shift did not come out of the blue of course; as noted above, it marked the culmination of a political critique of the public sector that had been developing since the 1970s. But longer-term challenges were also mounting, not least the demographic problems – faced by societies across Europe – of an ageing population and rising dependency ratios (see Sejersted 2011, 388–430).

What was remarkable, however, was not the demise of the Nordic welfare model that some had predicted, but its apparent resilience. At the turn of the new millennium, social scientists largely concurred that the twin challenges of globalisation and European integration had not significantly undermined the distinctiveness of the Nordic welfare states in a European context (Kautto et al. 2001; Kuhnle 2000). Popular support for the welfare state remained high, and political parties on both right and left presented themselves as the defenders of the unique Nordic welfare systems. Historian Pauli Kettunen (2011) has noted the paradox of the Nordic model in current debates: on the one hand, it requires defending against the threats of globalisation; on the other, it also offers the key to successful competition in a globalised world, underpinned by global league tables indicating the success of the Nordic countries in various criteria. An exception was perhaps Iceland, where politicians embraced an extreme version of neoliberal speculative capitalism during the early 2000s, but returned to elements of a more recognisable Nordic welfare model after the crash in 2008 (Ólafsson 2011).

There seems little doubt that the welfare state is now established as an essential element of the regional and national brand in the Nordic countries (Marklund 2016). After the turn of the millennium, and especially following the global financial crisis which began in 2008, international attention once more focused on the Nordic countries, with *The Economist* famously proclaiming the region to be 'the next supermodel' in 2013 (*The Economist* 2013). Nonetheless, the discourse of the welfare state has changed fundamentally. Foreign politicians now look to the Nordic countries not only as an example of social-democratic paradise (or dystopia), but also for examples of how to successfully introduce market reforms and competition into the provision of services such as healthcare and education (Hoctor 2017). In societies which are by any measure prosperous, welfare is no longer merely a matter of material security but also of well-being, where the different Nordic countries compete with each other for the accolade of 'world's happiest nation', but at the same time publicly debate concerns about rising levels of anxiety and stress.

Two challenges seemed to be especially prominent in 2019. The first concerns transnational mobility and citizenship. Who is the welfare state for? Mass immigration might logically seem to provide a potential solution to the challenge of an ageing indigenous population, but it is rarely regarded as such. Instead, in common with the rest of Europe, the Nordic countries have seen a steady rise in support for populist parties campaigning on a platform of 'welfare chauvinism' and nativism (Jungar and Jupskås 2014). These parties argue that access to the welfare state should be restricted to those holding full citizenship, which is moreover increasingly likely to be conceived in terms of cultural exclusivity.

A second challenge is the prospect of environmental crisis and responses to it. During the post-war period the welfare state was based on growing material prosperity and rising consumption (Andersson 2003), which was in turn based on the exploitation of natural resources, especially cheap energy. The first major challenge to the expansion of the welfare state came with the oil crisis of the early 1970s. Norway was exceptional in this respect, where the discovery of rich oil resources in the North Sea contributed to the country's exceptionally high levels of prosperity and welfare (Halvorsen and Stjernø 2008, 147–50). But it is also widely agreed that this is not sustainable in the long term. A major challenge for all the Nordic countries will be the need to adapt economies and societies based largely on fossil fuels, while also trying to maintain the high standards of living associated with the Nordic welfare model.

Will there continue to be a Nordic welfare model? The term is used to refer to common patterns in the development of social policies in the Nordic countries during the twentieth and twenty-first centuries – and even before – and the outcomes of these policies measured by social indicators such as equality. The Nordic countries are certainly not identical, whether in social policy or in any other field, but there do seem to be enough similarities between them to warrant analysis of them as a distinctive group in a European or global context. However, two observations may be made in conclusion. First, there was never a coherent blueprint for the development of the Nordic welfare states; as in other countries, social policy was formed piecemeal through a constant process of negotiation, conflict and compromise. Second, the Nordic welfare states are not, nor have they ever been, static constructions. The meanings of welfare and the policies needed to achieve it will doubtless continue to be a topic of heated debate for many years to come in the Nordic countries as in other societies.

Note

1. There are historical religious minorities in Norden, including small Jewish and Catholic communities, followers of the Orthodox Church in Finland and indigenous Sami religions, for example. From the eighteenth century the monopoly of the state Lutheran churches was challenged by pietism, with different consequences across the region. From the late twentieth century other religions such as Islam have also become more prominent. However, it would be hard to deny that at least until then the Nordic societies were religiously homogeneous to a much greater degree than most of the rest of Europe.

References

Åmark, Klas. 2004. 'Trygghet och tvång – två teman i aktuell nordisk välfärdsstatshistorisk forskning', *Arkiv för studier i arbetarrörelsens historia* 91: 1–18.

Åmark, Klas. 2005. *Hundra år av välfärdspolitik: Välfärdsstatens framväxt i Norge och Sverige*. Umeå: Boréa Bokförlag.

Andersson, Jenny. 2003. *Mellan tillväxt och trygghet: Idéer om produktiv socialpolitik i socialdemokratisk socialpolitisk ideologi under efterkrigstiden* (Uppsala Studies in Economic History 67). Uppsala: Uppsala Universitet.

Arter, David. 2016. *Scandinavian Politics Today*. 3rd ed. Manchester: Manchester University Press.

Baldwin, Peter. 1989. 'The Scandinavian Origins of the Social Interpretation of the Welfare State', *Comparative Studies in Society and History* 31 (1): 3–24.

Broberg, Gunnar and Nils Roll-Hansen, eds. 2005. *Eugenics and the Welfare State: Norway, Sweden, Denmark, and Finland*. Rev. ed. East Lansing: Michigan State University Press.

Broberg, Gunnar and Mattias Tydén. 1998. 'När svensk historia blev en världsnyhet: Steriliseringspolitiken och medierna', *Tvärsnitt: Humanistisk och samhällsvetenskaplig forskning* 3: 2–15.

Broberg, Gunnar and Mattias Tydén. 2005. 'Eugenics in Sweden: Efficient Care'. In *Eugenics and the Welfare State: Norway, Sweden, Denmark, and Finland*, edited by Gunnar Broberg and Nils Roll-Hansen, 77–150. Rev. ed. East Lansing: Michigan State University Press.

Christiansen, Niels Finn and Pirjo Markkola. 2006. 'Introduction'. In *The Nordic Model of Welfare: A Historical Reappraisal*, edited by Niels Finn Christiansen, Klaus Petersen, Nils Edling and Per Haave, 9–29. Copenhagen: Museum Tusculanum Press.

Dahlqvist, Hans. 2002. 'Folkhemsbegreppet: Rudolf Kjellén vs. Per Albin Hansson', *Historisk Tidskrift* 122 (3): 445–65.

Edling, Nils. 2006. 'Limited Universalism: Unemployment Insurance in Northern Europe 1900–2000'. In *The Nordic Model of Welfare: A Historical Reappraisal*, edited by Niels Finn Christiansen, Klaus Petersen, Nils Edling and Per Haave, 99–143. Copenhagen: Museum Tusculanum Press.

Einhorn, Eric S. and John Logue. 2003. *Modern Welfare States: Scandinavian Politics and Policy in the Global Age*. 2nd ed. Westport, CT: Praeger Publishers.

Emmenegger, Patrick, Jon Kvist, Paul Marx and Klaus Petersen. 2015. 'Three Worlds of Welfare Capitalism: The Making of a Classic', *Journal of European Social Policy* 25 (1): 3–13.

Esping-Andersen, Gøsta. 1990. *The Three Worlds of Welfare Capitalism*. Cambridge: Polity Press.

Frisk Jensen, Mette. 2018. 'The Building of the Scandinavian States: Establishing Weberian Bureaucracy and Curbing Corruption from the Mid-Seventeenth to the End of the Nineteenth Century'. In *Bureaucracy and Society in Transition: Comparative Perspectives*, edited by Haldor Byrkjeflot and Fredrik Engelstad, 179–203. Bingley: Emerald Publishing.

Goul Andersen, Jørgen. 2018. 'Globalisering og stigende økonomisk ulighed – økonomi eller politik?', *Økonomi og politik* 91: 46–64.

Gould, Arthur. 2001. *Developments in Swedish Social Policy: Resisting Dionysus*. Basingstoke: Palgrave.

Halvorsen, Knut and Steinar Stjernø. 2008. *Work, Oil and Welfare: The Welfare State in Norway*. Oslo: Universitetsforlaget.

Hilson, Mary. 2008. *The Nordic Model: Scandinavia since 1945*. London: Reaktion Books.

Hirdman, Yvonne. 1989. *Att lägga livet till rätta: Studier i svensk folkhemspolitik*. Stockholm: Carlsson.

Hoctor, Thomas. 2017. 'The Nordic Model and British Public Policy c. 1997–2015: Social Democratic Mythology or Free-Market Supermodel?'. PhD thesis, University College London.

Jalava, Marja and Bo Stråth. 2017. 'Scandinavia/Norden'. In *European Regions and Boundaries: A Conceptual History*, edited by Diana Mishkova and Balázs Trencsényi, 36–56. New York: Berghahn Books.

Jonsson, Gudmundur. 2001. 'The Icelandic Welfare State in the Twentieth Century', *Scandinavian Journal of History* 26 (3): 249–67.

Jungar, Ann-Cathrine and Anders Ravik Jupskås. 2014. 'Populist Radical Right Parties in the Nordic Region: A New and Distinct Party Family?', *Scandinavian Political Studies* 37 (3): 215–38.

Kautto, Mikko, Johan Fritzell, Bjørn Hvinden, Jon Kvist and Hannu Uusitalo, eds. 2001. *Nordic Welfare States in the European Context*. London: Routledge.

Kettunen, Pauli. 2001. 'The Nordic Welfare State in Finland', *Scandinavian Journal of History* 26 (3): 225–47.

Kettunen, Pauli. 2011. 'The Transnational Construction of National Challenges: The Ambiguous Nordic Model of Welfare and Competitiveness'. In *Beyond Welfare State Models: Transnational Historical Perspectives on Social Policy*, edited by Pauli Kettunen and Klaus Petersen, 16–40. Cheltenham: Edward Elgar Publishing.

Knudsen, Tim, ed. 2000. *Den nordiske protestantisme og velfærdsstaten*. Aarhus: Aarhus Universitetsforlag.

Koch, Lene. 2010. *Racehygiejne i Danmark 1920–1956*. 2nd ed. Copenhagen: Informations Forlag.

Koefoed, Nina Javette. 2017. 'Social Responsibilities in the Protestant North: Denmark and Sweden'. In *The Dynamics of Religious Reform in Northern Europe, 1780–1920, Volume IV: Charity and Social Welfare*, edited by Leen Van Molle, 251–80. Leuven: Leuven University Press.

Kuhnle, Stein. 2000. 'The Scandinavian Welfare State in the 1990s: Challenged but Viable', *West European Politics* 23 (2): 209–28.

Lewis, Jane and Gertrude Åström. 1992. 'Equality, Difference, and State Welfare: Labor Market and Family Policies in Sweden', *Feminist Studies* 18 (1): 59–87.

Markkola, Pirjo. 2011. 'The Lutheran Nordic Welfare States'. In *Beyond Welfare State Models: Transnational Historical Perspectives on Social Policy*, edited by Pauli Kettunen and Klaus Petersen, 102–18. Cheltenham: Edward Elgar Publishing.

Markkola, Pirjo. 2014. 'Focusing on the Family: The Lutheran Church and the Making of the Nordic Welfare State in Finland, 1940s to 1960s', *Journal of Church and State* 56 (1): 60–80.

Markkola, Pirjo and Ingela K. Naumann. 2014. 'Lutheranism and the Nordic Welfare States in Comparison', *Journal of Church and State* 56 (1): 1–12.

Marklund, Carl. 2013. 'A Swedish Norden or a Nordic Sweden? Image Politics in the West during the Cold War'. In *Communicating the North: Media Structures and Images in the Making of the Nordic Region*, edited by Jonas Harvard and Peter Stadius, 263–87. Farnham: Ashgate.

Marklund, Carl. 2017. 'The Nordic Model on the Global Market of Ideas: The Welfare State as Scandinavia's Best Brand', *Geopolitics* 22 (3): 623–39.

NordWel. n d. 'Nordic Centre of Excellence: The Nordic Welfare State – Historical Foundations and Future Challenges (NordWel)'. Accessed 5 July 2018. https://blogs.helsinki.fi/nord-wel/.

OECD COPE (Centre for Opportunity and Equality). 2016. 'Income Inequality Remains High in the Face of Weak Recovery'. Accessed 14 October 2019. https://www.oecd.org/social/OECD2016-Income-Inequality-Update.pdf.

OECD IDD (Income Distribution Database). 2019. 'OECD Income Distribution Database (IDD): Gini, Poverty, Income, Methods and Concepts'. Accessed 14 October 2019. http://www.oecd.org/social/income-distribution-database.htm.

Ólafsson, Stefán. 2011. 'Icelandic Capitalism: From Statism to Neoliberalism and Financial Collapse'. In *The Nordic Varieties of Capitalism*, edited by Lars Mjøset, 1–51. Bingley: Emerald Group Publishing.

Östberg, Kjell and Jenny Andersson. 2013. *Sveriges Historia, Volume 8: 1965–2012*. Stockholm: Norstedt.

Petersen, Jørn Henrik. 2016. *Fra Luther til konkurrencestaten*. Odense: Syddansk Universitetsforlag.

Petersen, Jørn Henrik. 2018. 'Martin Luther and the Danish Welfare State', *Lutheran Quarterly* 32: 1–27.

Petersen, Klaus and Klas Åmark. 2006. 'Old Age Pensions in the Nordic Countries, 1880–2000'. In *The Nordic Model of Welfare: A Historical Reappraisal*, edited by Niels Finn Christiansen, Klaus Petersen, Nils Edling and Per Haave, 145–88. Copenhagen: Museum Tusculanum Press.

Roll-Hansen, Nils. 2005. 'Conclusion: Scandinavian Eugenics in the International Context'. In *Eugenics and the Welfare State: Norway, Sweden, Denmark, and Finland*, edited by Gunnar Broberg and Nils Roll-Hansen, 259–71. Rev. ed. East Lansing: Michigan State University Press.

Runcis, Maija. 1998. *Steriliseringar i folkhemmet*. Stockholm: Ordfront.

Saarikangas, Kirsi. 1997. 'The Policies of Modern Home: Organization of the Everyday in Swedish and Finnish Housing Design from the 1930s to the 1950s'. In *Models, Modernity and the Myrdals*, edited by Pauli Kettunen and Hanna Eskola, 81–108. Helsinki: Renvall Institute for Area and Cultural Studies.

Sainsbury, Diane. 2001. 'Gender and the Making of Welfare States: Norway and Sweden', *Social Politics* 8 (1): 113–43.

Sejersted, Francis. 2011. *The Age of Social Democracy: Norway and Sweden in the Twentieth Century*, edited by Madeleine B. Adams; translated by Richard Daly. Princeton: Princeton University Press.

Sørensen, Øystein and Bo Stråth. 1997. 'Introduction: The Cultural Construction of Norden'. In *The Cultural Construction of Norden*, edited by Øystein Sørensen and Bo Stråth, 1–24. Oslo: Scandinavian University Press.

Spektorowski, Alberto and Elisabet Mizrachi. 2004. 'Eugenics and the Welfare State in Sweden: The Politics of Social Margins and the Idea of a Productive Society', *Journal of Contemporary History* 39 (3): 333–52.

Svendsen, Gunnar Lind Haase and Gert Tinggaard Svendsen. 2016. *Trust, Social Capital and the Scandinavian Welfare State: Explaining the Flight of the Bumblebee*. Cheltenham: Edward Elgar Publishing.

The Economist. 2013. 'Special Report: The Next Supermodel: Why the World Should Look at the Nordic Countries', *The Economist*, 2 February. http:www.economist.com/leaders/2013/02/02/the-next-supermodel.

Tilton, Tim. 1991. *The Political Theory of Swedish Social Democracy: Through the Welfare State to Socialism*. Oxford: Clarendon Press.

Timonen, Virpi. 2003. *Restructuring the Welfare State: Globalization and Social Policy Reform in Finland and Sweden*. Cheltenham: Edward Elgar Publishing.

WID (World Inequality Database). n.d. 'World Inequality Database'. Accessed 14 January 2019. https://wid.world.

Part II
Texts

6

The Trial of Bróka-Auðr: Invisible Bureaucracy in an Icelandic Saga

Richard Cole

A philistine might say that the Sagas of Icelanders (*Íslendingasögur*) are some of humankind's most elegant stories, told by some of humankind's clumsiest storytellers. True, their prose style reads much better in Old Norse than it does in English translation. Nonetheless, even when reading them in the original language, one cannot fail to notice that the mainstays of the modern narrative voice are either sparingly used or entirely absent from most *Íslendingasögur*: descriptive simile is almost unknown, as is the direct reporting of characters' thoughts, feelings or stream of consciousness (Hallberg 1962, 70–1, 76–80).[1] In contrast to modern literature, the maxim seems to be 'show, don't tell' – and even then, 'don't show too much'.

The object of our study, *Laxdæla saga*, is one of the *Íslendingasögur* most likely to be found on an introductory saga reading list, alongside *Egils saga*, *Hrafnkels saga*, *Grettis saga*, *Njáls saga* and, to a lesser extent, *Eyrbyggja saga* or *Gísla saga*. Written in Iceland around 1230–60, *Laxdæla saga* yields up more aesthetic treasures than the other six classics. As Magnús Magnússon and Hermann Pálsson put it: 'There is about it the air of a pageant – a style that luxuriates in descriptions of ornate occasions [...] a surface glitter' (1969, 41). But we would have to concede to our philistine that in the description of the tale of Bróka-Auðr, even *Laxdæla saga* has left a space in between what it tells us and how we imagine the characters must have felt. Such lacunae present excellent opportunities for literary criticism of the sagas. In what follows, we will recount the career of Auðr's marriage, the infraction she supposedly commits and the revenge she takes, and consider her consequent 'trial' alongside another perplexing literary trial: the possibly more widely known one narrated by Franz Kafka in his novel of the same name.

The Life and Times of Bróka-Auðr

Auðr is first introduced in chapter 32 of *Laxdæla saga* as the wife of the dashing Þórðr Glúmsson. The introduction is not promising: 'Þórðr átti systur þeira Þorkels, er Auðr hét; ekki var hon væn kona né gǫrvilig. Þórðr unni henni lítit; hafði hann mjǫk slœgzk til fjár, því at þar stóð auðr mikill saman' (*Laxd,* 87), (Þórðr was married to Þorkell's sister, who was called Auðr; she was not a beautiful woman nor an accomplished one. Þórðr had little love for her; he had really got married for money, because there was a great deal of wealth there.)[2] It could hardly have escaped an Old Norse-speaking audience that Auðr is also a noun, *auðr*, meaning 'riches, wealth, opulence' (Cleasby and Vigfússon 1874, 32). Her name underlines that Auðr is nothing more to her husband than a means of social advancement.

Þórðr meets Guðrún Ósvífrsdóttir: 'hon var kvenna vænst, er upp óxu á Íslandi, bæði at ásjánu ok vitsmunum [...] Allra kvenna var hon kœnst ok bezt orði farin' (*Laxd.,* 86). (She was the most beautiful woman who grew up in Iceland, both in appearance and by her wit [...] She was the cleverest and most eloquent of all women.) Things must take their course, it seems: the beautiful people of Iceland are destined to be together (for better or worse, in Guðrún's case), at the expense of anyone who has the misfortune to be perceived as average. The saga author, withholding their own judgement in typical saga style (Jón Helgason 1934, 135–6), only comments that: 'fell þar mǫrg umrœða á um kærleika þeira Þórðar ok Guðrúnar (93). There was much talk of love between Þórðr and Guðrún'.)[3]

But the affair is not only complicated by Þórðr's marriage to Auðr. Guðrún is also married, to Þorvaldr Halldórsson. The marriage is doomed from the start – Guðrún is just fifteen years old, is not consulted beforehand and her father seems to have arranged the match exclusively for money. Nothing positive is said of Þorvaldr, and at least one thing is said which indicates that the saga author did not intend him as a sympathetic character: He 'talaði óharðfœrliga' (spoke uncombatively) when presented with outrageous financial demands from Guðrún's father, implying a degree of spinelessness. A turning point soon comes when Þorvaldr commits an act of domestic violence against Guðrún (an act which probably did nothing further to endear him to audiences then, just as now):

On the same evening Þórðr came there. Guðrún told him of this humiliation and asked how she ought to repay it. Þórðr smiled and said: 'I know a good piece of advice here. Make a shirt for him with the neck-hole so wide that it is grounds for divorce, and declare yourself divorced for this reason'.

(Laxd., 94)[4]

The crucial detail here is that, in the world depicted by *Laxdæla saga*, if one's spouse cross-dresses, a divorce is to be automatically granted. (How far the world depicted by *Laxdæla saga* corresponded to the realities of late tenth-century Iceland is a different question, to which we will return.) Guðrún later suggests that the same legal principle be applied to Auðr:

> then Guðrún said: 'Is it true, Þórðr, that Auðr, your wife, is always going around in trousers with a codpiece, with legbindings tied all the way down?'[5] He said he hadn't noticed that. 'You're not paying her much attention then', says Guðrún, 'why else would it be that she is called Breeches-Auðr?' Þórðr said: 'I don't think she's been called that for very long.' Guðrún replies: 'The thing which will make more difference to her is whether she has this name for long from now on'.

(Laxd., 95)

While Þórðr actually *did* wear a shirt with too much décolletage, albeit unwittingly, everything in the above passage suggests that Auðr does *not* actually wear trousers. Auðr's innocence has been recognised by several commentators on the scene (e.g. Jesch 1991, 193; Meulengracht-Sørensen 1980, 26; Wolf 1997). Saga narratives often deploy a wry tone and *Laxdæla saga* especially so. When the author has Þórðr say that he has not noticed his wife's supposed trousers, and that people could not have been calling her 'Bróka-Auðr' (*brók* means 'trousers') for long, these are signs that Guðrún is starting a rumour rather than pointing out reality (Wolf 1997, 679). In this regard, Auðr's experience differs from Þorvaldr's. He was made a cross-dresser by accident. She was made a cross-dresser by accusation. She *does* wear trousers when she rides to inflict her revenge on Þórðr, but that is after the marriage is undone. The damaging nickname is given a chance to percolate, before events take the following turn:

> One day Þórðr Ingunnarson asked Guðrún what it would cost a woman if she went around in trousers like a man. Guðrún replies:[6] 'If women go about dressed as men they get the same treatment as

a man who has a shirt so low-cut that you can see his nipples. In both cases, it's grounds for divorce.' Then Þórðr said: 'What are you saying I should do, that I should declare myself divorced from Auðr here at the þing or in the district? And [if the latter] I could do so with the support of more people, because the sort of people who would consider this an offence are proud-minded.' A moment later, Guðrún answers: 'Time waits for no man.' Then Þórðr sprang to his feet at once and went to the Law-rock and named witnesses, that he was declaring himself divorced from Auðr, and gave as a reason that she wore seated-breeches like mannish women do.[7] Auðr's brothers didn't like this very much, but stay silent. Þórðr rides away from the þing with the sons of Ósvífr. And when Auðr found out this news, she then said: 'It's good to know. I have been left all alone'.

(*Laxd.*, 96)

Auðr's verse is short and simple, lacking the ostentatious impenetrability of 'good' skaldic poetry. Perhaps this was intended to reflect Auðr's mediocrity, although its directness also gives us insight into her anguish – indeed, by speaking plainly, Auðr at this moment seems to be the only sane person in a society that otherwise is acting rather absurdly.[8] Why have people chosen to believe a completely unsubstantiated rumour? Is the legal procedure nothing more than a declaration without investigation? Why do the people who should be sticking up for Auðr stay silent? Why are these transvestism laws in place anyway? We will return to all these questions, but for now the case of Bróka-Auðr continues:

The next summer the people of Hóll took to their summer pastures in Hvammsdalr. Auðr was at the summer pastures. The men of Laugar took to their summer pastures in Lambadalr […] Auðr asks the man who watched the cattle how often he met the shepherd from Laugar, 'and you must tell me, what people are in the winter houses or the summer pastures, and speak with Þórðr just as politely as you are supposed to.' The lad promises to do as she said. And in the evening, when the shepherd came back, Auðr asks him for news. The shepherd replies: 'I have found out some news which you'll like, that there is a wide landing between Þórðr and Guðrún's beds,[9] because she is at the summer pastures, and he is plugging away putting up outbuildings, and Ósvífr is with him at the winter-houses.' 'You've done a good job nosing about', she says, 'now, get two horses saddled while people are going to sleep'.

(*Laxd.*, 97)

If the reader suspects that Auðr is up to something, they are right:

> The shepherd lad did as he was told, and shortly before sunset Auðr mounted up, and she was certainly wearing trousers then. The shepherd lad rode the other horse and could hardly keep up with her, for she was spurring on her mount so fiercely. [Auðr arrives at Laugur]. She went into the kitchen and up to the bed-closet in which Þórðr lay sleeping. The door was drawn to, but the bolt was not. She got into the bed-closet, and Þórðr slept on, [turning out to be] sleeping on his back. Then Auðr woke Þórðr, and he turned over onto his side when he saw that a person had come in there. Then she drew her sword and struck at Þórðr and gave him a great wound which landed on his right arm. Then he was wounded across both his nipples. She struck so fiercely that the sword bit into the bed-stead.

Auðr makes her escape, and then:

> Þórðr tried to spring to his feet when he got the wound, but it didn't work out that way because he was weakened from blood-loss. At this Ósvífr woke up and asked what had been going on, and Þórðr said he had been wounded. Ósvífr asks if he knew who had done this to him, and got up and bandaged his wounds. Þórðr said he thought it had been Auðr who did it. Ósvífr offered to ride after her, saying she probably did not have many men with her, and that she deserved retribution. Þórðr said it could not go that way. He said she had done what she had to do. Auðr came home at sunrise, and her brothers asked her where she had been. Auðr said she had been to Laugar and told them what events had occurred during her journey. They responded happily to that and said not enough had been done.
>
> (*Laxd.*, 97–8)

Grounds for Divorce?

The law against cross-dressing which undoes first Þorvaldr and then Auðr is attested only in *Laxdæla saga*. Something reminiscent of it is found in the twelfth-century Icelandic law code *Grágás*, which is often understood to reflect elements of earlier jurisprudence: 'Ef maðr feldr ser til velar við kono [...] varðar þat fiorbavgs garð [...] Ef konor gerz sva af siða at þær ganga ikarlfötom eða hverngi carla sið […] varðar þat fiorbavgs garð' (*Grg*, 47). (If a man puts on a woman's headdress […] it is punishable by lesser outlawry […] If a woman makes it her custom to wear men's clothes or adopt any sort of manly habits […] it is punishable by lesser outlawry.)[10] However, while an outlawed person might well struggle to maintain a romantic relationship, this is not the same penalty as instant divorce. It has been suggested that the law as presented in *Laxdæla saga* is a remembering of a pre-Christian law, perhaps coloured by Christian legal culture (Einar Ól. Sveinsson 1934, 94 n3). However, this hypothesis is complicated by the fact that, while medieval Christians often took a dim view of cross-dressing (Bullough 1982, 43–54) canon lawyers did not discuss the issue with regards to marriage. Moreover, to maintain that *Laxdæla saga* remembers a tenth-century law correctly would necessitate that *Grágás* is remembering it incorrectly, or that there were in fact two laws and *Grágás* has entirely forgotten one. This proposition is unappealing, given that *Grágás* is older than *Laxdæla saga*.

Auðr's predicament becomes still more suspicious when we consider that, although Þórðr was the first to mention the law that a man could not wear a womanly shirt, he apparently does not know about the inverse principle. Guðrún has to point it out to him, even though he is supposedly an accomplished lawyer (Wolf 1997, 677). Has the thirteenth-century saga author made up a tenth-century law? Or have Guðrún and Þórðr made up a law, and everyone else has accepted it? In the latter case, the lovers' social capital would be the best explanation. Both are young, attractive, quick-witted and from good families. Auðr may be aristocratic but is considered ugly and unremarkable. Whether the law she breaks was spurious or not, there is nobody who publicly argues her cause.

The Trial

Anything we would now recognise as 'due process' is lacking in Auðr's divorce. Þórðr has only to declare publicly at the Law-Rock (*Lǫgbergr*) his accusation, and the marriage is terminated. There is apparently no scrutiny of his claims at all. He does 'nefna sér vátta' (name witnesses), but this is in order to attest that he was 'segir skilit við Auði' (declaring himself divorced from Auðr) (see also Dennis et al. 1980, 252). The saga does not suggest that these witnesses are supposed to have seen Auðr wearing trousers. Nor does Auðr have any chance to defend herself. *Grágás* is an imperfect comparandum to the Sagas of Icelanders, but it is striking that in *Grágás* a fairly comprehensive degree of arbitration and investigation is required in cases of marital separation: indeed, the whole case must be examined before both the local bishop (although this would obviously not apply in the pre-Christian period) and the Alþingi (*Grg,* 42–3).

Bróka-Auðr's 'trial', however, happens in the court of public opinion. Guðrún and Þórðr have sufficient social status that their claims seem to be accepted without question. True, Auðr has wealth and a good family, but Guðrun and Þórðr also have wealth through their marriages, and they have what Auðr does not: beauty and charisma. The people who should have demanded scrutiny of the allegation do nothing: Her brothers 'stay silent'. One critic (Byock 1993b, 254) interprets this inaction as the brothers being unable to get support from *goðar* (prominent chieftains with the right to bring cases at the Alþingi). But the fact the author says they are silent rather than unsuccessful indicates that they never made any attempt in the first place. Meulengracht Sørensen (1980, 26) thus says of Auðr's later, trouser-wearing revenge that 'she fulfils the duty which her male relatives have neglected'.

Why do the brothers remain tight-lipped? It is unlikely to be out of indifference, unless the saga author is being disingenuous, because they are said to be displeased by the situation. It might be cowardice, though two young men of good background would have less reason for timidity than most. The explanation may be that *Laxdæla saga* depicts a society where all must play their part – and the part of fraternal defender/avenger was not the only duty that fell to the brothers. The Icelandic Commonwealth was an unusual polity, in that it had a judiciary but no executive. There were no government agents of the sort one would recognise today, e.g. tax collectors, census takers, police, diplomats, etc. (Byock 1993a, 55–76). In a somewhat idealised model, it could be said that a society with policemen or bureaucrats pays 10 per cent of its population to fulfil those roles for 100 per cent of their public life. But in a world without officialdom, the need for the work officials perform does not disappear. Instead, 100 per cent of the people end up fulfilling those roles for 10 per cent of their public life (though it must be cautioned that even in highly bureaucratised states it is not just the bureaucrats who have to do bureaucratic chores; see Graeber 2015, esp. 45–66).

Similarly, Marion Poilvez has pointed out that, despite not having anything resembling a prison service, medieval Iceland became in effect a prison in itself: an island that an outlaw could not easily escape, with every single non-outlawed person whom they encountered becoming a potential warden (2016, 92, see also Foucault 1977, 231–3). I would suggest that something analogous is happening with the legal system as depicted by *Laxdæla saga*. The court room is not confined to the huddled conversations of the Alþingi: the whole society is the court room – and it is a corrupt one at that, charged not with upholding blind justice but with satisfying the desires of the people with the most social clout.

In this reading, it may be illuminating to draw a parallel between the trial of Bróka-Auðr and *The Trial* (*Der Prozess*, 1925) by Franz Kafka. Part of the horror of the 'Court of Inquiry' in Kafka's novel is that it is omnipresent in the world of Josef K, the accused. He can never quite grasp what is being done to him because anyone is potentially an official of the court. His own subordinates at the bank are mysteriously drafted in to keep an eye on him (Kafka 1968, 15, 33).[11] Even his uncle might be involved, given his suspicious familiarity with the court's workings (96). His personal relationships are always at risk of suddenly being transformed into impersonal ones. To make matters worse, the rules are arbitrary: on the one occasion K gets the opportunity to consult the court's law book, it turns out to be a pornographic novel (52). The analogy with K's trial suggests a way to understand both the angry silence of Auðr's brothers and the mystery of Þórðr's initial ignorance concerning the law against women wearing trousers. For Auðr, the court is neither fair nor transparent – but it is omnipresent, and when the population are called upon to become its enforcers by unspoken social codes, they must obey. If a bureaucrat is someone who carries out their official duties while alienated from their own opinions and desires (e.g. Cole 2019), then Auðr's brothers have found themselves in the curious position of becoming bureaucrats in a country without a state. We need not be mystified by their dereliction of duty to defend their sister if we consider that Iceland's peculiar political system has given them a greater, diametrically opposed duty: to marginalise the unremarkable when they stand in the way of the rich and beautiful.

The Trial Continues

Modern readers occasionally find themselves as compelled by Guðrún and Þórðr's allegation as the ninth-century Icelanders the saga depicts. Sometimes, it is not clear whether critics are validating the initial accusation or acknowledging Bróka-Auðr's later choice of clothing, (see Waugh 2011, 318; Miller 1990, 354). There are a few cases where the charge of cross-dressing appears to have been accepted by modern scholars, e.g. 'as her name implies, Auðr was known to be a cross-dresser and by implication was viewed as abnormal, a man in a woman's body in a man's clothes' (Acker 2006, 706), or simply 'she illegally dresses as man'

(Penack 1995, 65). Over the past thirty years, there has been a tendency for scholars to read the scene with an approving smile at Auðr's response to her situation – and to find a similar approval in the voice of the saga author or the minds of the saga audience (Clover 1993, 371–372; Jesch 1999, 199). When Bróka-Auðr bursts in to take revenge on Þórðr, one critic writes:

> The narrator's sympathy seems to be with Auðr all the way, although he/she has introduced her as something of a ne'er-do-well ('ekki görvilig'). Auðr is mentioned twice later on in the saga, both times in unequivocally positive contexts: first as a convivial hostess for the fugitive hero Kjartan, and later as a special friend of Kjartan's mother [...] But I maintain that even the first, and central episode in which she appears is meant to establish her as sympathetic [...] She is presented to us as something of a likeable rogue: neither fair of face nor addicted to the work ethic, but ready for action when she feels her honor trespassed upon.
>
> (Ballif Straubhaar 2001, 266)

Auðr's trial continues today. Only since the 1990s has she begun to get the cross-examination she deserves. We have seen that Guðrún and Þórðr's original charge is variously accepted or debated, but scholars also pose a new question: how far her retaliation against Þórðr constitutes an escape from patriarchal norms. Some have drawn attention to the fact that Auðr does not actually succeed in killing Þórðr, perhaps indicating that in a medieval Icelandic, patriarchal mindset, trousers alone do not a man make (Jochens 1996, 159; Jóhanna Katrín Friðriksdóttir 2013, 114, 151; Wolf 1997, 679). Importantly, Wolf points out that Bróka-Auðr, by donning male garb and picking up a sword is 'assimilating maleness, [and] accedes to male hegemony. This ambiguity or ambivalence in the portrayal of Auðr as a cross dresser [...] points to the "darker" side of the "poetics" of transgression that often inverts in order to reaffirm societal norms' (1997, 678–9). Put another way, one might say that if the only way for Auðr to express her dissatisfaction with a male-dominated society is for her to become male, then the anti-patriarchal cause has not been much advanced. That said, we must hasten to add that it would be slightly unfair to conscript Bróka-Auðr into standing for all women. Her divorce from Þórðr is readily interpreted as being more about her personal honour – or even emotions – than a wider political cause (Clark 1991, 8–9; Motz 1963, 164).

Auðr's Plight: Freedom and the Kafkaesque in Medieval Iceland

In closing, I want to consider Auðr's plight from a perspective adjacent to her gender: her personal liberty (see also chapter 7 in this volume). In doing so, I will also touch upon what her story tells us about the prospects and pitfalls of reading the Sagas of Icelanders in general. As Rikke Malmros notes, the idea that Early Medieval Scandinavian women enjoyed a peculiar degree of liberty has been around for some time and has appealed to people of differing ideological hues: 'Since the Swiss Paul-Henri Mallet published *Monuments de la mythologie et de la poésie des Celtes* [...] in 1756, European intellectuals have nursed the depiction of the proud, independent Nordic woman. She was originally also an inspiration for modern feminists' (Malmros 1998, 167; see also Jesch 1991 205–8; Jóhanna Katrín Friðriksdóttir 2013, 1–12). This presumption has been dispelled among saga scholars, but it remains prevalent both in other disciplines and beyond the walls of the university. Online searches will reveal both far-right 'Traditionalists' and eco-friendly anarchists who eagerly claim the identity of the empowered, Viking-Age woman. Indeed, an unfortunate perception of medieval Iceland as being particularly liberal, both for women and men, is a recurrent theme amongst novices to Old Norse.

The reasons for this persistent belief are mutifaceted (on the historic notion of 'Germanic liberty', see O'Donoghue 2014, 28–33; Zernack 2018). But one factor is probably that the Sagas of Icelanders are potent ideological concoctions. They pretend to depict the ideological currents of the tenth century where they are set. Sometimes they may be accurate in this, often not. But they also contain the ideological currents of the thirteenth century when they were written (Foote 1984; Harris 1986, esp. 213–6). They may intend to deprecate the Icelandic Commonwealth and tacitly support the status quo of the 1200s, or the inverse may be true. The reader must always keep in mind that not only are the sagas trying to 'sell' their ideologies to us, they are also detailed pictures of tenth-century people practicing ideologies of their own, which may be fictional as well as historical. Some anarcho-capitalists praise tenth-century Iceland for being bureaucracy-free – and even suggest our own society could be remodelled to be more like it (e.g. Friedman 1979, 414–5, who advocates for privatised blood feud agencies). In doing so, they are allowing themselves to be sold one ideological layer of the text while disregarding the others. A given saga character (imagined to exist in the tenth century) may not represent the saga author's own feelings (writing in the thirteenth century).

Auðr's story stands very much opposed to any notions of medieval Iceland's supposed freedom or fairness. It is not only that the characters of *Laxdæla saga* are not free to wear what they want without penalty. There is also an unpleasant, indeed Kafkaesque, sense of claustrophobia in the saga (and many other sagas, for that matter). In *The Trial*, K faces a society which pretends to have an extensive, transparent and ordered legal praxis. But in reality, power is exercised arbitrarily and inconsistently. In K's world, the principle of 'the people' before 'the law' is a fiction. Judge, lawyer, warden, citizen, courtroom, living room etc. have all become blurrily mixed: Everyone is so alienated that anyone can be called upon at a moment's notice to enforce rules they barely understand. Each one of these horrors faced by K is also faced by Auðr.

One might say that Auðr escapes her nightmare when she rides to inflict vengeance on Þórðr; that the story has an odd sort of 'happy ending' in that she gets revenge on someone who has shamelessly wronged her. But here we should remember Wolf's concerns about Auðr's participation in masculine norms. The retribution scene can only be read as emancipatory if we grant that Bróka-Auðr secretly desired to wear trousers and wield a sword all along. If she never wanted to be a man in the first place (and only Guðrún and Þórðr's allegation imply she did) then it is difficult to see how her performance of a male role in male costume could be considered liberating. If we think of the world of *Laxdæla saga* as a Kafkaesque setting, where all are obligated to play their part in a complicated pantomime, Þórðr's resigned statement takes on a different meaning. That 'she had done what she had to do' does not just mean that Auðr did what was right for her own emotional well-being, but that she had mechanically fulfilled the role allotted to a woman who had been arbitrarily turned into a man.

It is worth noting that Auðr does not disappear from the saga after her attack on Þórðr. Her final appearance comes immediately before the saga's climax.[12] Kjartan Óláfsson and Bolli Bollason have become rivals for the affection of the same Guðrún who was the architect of Auðr's humiliation. Kjartan spends the night at the farmstead Hóll. In the dead of night, a smith called Án wakes, having had a terrible dream of being disembowelled and having his entrails replaced with brushwood by an ogress. Kjartan and his men make light of the nightmare. Then the saga author suddenly reveals that Bróka-Auðr was amongst them the whole time. It has been suggested that she was playing the role of a 'convivial hostess' (Ballif Straubhaar 2001, 266) though again, this is a matter of interpretation because the saga author does not say as much. She considers the dream to be a serious portent:

> Then Auðr said: 'You needn't mock this so much. My suggestion is that Kjartan should do one of two things, that he stays here longer, or, if he must ride on, he rides with more men than he came with.' 'Perhaps you find Án Brushwood-belly perceptive, when he is sitting around all day chatting with you, and you find wisdom in everything which he dreams up, but I'm going as I planned to, regardless of this dream.' Kjartan prepared for his journey […] together with Þorkell the Pup and Knútr, his brother, according to Auðr's advice.
>
> (*Laxd.*, 149)

Kjartan and his men pour scorn on Auðr's counsel, but they do actually follow it. The normal logic of the Sagas of Icelanders is that women might well have a role as inciters of violence, but their practical expertise in martial matters is generally disregarded (Jochens 1996, 158–61).[13] One wonders if the reason Bróka-Auðr's advice is acted upon is that she was still regarded as male to some extent, even though this scene occurs many years after her divorce. Is she wearing trousers as she voices her opinion? The saga author does not say.

Few are satisfied by the end of the tale of Bróka-Auðr. Her brothers rejoice at her vengeance, presumably because it lets them off the hook and thereby resolves the tension between their role as fraternal protectors and their role as subservient citizens. Guðrún and Þórðr are happily married for a while, but Guðrún is soon widowed when Þórðr aggravates a witch, who conjures a storm to drown him while he is at sea. As for Auðr herself, the fate of being forced to live in a gender with which one does not identify, owing to a process which is wickedly unfair, cannot be seen as overly enviable. But it should not be overlooked that there is never a sense of docile resignation in either her words or actions. At the end of *The Trial*, K dies with a knife in his heart (Kafka 1968, 223–9). Auðr lives with a sword in her hand.

Notes

1. Other Old Norse genres – particularly hagiography and miracle tales – are capable of interiority, e.g. *MaS*, 881.
2. All translations are my own. Scholarship originally published in Danish has been silently translated for reasons of space.

3. In this study I have opted to use 'they' as a grammatically neuter personal third-person pronoun, when a person's gender is unknown or unimportant. I have previously used 'his/her' to fill this gap in English grammar but it is clumsy and I have recently encountered arguments against it by Spencer-Hall and Gutt (2020). The use of 'they' is also appropriate here because, regrettably, there is no space to treat the fascinating suggestion that *Laxdæla saga* may have been written by a woman. A convenient and current summary of the arguments is offered by Callow (2017, 23, 31 n82–5).

4. Similarly, for reasons of space, the original Old Norse is not cited when in indented quotes. The citation '*Laxd.*' refers to is the Íslenzk Fornrit edition. All translations are my own, unless otherwise stated.

5. The codpiece as conjured by the mind's eye would be anachronistic. Old Norse *setgeiri* does not have a precise equivalent in colloquial English. Jochens (1991, 252) proposes 'pants with inserted gores'. I submit that the *setgeiri* was a piece of material inserted in the front of either half of the pants in order to accommodate the male genitalia.

6. The reader will notice the gambol between tenses. This is common in saga style (Johnston 1957–61, 396–98). For explanations and analogues see: Zeevaert (2018, 152–7, 16–74).

7. *Karlkona,* literally 'man-woman', is wonderfully descriptive. It may be a coinage by the author or a slip by a later scribe (Cleasby and Vigfússon 1874, 332). Another manuscript has *karlmaðr* (Einar Ól. Sveinsson 1934, 96 n3) and the word is not listed outside of *Laxdæla saga* in the *Ordbog over det norrøne prosasprog* (s.v. *karl·kona*).

8. The verse has also been interpreted as deceptive, i.e. that Auðr is pretending she is happy to hear the news, '[but her] words mask her real feelings, and her wounded pride and honor merely go underground for months until they surface' (Clark 1991, 9). I understand the verse as deliberately sarcastic. Here again we have just the kind of gap between depiction and interpretation which makes the sagas such exciting literary endeavours.

9. The shepherd speaks figuratively, i. e., that they are in different building complexes: Guðrún at the summer pastures and Þórðr at home. The sense of the Norse is that the couple's notional bed-closet (*hvílugólf*) must be very wide because the two beds it contains are so far apart.

10. *Fjǫrbaugsgarðr* 'lesser outlawry' was a difficult concept, originally consisting of a period of exile with an initial period to prepare before going abroad. It has been shown that saga authors frequently misrecalled its details (Jones 1940, 162–3), although confusing a form of outlawry for grounds of divorce seems a step beyond reasonable misunderstanding.

11. One might also think of the Agent Smith character in *The Matrix* films. The agent can inhabit the body of any citizen at any time.

12. While chapter 48 is the last time the audience are presented with a scene where Auðr is physically present, her name is briefly mentioned by the narrative voice in chapter 53, where it is said that Þorgerðr Egilsdóttir (Kjartan's mother) is going '*at hitta Auði, vinkonu sína*' (to meet her friend, Auðr) (*Laxd.* 161). This is puzzling as no other information is given about the history or nature of their acquaintance (Van Deusen 2014, 58).

13. This is not true of other, more fantastical genres of Old Norse prose, e.g. the *Fornaldarsögur* (Jóhanna Katrín Friðriksdóttir 2013, 112–16).

References

Acker, Paul. 2006. 'Horror and the Maternal in *Beowulf*', *PMLA* 121 (3): 702–16.

Ballif Straubhaar, Sandra. 2002. 'Ambiguously Gendered: The Skalds Jórunn, Auðr and Steinunn'. In *Cold Counsel: Women in Old Norse Literature and Mythology*, edited by Sarah M. Anderson and Karen Swenson, 261–71. New York: Routledge.

Bullough, Vern L. 1982. 'Transvestism in the Middle Ages'. In *Sexual Practices and the Medieval Church*, edited by Vern L. Bullough and James Brundage, 43–54. Buffalo, NY: Prometheus Books.

Byock, Jesse L. 1993a. *Medieval Iceland: Society, Sagas, and Power*. Enfield: Hisarlik.

Byock, Jesse L. 1993b. *Feud in the Icelandic Saga*. Berkeley: University of California Press.

Callow, Chris. 2017. 'Dating and Origins'. In *The Routledge Research Companion to the Medieval Icelandic Sagas*, edited by Ármann Jakobsson and Sverrir Jakobsson, 15–33. London: Routledge.

Clark, Susan. 1991. '"Cold Are the Counsels of Women": The Revengeful Woman in Icelandic Family Sagas'. In *Women as Protagonists and Poets in the German Middle Ages: An Anthology of Feminist Approaches to Middle High German Literature*, edited by Albrecht Classen, 1–27. Göppingen: Kümmerle Verlag.

Cleasby, Richard and Gudbrand Vigfusson. 1874. *An Icelandic–English Dictionary*. Oxford: Clarendon Press.

Clover, Carol J. 1993. 'Regardless of Sex: Men, Women, and Power in Early Northern Europe', *Speculum* 68 (2): 363–87.

Cole, Richard. 2019. 'Bureaucracy and Alienation: Some Case Studies from *Hákonar saga Hákonarsonar*', *Saga-Book* 43: 5–36.

Dennis, Andrew, Peter Foote and Richard Perkins. 1980. 'Guide to Technical Vocabulary: Annotated Glossary'. In *Laws of Early Iceland: Grágás I*, translated by Andrew Dennis, Peter Foote and Richard Perkins, 239–62. Winnipeg: University of Manitoba Press.

Einar Ól. Sveinsson. 1934. Notes to *Laxdæla saga*.

Foote, Peter. 1984. 'The Audience and Vogue of the Sagas of Icelanders – Some Talking Points'. In *Aurvandilstá: Norse Studies*, edited by Michael Barnes, Hans Bekker-Nielsen and Gerd Wolfgang Weber, 47–55. Odense: Odense University Press.

Foucault, Michel. 1977. *Discipline and Punish: The Birth of the Prison*, translated by Alan Sheridan. New York: Vintage Books.

Friedman, David. 1979. 'Private Creation and Enforcement of Law: A Historical Case', *Journal of Legal Studies* 8 (2): 399–415.

Graeber, David. 2015. *The Utopia of Rules: On Technology, Stupidity, and the Secret Joys of Bureaucracy*. Brooklyn, NY: Melville House.

Grg = Anon. 1852. *Grágás: Islændernes lovbog i fristatens tid, udgivet efter det kongelige Biblioteks Haandskrift, Volume 2*, edited by Vilhjálmur Finsen. Copenhagen: Brødrene Berlings Bogtrykkeri.

Harris, Joseph. 1986. 'Saga as Historical Novel'. In *Structure and Meaning in Old Norse Literature: New Approaches to Textual Analysis and Literary Criticism*, edited by John Lindow, Lars Lönnroth and Gerd Wolfgang Weber, 187–219. Odense: Odense University Press.

Jóhanna Katrín, Friðriksdóttir. 2013. *Women in Old Norse Literature: Bodies, Words, and Power*. New York: Palgrave Macmillan.

Jesch, Judith. 1991. *Women in the Viking Age*. Woodbridge: Boydell Press.

Jochens, Jenny. 1991. 'Before the Male Gaze: The Absence of the Female Body in Old Norse'. In *The Eighth International Saga Conference, Göteborg 11–17 August 1991: The Audience of the Sagas, Preprints I–II*, edited by Lars Lönnroth, 247–56. Gothenburg: Gothenburg University.

Jochens, Jenny. 1995. *Women in Old Norse Society*. Ithaca, NY: Cornell University Press.

Jochens, Jenny. 1996. *Old Norse Images of Women*. Philadelphia: University of Pennsylvania Press.

Johnston, George. 1957–1961. "On Translation II." *Saga-Book* 15: 394–402.

Jón, Helgason. 1934. *Norrøn litteraturhistorie*. Copenhagen: Levin og Munksgaard.

Jones, Gwyn. 1940. 'Fjörbaugsgarðr', *Medium Ævum* 9 (3): 155–63.

Kafka, Franz. 1968. *The Trial*, translated by Willa Muir and Edwin Muir. New York: Schocken Books.

Laxd = Anon. 1934. *Laxdœla saga: Halldórs þættir Snorrasonar: Stúfs þáttr* (Íslenzk Fornrit 5), edited by Einar Ól. Sveinsson. Reykjavík: Hið íslenzka fornritafélag.

Magnus Magnusson, and Hermann Pálsson. 1969. 'Introduction'. In *Laxdæla saga*, translated by Magnus Magnusson and Hermann Pálsson, 9–42. Harmondsworth: Penguin.

Malmros, Rikke. 1998. 'Book Review – *Old Norse Images of Women*, by Jenny Jochens (1996)', *Historie: Jyske Samlinger* 1: 167–8.

MaS = Anon. 1871. *Mariu saga: Legender om jomfru Maria og hendes jertegn*, edited by C.R. Unger. Christiana: Brögger & Christie.

Meulengracht Sørensen, Preben. 1980. *Norrønt nid: Forestillingen om den umandige mand i de islandske sagaer*. Odense: Odense Universitetsforlag.

Miller, William Ian. 1990. *Bloodtaking and Peacemaking: Feud, Law, and Society in Saga Iceland*. Chicago: University of Chicago Press.

Motz, Lotte. 1963. 'Female Characters of the Laxdoela Saga', *Monatshefte* 55 (4): 162–66.

O'Donoghue, Heather. 2014. *English Poetry and Old Norse Myth: A History*. Oxford: Oxford University Press.

Ordbog over det norrøne prosasprog. 1989–, edited by Helle Degnbol, et al. Copenhagen: Den Arnamagnæanske Samling.

Pencak, William. 1995. *The Conflict of Law and Justice in the Icelandic Sagas*. Amsterdam: Rodopi.

Poilvez, Marion. 2016. '*Vár lǫg*: Outlaw Communities from *Jómsvíkinga saga* to *Harðar saga*', *Średniowiecze Polskie i Powszechne* 8 (12): 90–107.

Spencer-Hall, Alicia and Blake Gutt. 2020 [forthcoming]. 'Trans and Genderqueer Studies Terminology, Language, and Usage Guide'. In *Trans and Genderqueer Subjects in Medieval Hagiography*, edited by Alicia Spencer-Hall and Blake Gutt. Amsterdam: Amsterdam University Press.

Van Deusen, Natalie M. 2014. 'Sworn Sisterhood? On the (Near-) Absence of Female Friendship from the *Íslendingasǫgur*', *Scandinavian Studies* 86 (1): 52–71.

Waugh, Robin. 2011. 'The Foster Mother's Language: Anti-Representation, Pseudo-Feminization, and Other Consequences of a Mistake of Gender Charm in *Heiðarvíga saga*', *Scandinavian Studies* 83 (3): 307–64.

Wolf, Kirsten. 1997. 'Transvestism in the Sagas of Icelanders'. In *Sagas and the Norwegian Experience: 10th International Saga Conference, Trondheim, 3–9 August 1997*, edited by Jan Ragnar Hagland, 675–84. Trondheim: Senter for Middelalderstudier.

Zeevaert, Ludger. 2018. 'The Historical Present Tense in the Earliest Textual Transmission of *Njáls Saga*. An Example of Synchronic Linguistic Variation in Fourteenth-Century Icelandic *Njáls saga* Manuscripts.' In *New Studies in the Manuscript Tradition of* Njáls saga. *The* historia mutila *of* Njála, edited by Emily Lethbridge and Svanhildur Óskarsdóttir, 149–78. Kalamazoo: Medieval Institute Publications.

Zernack, Julia. 2018. 'Pre-Christian Religions of the North and the Political Idea of Liberty'. In *The Pre-Christian Religions of the North: Research and Reception, Volume I: From the Middle Ages to c. 1830*, edited by Margaret Clunies Ross, 255–66. Turnhout: Brepols.

7

Nora: The Life and Afterlife of Henrik Ibsen's *A Doll's House*

Elettra Carbone

In Nordic literary history the time-span stretching roughly between the 1870s and 1890s is known as The Modern Breakthrough (*Det moderne gennembrud*). Coined by the Danish literary critic Georg Brandes (1842–1927) in 1883, the term is used to refer to the strong naturalist and social-realist movements that spread throughout the Nordic countries and beyond, particularly thanks to the works of Henrik Ibsen (1828–1906).

The lectures on the main currents in European literature given by Brandes at the University of Copenhagen in 1871, and his successive publication *Main Currents in Nineteenth-Century Literature* (*Hovedstrømninger i det nittende Aarhundredes Litteratur*, 1872–75), are often the events used to mark the beginning of this period. Brandes stated that Denmark and, for that matter, the other Nordic countries had not kept pace with other European countries as far as literary trends were concerned. He therefore championed a socially involved literature that raised and discussed topical issues.

Taking as its starting point Brandes' cry for an engaged literature and Ibsen's renowned play *A Doll's House* (*Et dukkehjem*, 1879), this chapter explores how Nora, the play's iconic main character, and her slamming of the door have been central in debates on gender roles and on the relationship between the individual and society to the present day.[1] As Ibsen wrote in the preliminary notes for the play in 1878, the drama sets out to investigate why a woman cannot be herself in his contemporary male-dominated society (Ibsen 1961, 436–7).

In the play itself we follow the crucial events that lead to Nora's final decision to leave her family in order to make something of herself.

In Act I, Nora is blackmailed by Krogstad, a man who has secretly lent her the money to take Torvald, her once ill husband, on a restorative trip to Italy. Krogstad, who knows that Nora has forged her father's signature to obtain the loan, threatens to tell Torvald about her actions if she does not help him regain his job at the bank where Torvald is now the manager. Nora becomes increasingly distressed and, when it becomes clear that Torvald is about to find out her secret, she decides to commit suicide as she does not want her husband to publicly take the blame for her actions.

However, Nora changes her mind when Torvald, having finally found out about the loan and forgery, reacts differently to how she had expected: first he blames her for ruining his life and reputation with her scandalous actions, and later, once Krogstad has had a change of heart and returns the forged document, forgives her. Realising her husband's true character for the first time, Nora leaves him and her children.

This drama – which was controversial in its own time – raises several questions, of which three are considered below: To what extent does *A Doll's House* cast light on the family dynamics of the emerging middle class? What are Nora's roles in relation to her family within the play, and which ones does she decide to prioritise? The first part of the chapter will answer these questions while considering Toril Moi's statement that '*A Doll's House* is about Nora's painful entrance into modernity' as she transforms from generic family member (wife, daughter, mother) to individual (Nora) (2006, 258).

The second part of this chapter will then briefly examine the afterlife of *A Doll's House* and its main character, reflecting on how Ibsen's play has travelled across space, cultures and time. Nora's slammed door continues to reverberate 'across the roof of the world', but how did the play manage to achieve its international status? (Huneker 1905, 65). As Ståle Dingstad points out, 'Ibsen was not the most central agent in this success story', as he was helped by 'a variety of sources throughout several generations' (Dingstad 2016, 104). *A Doll's House* was translated and adapted immediately following its first publication and has been disseminated through numerous printed editions and performances. Besides being one of the most staged plays in the world, the play has also inspired and continues to inspire sequels speculating on Nora's and Torvald's 'post-slam' existences.[1] Using the famous case of the play's so-called 'German ending', namely the alternative ending written by Ibsen himself for the German audiences in 1879, and examples of the play's recent adaptations and sequels, the chapter will conclude by reflecting on Nora's global impact.

A Daughter of Her Time

As Egil Törnqvist has argued, if Brandes was responsible for initiating the debate around social problems in the 1870s, Ibsen's plays *A Doll's House* and later *Ghosts* (*Gengangere*, 1881) were instrumental during the second wave of this debate in the 1880s, dealing with controversial topics such as gender roles and sexual morality (Törnqvist 1995, 5). Considered his second social play following *The Pillars of Society* (*Samfundets støtter*, 1877), *A Doll's House* is often referred to as a *titteskapsdrama*, a 'drama of the interior' where the reader/spectator is invited to gaze into the middle-class family home and examine the marriage at its centre, in this case that of the Helmers (Grene 2014, 16–7).

The setting is indicative of a key aesthetic shift in late-nineteenth-century European theatre from 'a popular theatre of romantic spectacle to a theatre reflecting the everyday domestic life of the bourgeoisie' (Holledge 2008, 14; Moi 2006). The whole play is set in the living room, which, despite references to the rest of the flat and to the outside world from which the limited set of characters arrive, remains the focus and becomes the intersection between the private and social sphere (Grene 2014, 18). The ideal of the bourgeois family structure and dynamics sketched out in the opening scenes of *A Doll's House* is somewhat similar to that portrayed in the Danish artist C.W. Eckersberg's (1783–1853) painting *The Nathanson Family* (*Familien Nathanson*, 1818; see Figure 7.1), often considered a representation of the growing economic and political power of the middle class in the Nordic countries. In the painting, the children with the maid are gathering around the mother, who has just come home from a function. Although she has been out, she is clearly positioned within the living room, unlike her husband, who has one foot inside the room and one foot on the outside, symbolising his role as the link between the outside world and the home.

At the beginning of Act I, Ibsen's play strives to achieve an appearance of cosiness and neatness not just through the detailed stage directions but also through its references to the preparations for the Christmas celebrations and Nora and Torvald's initial interaction. Both Grene and Ørjasæter remind us in this respect that *A Doll's House* was used to indicate a cosy and neat home and not a house or home for dolls, a meaning it only acquires by the end of the play when Nora declares that she has been passed on from her father's hands to Torvald's like a doll (Grene 2014, 16; Haugen 1979, 103; Ørjasæter 2005, 29). The first extensive stage direction tells us that the play takes place in '[a] comfortably and tastefully, though not expensively, furnished room' (Ibsen 2016, 109).

Figure 7.1 The painting 'The Nathanson Family' ('Familien Nathanson', 1818) by the Danish painter C.W. Eckersberg (1783–1853), today considered a representation of a typical middle-class family in the Nordic countries in the nineteenth century. Source: Statens Museum for Kunst.

This is the heart of the Helmers' family life: it is a symbol of Nora's dream of security in the home and a space that she attempts to protect even at difficult times. The Christmas tree – a status symbol of the middle class – is an example of this: Nora continues to decorate the tree – brought in by the porter when she arrives home in the opening scene – even when she is preoccupied by Krogstad's blackmails and concludes '[t]he Christmas tree is going to be lovely' (Grene 2014, 20; Ibsen 2016, 137). Nothing can possibly spoil what appears to be a family idyll.

The initial interaction between Nora and Torvald also suggests that we are in the presence of a happily married couple, while at the same time reflecting the traditional gender dynamics between husband and wife. Nora's subordination to Torvald is made evident through his pet names for her: Nora is a 'song-lark' who chirrups, a 'squirrel' who rummages, and, most importantly, a 'spending-bird' and 'spendthrift' who fritters money away before Christmas (Ibsen 2016, 110–1). She is dependent on him for money as well as ethical and aesthetic principles. Torvald gives her money for housekeeping and expects her to share his ideas, such as his hatred of loans and debts, and his taste in furnishings (Ibsen 2016, 111, 182).

Nora is embedded in the typical spaces and family structures of the middle class. Following great economic growth in the course of the nineteenth century, the bourgeoisie (or *borgerskap* in Norwegian) emerged and grew as a powerful and complex new class, defining itself against the supremacy of the *embetsmenn* (the higher civil servants), who had ruled Norway since 1814. The middle class was far from homogeneous as it encompassed a range of occupations including entrepreneurs, functionaries, artisans and shopkeepers (Myhre 2008, 240–1). As a newly appointed bank manager, Torvald belongs to the white-collar, middle-class functionaries who separated themselves from the working class by 'more long-ranging employment terms' and occupations that demanded education rather than training (Myhre 2008, 243). From a financial point of view, Torvald and Nora embody the hopes and fears of this class, which aspired to upward mobility and dreaded social descent (Myhre 2008, 245). We see this clearly in Torvald and Nora's initial dialogue when Nora says she is looking forward to being able to spend Torvald's 'big salary' and Torvald worries about the consequences of overspending (Ibsen 2016, 110). Their initial attitudes towards money also make the setting a 'sexualised economic space', which reinforces the dichotomy between male and female represented in Eckersberg's painting. As Anna Westerståhl Stenport has argued in her 'Sexonomics of *Et dukkehjem*', 'Production in the form of entrepreneurship [...] became a male-gendered virtue', while 'female consumption is coded socially as an unnecessary luxury' (Westerståhl Stenport 2006, 343).

From the point of view of the composition of the drama, the set-up of *A Doll's House* is in line with Ibsen's use of the 'retrospective technique', according to which the past events leading to the climax are progressively unveiled through the words and acts of the characters in the course of the play. Plays employing this technique often start with a scene where the life of the characters appears 'normal and happy' before a 'discordant note' is introduced, often through the arrival of a stranger or an old friend, in this case Mrs Linde and later Krogstad (Haugen 1979, 64–6). Following the encounter with these characters, the real state of affairs behind the harmonious appearance – a state of affairs caused by events that have happened before the start of the play – begins to be revealed to the reader/spectator. This finally leads to the play's climax and leaves the main character or characters facing a dilemma, in this case Nora's choice to stay or leave (Haugen 1979, 64–6).

As the drama unfolds, it becomes evident that Nora is only pretending to be her husband's doll-wife in order to fulfil 'her ambition of creating a loving and well-functioning family' (Ørjasæter 2005, 29). In addition to secretly subverting the 'consumption-production pattern within the Helmeran domestic economy', Nora uses her power to save, as well as to manipulate, Torvald (Grene 2014, 20; Westerståhl Stenport 2006, 343). As we find out in Nora's dialogue with Mrs Linde in Act I, Nora has secretly borrowed money from Krogstad in order to take Torvald on a trip to Italy to save him from a life-threatening medical condition. To bypass the law, which would have prevented her from borrowing money without her husband's consent, she has forged her father's signature. In the eyes of the law, she has committed two crimes because, as Krogstad points out, 'the law doesn't ask about motives' (Ibsen 2016, 135). In her own eyes, she has simply done her duty towards her family, taking care of her husband's welfare and health (Ørjasæter 2005, 31). While doing this, she has also acquired a taste for entrepreneurial tasks traditionally associated with men (Westerståhl Stenport 2006, 344). She has become, as she states herself, 'a wife with a touch of business flair – a wife who knows how to go about things a little cleverly' and who knows about 'quarterly interest, and something called instalments' (Ibsen 2016, 121). In order to repay the money she owes Krogstad, she has had to put aside some of Torvald's housekeeping money but also to earn money by taking on copying work, something which has almost made her feel like a man. By the end of the play, however, Nora comes to the realisation that the family idyll she has continuously attempted to protect is just a charade.

The change in her attitude is represented in the shifting meaning of her use of the expression 'the miraculous thing' (or, in Norwegian, 'det vidunderlige', literally 'the wonderful thing'). At the beginning she uses this expression to refer to her expectation that upon finding out about her crime, Torvald will rescue her and take the blame. Throughout the play, Nora is both looking forward to and dreading this 'miraculous thing': on the one hand, Torvald's sacrifice would be a demonstration of his love for her; on the other, it would compromise his reputation and thus the future of the family, something Nora wants to avoid by committing suicide (Moi 2006, 264). As Nora is about to leave Torvald, the 'miraculous thing' has changed meaning: disillusioned by Torvald's reaction to her revelations, Nora declares that, if Torvald is to be more than a stranger to her, 'the most miraculous thing' would have to happen, namely that their 'living together could become a marriage' (Ibsen 2016, 188). 'Marriage' here stands for an 'ideal marriage', along the lines of the Norwegian writer Camilla Collett's (1813–95) definition of the term, namely a partnership where both husband and wife are committed to mutual growth (Ørjasæter 2005, 25). Nora's rejection of her identities of 'doll' and 'wife and mother' should therefore be seen as an exemplary case of women's rejection of a patriarchal and sexist family structure, which would other-wise see her tied to a man she does not love any more (Moi 2006, 278). While before Torvald's final reaction, Nora is prepared to leave her children motherless in order to spare them from the fog of lies she thinks she has created, by the end of the play she chooses to leave them because she has come to the realisation that she cannot educate them without educating herself first (Moi 2006, 278).

Throughout the play, Nora is represented as a product of her heredity as well as of her environment. Torvald and Mrs Linde both mention that Nora takes after her father since she has committed the same type of crime he once committed, a crime that Torvald has had to cover up. Her behaviour is, however, also clearly conditioned by the social norms of the environment around her. By making Nora aware of the role her father, her husband and, more generally, society have played in shaping her life, the play addressed the contemporary debate around women's con-sciousness and whether femininity was instinctive or a social construct (Shepherd-Barr 2015, 101).

Just a Human Being

Many scholars have discussed the question of Ibsen's relationship to femi-nism, both as a movement and as an ideology. As Giuliano D'Amico points out, Nora confronted 'the general values of the European Bourgeoisie of the late nineteenth century', encouraging the audience to consider and eventually challenge the family law that legally regulated the relation-ship between husband and wife and saw the woman as the losing party (D'Amico 2013, 81; see also Janss 2017, 17). *A Doll's House* was part of broader movements that attempted to cast light on women's rights. Nora's statement that she is not fit to be a wife and mother if she does not first fulfil her duty to herself echoes 'frontline figures of the women's rights movement such as Mary Wollstonecraft, Fredrika Bremer, Har-riet Martineau and Camilla Collett' (Ørjasæter 2005, 21; see also Finney 1994; Templeton 1997). As Ørjasæter points out, Nora's struggles are embedded within the debates around women's capacity for reasonable thinking and the role of women in the family. These were only two of the main issues with which the early generation of feminists had to engage while battling Jean-Jacques Rousseau's established claim that women were naturally subordinate to men, and Hegel's definition of the family, which did not allow women to exist as self-conscious individuals (Moi 2006, 276–7; Ørjasæter 2005, 21–3). John Stuart Mill's (1806–73)

The Subjection of Women (1869) was instrumental in spreading the view that the oppression of women was not based on any scientific ground and was therefore unjust (Janss 2017, 18; Ørjasæter 2005, 24).

Changing established views on these matters was, however, not an easy task. As Shepherd-Barr has observed, works like Mill's were 'countering culturally embedded biases shared by even the best-educated and most scientific men', including Charles Darwin (1809–82), who, while supporting the cause of women's right to education, argued that women were biologically disadvantaged compared with men outside the domestic sphere (Shepherd-Barr 2015, 95).

There is general consensus that Ibsen supported the women's cause, but that this was part of his broader interest in freedom and self-determination that cut across class as well as gender (Finney 1994, 89; Törnqvist 1995, 5–6; Ørjasæter 2005, 40–1). In a speech given to the Women's League in 1898, Ibsen stated that rather than having deliberately worked for women's rights, he had been preoccupied with human rights and with the task of describing mankind. Taking their starting point in this statement, a number of critics have dismissed or downplayed Ibsen's feminist agenda (Templeton 1997, 111). From the 1880s, Ibsen's Nora inspired a large number of essays discussing the 'woman question' in light of the play (Templeton 1997, 126). Ibsen himself was actively engaged in the battle for women's rights by, for instance, signing the petition by the Norwegian Women's Rights League, founded in 1884, 'urging the passage of a bill making obligatory separate property rights for married women' while also openly supporting the campaign for universal suffrage (Templeton 1997, 127).

As Ørjasæter has pointed out, Ibsen's declaration at the Women's League does not in any way diminish the powerful feminist message of the play, which takes important steps towards 'regarding women as dignified humans' (Ørjasæter 2005, 40). *A Doll's House* is the 'dramatization of the flowering of one woman's consciousness' (Templeton 1997, 141): in her final dialogue with Torvald, reminded by him of her duties to her husband and her children, she asserts the sacred nature of her duties towards herself adding that she is 'first and foremost a human being' (Ibsen 2016, 184). The play can thus be seen as representing an individual's attempt to challenge society as a whole, demonstrating that there is no opposition between 'humanity' and 'femininity' (Moi 2006, 275). Moi argues that this is particularly clear in the tarantella scene, which she sees as a display of Nora's humanity, 'a graphic representation of a woman's struggle to make her existence *heard*, to make it *count*' (Moi 2006, 269).

The scene was a late addition to the early draft in which Nora was supposed to sing and dance 'Anitra's Song' from Ibsen's own play *Peer Gynt* (1867) to the incidental music composed by the Norwegian composer Edvard Grieg (1843–1907) in 1876 (Grene 2014, 26). Aware that her secret will soon be revealed, in the final version of Act II Nora rehearses the tarantella, the Neapolitan folk dance she had learnt during her stay in Italy, which is characterised by an upbeat tempo and usually accompanied by tambourines (see Figure 7.2). She is to perform the dance the following night at the Stenborgs' party. Nora's exotic and seductive dance becomes increasingly violent, to the extent that Torvald exclaims:

Figure 7.2   Adeleide Johannesen performing Nora's tarantella scene in the first staging of the play at Den Nationale Scene (The National Stage) in Bergen in 1880. Source: National Library of Norway.

'But, my dear sweet Nora, you're dancing as if your life depended on it' (Ibsen 2016, 163). Nora's immediate aim with the rehearsal is to distract Torvald from the mailbox containing Krogstad's letter by keeping him busy correcting and guiding her. Yet her performance may also be interpreted as a mirror of her state of mind, as, unable to keep up appearances any more, she displays her distress (Moi 2006, 269).

The tarantella scene has had mixed reactions and interpretations in the countless stagings of the play. Located in this tension between melodrama – a typically sensational dramatic piece well-known for prioritising action over character and designed to appeal to the spectators' emotions – and authenticity, with its display of the woman's dancing body, Nora's tarantella remains one of the most powerful scenes of the drama. In their comparative study of Ibsen performances worldwide, Holledge, Bollen, Helland and Tompkins have uncovered how this scene has either been substituted or adapted to reflect or critique specific views on the role and use of women's bodies within society (2016, 157–96). They refer, for instance, to the practice, common in productions in or for Islamic cultures, of cutting or transforming the tarantella into a 'social

Figure 7.3   Photograph of Helmer and Svetlana, the Helmers' au pair, in *Helmer Hardcore – A Doll's House 2* by Jakob Weis (1970–). The play, which appeared in Danish in 2007, was translated into English by Paul Russell Garrett and produced by [Foreign Affairs] theatre company in 2015, featuring Krzysia Balińska and Will Timbers. © Camila França Photography.

dance', of exchanging the tarantella for other local ritual dances (such as the traditional *vimbuza* dance in the Malawi production) or of using images of film icons (such as Angelina Jolie as Lara Croft or Marilyn Monroe) to suggest how women are influenced by the media in some Western productions (2016, 166–77).

Ultimately, together with the ending, the tarantella scene reveals the potential present within *A Doll's House* as the text presents theatre directors with the challenge to 'reproduce and then break free of the conventions' used to represent 'the aesthetically desirable female performing body' in other cultures (2016, 190).

Nora's Afterlife

A Doll's House was a great success as many recognised the explosive and subversive quality of the ending and the power of Nora's door slamming. On 23 January 1891, Ibsen himself wrote in a letter to his Russian translator, Moritz Prozor: 'I might honestly say that it was for the sake of the last scene that the whole play was written' (Templeton 1997, 120). The play premiered at the Royal Theatre in Copenhagen on 21 December 1879, only two weeks after it was published, and by the early twentieth century it had been performed in forty-six countries (Törnqvist 1995, 63; Holledge et al. 2016, 29). Dingstad reports that in the Nordic countries the play had an unprecedented popularity: published in three editions, it sold 13,500 copies in three months, was reviewed in all newspapers and performed multiple times in Copenhagen, Oslo and Stockholm, triggering extensive debates (Dingstad 2016, 111). The same was not true, however, of all the countries it reached. First of all, it is worth bearing in mind that, as D'Amico has argued, with the exception of Germany, England and France, many European and non-European countries did not receive the *Norwegian* Ibsen, but 'an already received, elaborated and domesticated *international* Ibsen' mediated through one of these three countries.

Moreover, the lack of a comprehensive copyright law protecting intellectual property meant that Ibsen's plays could be changed as publishers and directors pleased (Dingstad 2016, 114; Fulsås and Rem 2018, 67–71, 186–7). Unlike other European countries, Denmark – to which Ibsen's works legally belonged since he published them with Gyldendal in Copenhagen – did not join the Berne Convention for the Protection of Literary and Artistic Works of 1886 until 1903 (D'Amico 2014, 23). The consequences of this lack of bilateral agreements became particularly evident in Germany, the first non-Scandinavian country into which Ibsen was introduced (D'Amico 2014, 11). Here unauthorised translations and performances were a common occurrence (D'Amico 2014, 23). Under pressure from a number of agents – including his translator Wilhelm Lange (1849–1907) – who feared the reactions of unprepared audiences steeped in conservative convictions, Ibsen reluctantly agreed to write an alternative ending for the play, known as the 'German ending', in 1879 in the attempt to make the play acceptable to German audiences while maintaining some control over his own work and avoiding further changes and intrusions (Dingstad 2016, 116; Janss 2017, 6–7, 9, 11, 20).

While it does not bring reconciliation between Nora and Torvald, the alternative ending rebalances the dynamics among Nora's different identities as mother, wife and human being since she decides to stay for her children's sake in order not to leave them 'motherless'. Torn between self-respect and the 'holy task' of motherhood, Nora chooses the latter (Ørjasæter 2005, 27–8). On the one hand, in this version of the ending Nora is attempting to give her children what she did not have – as she grew up without her mother. Worried about the consequences of a childhood without a mother, she expresses her concerns for her children earlier in the play when she asks the nanny: 'Do you believe they'd forget their mummy if she was gone altogether?' (Ibsen 2016, 142). The sacrifice she makes for her children by staying is justified within the play, particularly considering that, as Ørjasæter has pointed out, Nora's relationship with her children is portrayed in the play as much closer and stronger than what was expected of women in a similar social position at the time: despite hiring a nanny for them, Nora plays and spends time with her children and is concerned about their welfare (Ørjasæter 2005, 37).

On the other hand, the conciliatory ending emphasises a dichotomy between being a mother and being a self-respecting human being, thus perpetuating the myth that these two roles are mutually exclusive (Ørjasæter 2005, 36–7). The dramatic change of the ending, which Ibsen saw as a 'barbarous outrage' against his own work and which was only one example of similar requests for softer endings made to Scandinavian authors, removes the most explosive element in the play, namely the slam that made Ibsen a champion of women's liberation (Dingstad 2016, 116; Janss 2017, 4). The conciliatory ending continued to be used and published side-by-side with the original ending both in Germany and beyond, but was never introduced in Scandinavia despite the fact that Nora's transformation at the end of the play was seen by some critics as 'psychologically unexplainable' (Janss 2017, 9–16).

As the project *A Global Doll's House* has recently concluded, a comparative study of performances of Ibsen's *A Doll's House* shows that Ibsen was right in imagining that, in the long run, the original ending would prevail (Holledge et al. 2016, 143). This does not mean, however, that Nora's departure from Torvald has not been subjected to any more changes and adaptations. The history of the play's performance showcases a wide range of interpretations, varying from endings which allow for the door to be left ajar — such as the 2006 Egyptian production directed by Gamal Yakout, which does not want to exclude Nora's return and Torvald's ability to change — to definitive endings where there is no hope of reconciliation — such as Thomas Ostermeier's 2002 German production, in which Nora shoots Torvald (Holledge et al. 2016, 143–4).

On the whole, it is difficult to establish which elements in *A Doll's House* have made it so successful across time and cultures (Holledge 2008, 17). Julie Holledge has suggested that in order to understand the popularity of the play as a global phenomenon, we should focus less 'on both aesthetic innovation and the audience's identification and empathy with Nora as the embodiment of a modernist female subject' and more on 'the sites of anxiety surrounding the abandonment of children and the masquerade of femininity' (Holledge 2008, 24). This is what, in Holledge's opinion, has allowed 'an infinite variety of cultures to explore the consequences of rupturing a gendered binary that supports and maintains an unequal distribution of social power', regardless of cultural particularities (Holledge 2008, 24). A number of adaptations and sequels have attempted to do this in creative and provocative ways.

In the 2003 production by Lee Breuer called *Mabou Mines Dollhouse*, all the male actors were less than four-feet-six-inches tall, while all the actresses were of average height. The miniature setting was shaped to fit the men but not women, who had to physically adjust in order to live in a man-sized world (Holledge et al. 2016, 187). Gender roles are also at the centre of the 2009 performance by Toneelgroep ADODVS, *Een Poppenhuis*, directed by Manon van Gelder, in which the genders of the characters were swapped as Torvald the house husband attempted to reclaim his masculinity from Nora the career woman (Holledge et al. 2016, 181). The question of masculinity is also addressed by *Helmer Hardcore*, a sequel to *A Doll's House* written by the Danish playwright Jakob Weis in 2007 (see Figure 7.3). Entirely set in the Helmers' bathroom, the play focuses on Torvald as we follow his hopeless attempt to live as a single father without his wife. Despite their different takes on Ibsen's text, what all these productions have in common is a claim to originality, possibly in the attempt to continue to shock and provoke their audiences in the same way that Ibsen did with his ending in 1879 (Holledge et al. 2016, 144).

Local and Global

By leaving Torvald, Nora sets off on a quest to find out who is right, society or her. As she admits in her final dialogue with Torvald, she does not understand the society that has transformed her into a doll by refusing to acknowledge her duties to herself. Nora finds society contradictory as, on the one hand, it requires women to sacrifice themselves for their families by 'putting other people's well-being above their own' but, on the other, punishes them when, like her, they do this without their husbands' consent (Ørjasæter 2005, 35). By portraying the struggle of a middle-class woman attempting to find her identity in nineteenth-century Norwegian society, *A Doll's House* addressed social issues of its time that were directly linked to the emergence of the middle class and women's rights, as Brandes had advocated. There is, however, no doubt that *A Doll's House*, its performances and responses quickly became, and continue to be, a global phenomenon, as they refer to and advance debates on modernisation and modernity that are relevant in different temporal, geographical and cultural contexts (Fisher-Lichte 2011, 3).

Note

1. The play ends as Nora shuts the door of her home behind her. Nora's slamming of the door has therefore become an iconic scene, which is essential not only for the interpretation of Nora's change within the play but also for the understanding of the impact *A Doll's House* as a whole on world literature and society.

References

D'Amico, Giuliano. 2013. *Domesticating Ibsen for Italy: Enrico and Icilio Polese's Ibsen Campaign*. Bari: Pagina.

D'Amico, Giuliano. 2014. 'Six Points for a Comparative Ibsen Reception History', *Ibsen Studies* 14 (1): 4–37.

Dingstad, Ståle. 2016. 'Ibsen and the Modern Breakthrough: The Earliest Productions of *The Pillars of Society, A Doll's House*, and *Ghosts*', *Ibsen Studies* 16 (2): 103–40.

Finney, Gail. 1994. 'Ibsen and Feminism'. In *The Cambridge Companion to Ibsen*, edited by James McFarlane, 89–105. Cambridge: Cambridge University Press.

Fischer-Lichte, Erika. 2011. 'Introduction'. In *Global Ibsen: Performing Multiple Modernities*, edited by Erika Fischer-Lichte, Barbara Gronau and Christel Weiler, 1–16. New York: Routledge.

Fischer-Lichte, Erika, Barbara Gronau and Christel Weiler, eds. 2011. *Global Ibsen: Performing Multiple Modernities*. New York: Routledge.

Fulsås, Narve and Tore Rem. 2018. *Ibsen, Scandinavia and the Making of a World Drama*. Cambridge: Cambridge University Press.

Grene, Nicholas. 2014. *Home on the Stage: Domestic Spaces in Modern Drama*. Cambridge: Cambridge University Press.

Haugen, Einar. 1979. *Ibsen's Drama: Author to Audience*. Minneapolis: University of Minnesota Press.

Holledge, Julie. 2008. 'Addressing the Global Phenomenon of *A Doll's House*: An Intercultural Intervention', *Ibsen Studies* 8 (1): 13–28.

Holledge, Julie, Jonathan Bollen, Frode Helland and Joanne Tompkins. 2016. *A Global Doll's House: Ibsen and Distant Visions*. London: Palgrave Macmillan.

Huneker, James. 1905. *Iconoclasts: A Book of Dramatists*. New York: Charles Scribner's Sons.

Ibsen, Henrik. 1961. *The Oxford Ibsen, Volume V*, edited and translated by James Walter McFarlane. London: Oxford University Press.

Ibsen, Henrik. 2016. *A Doll's House and Other Plays*, edited by Tore Rem; translated by Deborah Dawkin and Erik Skuggevik. London: Penguin.

Janss, Christian. 2017. 'When Nora Stayed: More Light on the German Ending', *Ibsen Studies* 17 (1): 3–27.

McFarlane, James, ed. 1994. *The Cambridge Companion to Ibsen*. Cambridge: Cambridge University Press.

Moi, Toril. 2006. '"First and Foremost a Human Being": Idealism, Theatre, and Gender in *A Doll's House*', *Modern Drama* 49 (3): 256–84.

Myhre, Jan Eivind. 1994. 'Finding the Middle-Class: Norway in a Comparative Perspective, c. 1870–1940', *Scandinavian Journal of History* 19 (3): 237–49.

Ørjasæter, Kristin. 2005. 'Mother, Wife and Role Model: A Contextual Perspective on Feminism in *A Doll's House*', *Ibsen Studies* 5 (1): 19–47.

Shepherd-Barr, Kirsten E. 2015. *Theatre and Evolution from Ibsen to Beckett*. New York: Columbia University Press.

Stenport, Anna Westerståhl. 2006. 'The Sexonomics of *Et dukkehjem*: Money, the Domestic Sphere and Prostitution', *Edda* 106 (4): 339–53.

Templeton, Joan. 1997. *Ibsen's Women*. Cambridge: Cambridge University Press.

Törnqvist, Egil. 1995. *Ibsen: A Doll's House*. Cambridge: Cambridge University Press.

8
Nordic Noir

Anne Grydehøj

In the twenty-first century, Scandinavian crime fiction has become an international publishing phenomenon, generating an unprecedented number of literary translations, films and TV series from the Nordic region. It has concurrently become a research object for academics addressing the question of why there is such an exceptional interest in grim narratives from countries otherwise perceived as some of the most socially successful in the world. This chapter will explore what stories crime narratives tell of life in the Scandinavian countries, and advance some potential reasons behind the appeal of these narratives to an international audience.

Taking its starting point in a view of crime fiction as a genre which responds to and develops alongside shifting social conditions, the chapter will first provide a brief historical introduction to the Scandinavian variant of the crime fiction genre, from its consolidation during what is perceived as the golden age of social democracy in the 1960s to narratives from the early 1990s and onwards that depict welfare societies undergoing dramatic change. In the second part of the chapter, a closer reading of Swedish author Henning Mankell's novel *Mördare utan ansikte* (1991, *Faceless Killers*, 1997) will be used to examine in more detail key themes and features and their mediation of societal change in the (post-)welfare state. Of special interest is the role the novel plays in the depiction of relationships between the state and the citizen, geographical centres and peripheries, and of migration, racism and transnational crimes.

Origins

The origin of what was later to become known as Nordic Noir is undoubt-edly to be found in the ten-novel series written by the Swedish writer couple Maj Sjöwall (1935–) and Per Wahlöö (1926–1975) between 1965 and 1975. This is not to say that crime fiction did not exist in the Nordic region before the 1960s – Sweden in particular had a thriving detective fiction industry with authors such as Stieg Trenter and Maria Lang in the 1940s and 1950s – but Sjöwall and Wahlöö conceived a modern template for the Scandinavian crime novel. This initial version took the form of police procedurals (crime narratives focusing on the investigative procedures of the police) with a strong element of social critique that radically broke with the earlier Swedish *pusseldeckar* tradi-tion (whodunnits in the fashion of English golden-age detective fiction). This early tradition placed most of its crimes within the close confines of a bourgeois milieu to a large extent inhabited by characters oblivious to pressing societal issues.

Sjöwall and Wahlöö's series, collectively entitled *Roman om et brott* ('Novel of a Crime'), features detective inspector Martin Beck, who, with a team of colleagues in Stockholm, solves crimes which, by contrast, reveal fundamental social problems within the Swedish welfare state. A further important change from the golden-age novel is the shift in focus onto the investigative group's organic structure. While Martin Beck plays a central role in the novels, his colleagues – in particular Gunvald Larsson, Lennart Kolberg and Einar Rönn – are equally fully developed characters with pri-vate lives, who invariably take on both the narrative point of view and the investigatory lead. Sjöwall and Wahlöö emphasise this collective dimen-sion in their literary manifesto article 'Kriminalromanens fornyelse' (The Renewal of the Crime Novel), first published in the Danish newspaper *Politiken* (30 July 1971): 'We do not believe that the so-called ordinary novel with its orientation around individuals is suitable for an analysis of our society. The crime novel has contrarily from an early stage been conscious of the fact that individuals belong to a group'.[1]

The legacy of Sjöwall and Wahlöö's series on contemporary Scandinavian crime fiction is still very much in evidence, and, albeit with certain modifications, the genre continues to employ a highly influential template: the police procedural with its team of investigators; Martin Beck as prototypical model for male (and, later, female) protagonists who strug-gle to maintain interpersonal relations in their private lives; the authors' use of a widely-copied variant of literary realism; and socially engaged themes which raise questions about and criticise society's malaises.

The Disintegration of the Nordic Welfare State

A great amount of scholarship has consisted of socio-historical readings of the Scandinavian variant of the crime fiction genre, and has seen its premise and development as according with the perceived dissolution of the welfare state (e.g. Nestingen 2008, Arvas and Nestingen 2011, Bergman 2014a, Stougaard-Nielsen 2017; see also chapter 5 in this volume). Andrew Nestingen, in his introduction to *Crime and Fantasy in Scandinavia* (2008), promotes the idea that popular culture reflects a transformation of 'the background understanding of the Nordic welfare state' (2008, 5) and that it has increasingly 'become a forum for struggling over these changes by creating, discussing, and contesting the self-representation of the nation' (2008, 7). In Nestingen's analysis, these changes are due to the introduction of neoliberal values and policies from the 1980s onwards, which caused a gradual dissolution of the post-war Scandinavian social-democratic continuum. An important premise for the relevance of studying popular culture, according to Nestingen, is the fact that the issues being debated by the public, media and politicians in the Nordic region since the 1990s are by and large the same as the issues raised in popular fiction – Nestingen mentions individuality, equality, heterogeneity, transnationalism and gender (9). The same synthetic conclusions are applied more specifically to crime fiction from Scandinavia in Nestingen and Arvas's introduction to *Scandinavian Crime Fiction* (2011), where the authors emphasise the political imperatives of the genre, arguing that it is 'one of the great popularizers of criticism of neoliberalism' (2011, 9). In light of the popularity of Scandinavian crime fiction nationally and internationally, the contribution of these socially engaged texts is significant for a debate about and redefinition of Nordic national identities.

Where Sjöwall and Wahlöö in their *Roman om et brott* were able, from their Marxist position, to directly engage with what they saw as the shortcomings of *Sveriges socialdemokratiska arbetarparti* (the Swedish Social Democratic Party) in accommodating the working class, crime fiction from the beginning of the 1990s articulates additional concerns. Rather than being concerned primarily – as Sjöwall and Wahlöö's works were – with questions of social and economic inequality and of care for individuals within the boundaries of the welfare state, more recent novels such as Henning Mankell's are preoccupied with issues of national identity, isolation, bigotry and xenophobia within an atmosphere of change caused by globalisation and immigration. That is, to borrow the terms of political philosopher Nancy Fraser, the Swedish crime novel might be seen to have undergone a shift from a paradigm of 'redistribution' to a paradigm of 'recognition' (Fraser 1997).

The Social Body

Sjöwall and Wahlöö's underlying Marxist agenda and their critique of successive Social Democratic governments' failures were clear. As Per Wahlöö discloses in an essay: 'We [...] had this special idea together: to use the crime novel in its pure form as a scalpel to slit open the belly of the ideologically pauperized and morally debatable so-called welfare state of the bourgeois type' (Wahlöö 1967, 176). The quotation's reference to surgical (or perhaps, forensic) medicine – alluding to crime fiction's ability to dissect with precision – contains further implications when viewed in relation to the series' use of strong and persistent metaphors of the corporeality of society. Society as an organism is brought into relation not only with the bodies of murdered victims, but also with the investigators' own bodies. When Martin Beck and his colleagues throughout the series are tired, suffer from insomnia, sneeze, have flu or upset stomachs, their physical state reflects the larger scale processes of a malfunctioning social body, 'their bodies [being] metaphors for a sick and decaying society' (Tapper 2011, 23).

This interconnectedness between the individual and the societal body becomes a recurring attribute of Scandinavian crime fiction, with multiple examples stressing the (troubled) relationship between citizen and polity in decay. Swedish author Arne Dahl, for example, establishes an undisguised analogy with the human body in a conversation between his main investigator Paul Hjelm and his superior, in which the latter affirms the essential role of the police as a protective membrane of social cohesion: '[T]he skin holding society's fragile body together is the forces of order. We are the outliers closest to the sources of anxiety, and therefore we are also the most exposed of all. If the skin tears open in a critical place, the innards of the social body will spill out' (Dahl 2010 [1999], 33).

Another instance of the metaphor of the sick human body is found in Mankell's stand-alone novel *Danslärarens återkomst* (2000, *The Return of the Dancing Master*, 2003). Here, Stefan Lindman, a younger police officer, is diagnosed with tongue cancer. In this novel's treatment of the historical heritage of Nazi ideology and the origins of Swedish neo-Nazism, the cancerous illness in the speech organ becomes a signifier for the difficulty of talking about a wartime Sweden in which pro-Nazi sentiments were pervasive.

The human body as metaphorical expression of social pathology is also ubiquitous in Stieg Larsson's *Millennium* trilogy, where the juxtaposition of the investigator's body and of what Gregersdotter (2013) calls 'the commodified bodies of the victims of rape and the trafficking industry' reveals the symptoms of 'the globalized economy and the transformation of the welfare state' (83).

While bodily illness as a metaphor for social illness has frequently been exploited in individual works of literary fiction (for example, Charles Dickens' *The Old Curiosity Shop* [1841], Honoré de Balzac's *La Cousine Bette* [1846] and Albert Camus' *La Peste* [1947]), the prominence of the analogy in the contemporary Nordic variant of the crime fiction genre provides a fundamental interpretative framework for the genre's texts collectively. Central to an understanding of this metaphorical equivalence between society and individual body is the trope of the investigator being an interpreter of the illness while simultaneously being contaminated by it.

The Success of Nordic Noir

Besides the history of the origins of the modern Nordic crime novel and its common features, there is another development which has prompted at least as much attention and examination in the media and academia: the story of how, when and why crime fiction from the Nordic region came to take centre stage in the international marketplace of cultural production. It might here be beneficial to employ separate terminology to distinguish the literary development of 'Scandinavian crime fiction', i.e. the genre per se, from the publishing phenomenon of 'Nordic Noir', a catchy tagline proven to be very exploitable for marketing purposes. Broadly speaking, the study of Scandinavian crime fiction tends to be concerned with the literary representation of the dysfunctionality of societies undergoing transformation, while the study of Nordic Noir can be said to deal with reception and cultural transfer (translation, cultural export, marketing, branding, readership/audience, fandom, mediatisation).

While it has been argued that '[t]he geographical relocation of the crime genre northwards was initiated by [...] Peter Høeg's *Miss Smilla's Feeling for Snow*' (Forshaw 2012, 5), and while Mankell's role in modifying the key themes of Scandinavian crime fiction cannot be underestimated, it is unquestionable that the vital contribution to the publishing success of Nordic Noir is Stieg Larsson's *Millennium* trilogy, published in English as *The Girl with the Dragon Tattoo* (2008 [2005]), *The Girl Who*

Played with Fire 2009 [2006]) and *The Girl Who Kicked the Hornet's Nest* (2009 [2007]).

The success of Stieg Larsson's *Millennium* trilogy spurred an inundation of Scandinavian crime narratives in the form of novels, television series and films on the international market. What became known as 'the Larsson effect' (Bergman 2014b) or 'the Larsson phenomenon' (Forshaw 2012, 64), with the international publishing industry looking for the NSL ('Next Stieg Larsson'), subsequently generated considerable academic attention. Book-length academic titles such as *Scandinavian Crime Fiction* (Nestingen and Arvas 2011), *Death in a Cold Climate* (Forshaw 2012), *Swedish Crime Fiction* (Bergman 2014a) and *Scandinavian Crime Fiction* (Stougaard-Nielsen 2017) have been concerned with the origins of the modern Scandinavian crime novel and its specific generic features, as well as with its intertwined relationship with the development and decline of the welfare state. A particular preoccupation of such scholarship, however, has been the investigation of how and why dark tales from the far corner of the Northern Hemisphere have attracted global attention.

Historically, crime fiction has been a genre which has moved easily from one cultural sphere to another (see e.g. Platten 2011, 29). Frequently, in the specific case of Scandinavia, such mobility has been facilitated by appeals to exoticism and, perhaps paradoxically, to the troubling of preconceived ideas about a Scandinavian social utopia; the transnational success of Scandinavian crime fiction has been no exception in this regard. Crime novels emerging from the Nordic countries have captured their international readership with exotic (and exoticising) snow-covered, desolate landscapes on their covers, while at the same time challenging and disturbing the widespread image of the region as consisting of well-functioning, exemplary nation states.

On a practical level, while the publishing industry and individuals in the form of academics and translators have certainly played a part in promoting crime fiction from the Nordic countries, it is also noteworthy that the surge of interest in crime fiction from the region has happened at a moment when the positive international image of the Nordic welfare model is in decline. The 'Nordic model' has been an internationally acclaimed social model, and Sweden especially has been regarded as a 'paragon welfare state in its realisation of universalist principles and an institutional welfare model' (Sunesson et al. 1998, 19; see chapter 5 in this volume). However, since the early 1990s, the Scandinavian welfare state has been profoundly transformed, and this has been reflected in crime fiction from the region. It is therefore unsurprising that a key factor in the reception of Nordic Noir has been acknowledgement of the problematics in adjusting to the transformation of societies previously founded on a social solidarity of which ethnic and cultural homogeneity – now things of the past – were seen precisely as the bedrock. These existing themes in Scandinavian crime fiction were brought to the attention of an international audience through Nordic Noir.

A further consideration is that the Nordic Noir phenomenon is based on a geographical categorisation conflating Denmark, Norway and Sweden – as well as the wider Nordic region including Finland, Iceland and the Faroe Islands – into one entity. At a time of globalisation, when cultural products become more and more fluid and transnational, does it make sense to make genre definitions based on nationally defined categories? The label Nordic Noir is itself a product of international success, and one which has been exploited efficaciously as a recognisable brand in the marketing of crime novels produced in the Nordic countries. In many ways, it is clearly problematic to categorise distinct authorial voices within a rather inflexible and predetermined classification. In this regard, it is significant that the concept of Nordic Noir can best be understood as having been constructed *outside* the region; as Stougaard-Nielsen suggests: 'Scandinavian crime fiction is perhaps "only" Scandinavian when viewed or read from abroad' (2017, 206).

Indeed, scholarly criticism dealing with the publishing phenomenon of Nordic Noir accordingly often modifies the regional epithet and points to both commonalities and particularities within the Nordic region's five countries, for instance by dealing with them in separate chapters (e.g. Maricourt 2010, Arvas and Nestingen 2011, Forshaw 2012). Kerstin Bergman, while agreeing that it makes sense to talk about 'Nordic crime fiction as a common, regional phenomenon', also argues that the different 'national crime fiction traditions display their own specificities and preferences – often based on national historical conditions rather than mainstream literary history' (2014a, 173). This tendency to specificity, Bergman contends, is frequently ignored in the international reception. It may also be worthwhile to consider in what ways the amalgamation of the Nordic countries into a fixed set of commonly described features feeds back into the creative production of writers and television and film producers who – consciously or not – might aim to please the encoded expectations of an international readership.

Faceless Killers

Between 1991 and 2013, Henning Mankell (1948–2015) published eleven novels, one short story collection and a novella, all featuring police investigator Kurt Wallander. Mankell's works about Wallander have sold more than 40 million copies and have been translated into forty-one languages, and have additionally been serialised in three different television productions, making them a prominent example of the transposition of a local cultural sphere to an international audience, highlighting different aspects of the processes of translation, adaptation and mimicry.[2] Mankell's novels, having become 'the standard bearer for foreign crime in translation' (Forshaw 2012, 21), have demonstrably been read within the paradigm of Nordic Noir, with a focus on reception and mediatisation (e.g. Tapper 2009, Waade 2012, Peacock 2012, Waade and Toft Hansen 2017, Gregorek 2017). At the same time, the *Wallander* series has been read as an important contribution to the literary history of Scandinavian crime fiction in readings where the focus is on the legacy of Sjöwall and Wahlöö and the socio-historical backdrop of the narratives (e.g. Nestingen 2008, McCorristine 2011, Stougaard-Nielsen 2017).

It is worth bearing in mind that this socio-historical backdrop is not uniform or continuous. While the *Wallander* narratives in many respects generically point backwards to Sjöwall and Wahlöö's 'Novel of a Crime', Mankell's stories are determinedly placed in a historical sphere of *post*-welfarism. The interval between the publication of the last novel in Sjöwall and Wahlöö's series, *Terroristerna* (*The Terrorists,* 1975), and that of Mankell's first *Wallander* novel also coincides with a significant socio-economic shift in Sweden: 'The period 1975–1991 was a transition period from welfare-state industrialism to a post-industrial economy with neo-liberal features' (Tapper 2009, 64). Retrospectively reflecting on the questions which governed his writing of the *Wallander* series in his introduction to *Pyramiden* (1999 [2009]), Mankell himself situates his writing against the context of societal change: 'What is happening to the Swedish welfare state in the 1990s? How will democracy survive if the foundation of the welfare state is no longer intact? Is the price of Swedish democracy today too high and no longer worth paying?' (Mankell 2009, 1).

Faceless Killers – the first instalment in the series – opens in January 1990 in a bucolic Scanian setting where an elderly farmer couple, the Lövgrens, are brutally attacked and tortured by unknown intruders. The crime is discovered by their neighbours, the Nyströms, who have lived on the farm next door to them for the past 40 years. Before Nyström discovers that a crime has been committed, the old man senses that something is wrong and ponders: 'Something is different. Something has changed' (Mankell 2002, 1). He then questions his own ability to comprehend the situation: 'I'm an old man who can't figure out what's really happening anymore' (5). The text decisively insists on the period 1950–1990 (by mentioning '40 years' three times on the novel's first two pages) as one characterised by the neighbours' shared rural identity and history, daily rhythms and annual routines of seasonal festive celebrations, communal spirit and mutual assistance. The murder of Nyström's neighbours is an abrupt disruption of life as it has been known, and by extension a metaphor for the collapse of the supposedly harmonious, idyllic Swedish society of the post-war settlement, with the ensuing uncertainty about what the future will bring. The woman survives the initial attack and manages, before she dies a couple of days afterwards, to utter the word 'foreigner' (41). The subsequent investigation focuses on various interpretations of this word, and not least on how the word can be misinterpreted by the press and public opinion and reinforce already existing xenophobic attitudes, significantly because of the refugee camp which is situated in the vicinity of the Lövgrens' farm.

The opening chapter functions as a *mise en abyme*.[3] First, it is mirrored in the rest of the novel; second, it reflects the *Wallander* series – which Mankell retrospectively titled 'Novels about the Swedish anxiety' (Mankell 2009, 1); and third, it can also be seen more widely as the incipit, if not the manifesto, for Nordic crime fiction, which broadly from the 1990s onwards addresses questions of national identity, globalisation, immigration and the crisis of the welfare state. What finally triggers the neighbour's realisation that something is wrong in the house next door is an open window: 'he looks at the window again, and now he is sure that it is open. A window that has always been closed at night is open' (Mankell 2002, 3). The neighbour's family name, Nyström (suggesting new current or flow) represents a possible allusion to a metaphor of liquidity or fluidity to characterise the incoming of refugees and immigrants to a previously ethnically and culturally homogenous country – as well as perhaps to new currents in a more general sense indicating changing times and drifts. This metaphor of openness is also reflected in Wallander's anti-immigrant opinions, which are revealed later in the novel in internal monologues concerned with Sweden's open-border policy: 'I really hope that the killers are at the refugee camp. Then maybe it'll put an end to this arbitrary, lax policy that allows anyone at all, for any reason at all to cross the border into Sweden' (44). Wallander's ambivalent relationship with the foreign other is further accentuated in his recurrent erotic and exotic dreams of a black woman with whom he is 'making fierce love' (7) – 'the ultimate colonial fantasy' (Westerståhl Stenport 2007, 4).

Situated on the fringes of Sweden on the Baltic Sea, Ystad, in the region of Skåne (Scania), is a suitable location for Wallander's home town: 'an in-between space where a provincial, almost backward-looking, Sweden meets the modern cosmopolitan world' (McCabe 2015, 757). With ferry crossings to mainland Europe (Denmark, Germany and Poland), the region's function as a borderland and entry point to Sweden for asylum seekers and European immigrants has also made it prone to extreme right-wing factions and xenophobic sentiment. It also thus stands symbolically on a historical cusp between a stable and homogenous past and a volatile multicultural present. It is therefore unsurprising that Wallander, who functions as a liminal, intermediate figure, finds himself articulating nostalgic unease about the transitions the region is undergoing, which affects him personally and professionally as much as it affects society. In an echo of the elderly Nyström in the opening chapter, Wallander reflects on the unnerving shift in socio-cultural contexts for crimes and their investigation: 'A new world had emerged, and he hadn't even noticed it. As a policeman, he still lived in another older world. How was he going to learn to live in a new? How would he deal with the great uneasiness he felt at these changes, at so much happening so fast?' (231).

Wallander, therefore, straddles two socio-historical paradigms, just as in family terms – as a middle-aged man – he stands between two generations, that is, between his progressive daughter travelling the world and whose boyfriend, Herman Mboya, is a Kenyan medical student, and his father, who is locked in a capsule of bygone time, symbolically depicted as repeatedly repainting the same pastoral autumn landscape motif he has painted all his life. His dementia-ridden father's persistent – and, to Wallander, annoying – phone calls are contrasted with his daughter Linda's reluctance to speak to him. The corrosion and breakdown of his marriage and his inability to engage in new sexual relationships adds further to a generalised sentiment of despair; if there are cross-generational communication problems, there is also alienation and anomie within his own generational group, struggling to find its place in a transformed social environment.

Criticism has acknowledged Wallander's status as an embodiment of social and professional disenchantment in the present, combined with an uneasy nostalgia for lost times. He is variously 'the melancholic policeman' (Tapper 2011, 418), 'the burnt-out policeman' (Nestingen 2008, 223), 'a modern nostalgic' (Stougaard-Nielsen 2017, 124), or, in more explicitly political terms, a consciousness emblematically engaged in 'contemplation of the transformation of the welfare state' (Gregersdotter 2013, 82). Wallander, however, is not naïve, observing internally, with a nostalgia that is clearly qualified, that: 'We live as if we are mourning for a lost paradise [...]. But those days have irretrievably vanished, and nor is it certain that they were as idyllic as we remember them' (Mankell 2002, 232).

Like his predecessor, Martin Beck in Sjöwall and Wahlöö's crime narratives, Wallander can be categorised within the group of Scandinavian detectives belonging to the 'Ulcer school' (based on Bo Lundin's characterisation of Beck [1981, 10]). Aware of the effects that his alcohol consumption, poor diet of fast food and lack of sleep has on his general physio-mental state, Wallander is conscious that he must do something about his bodily neglect, but constantly defers it: 'I'll change my eating habits tomorrow. [...]. He ate a hamburger special. He ate it so fast that it gave him diarrhoea. As he sat down on the toilet he noticed that he ought to change his underwear' (Mankell 2002, 34). His self-inflicted physical decline ends with a diagnosis of Type-2 diabetes in the seventh novel, *Steget efter* (1997, *One Step Behind,* 2002), a revelation that leads to a feeling of guilt:

> He realised he only had himself to blame. The foods he ate, his lack of exercise, and his on-and-off dieting had all contributed to the disease [...]. A sense of failure and disgust came over him. He knew there was no way out. He had to do something about his lifestyle.
> (Mankell 2008, 42)

Wallander can easily be interpreted as a micro-level representation of his struggling country: 'The firm and muscular body of the past has withered away under malnourishment and diabetes, and [Wallander] has an empty, despairing soul to match. [He] is a monument of the diseased consumer society, working overtime and fattening his body with a cholesterol overload' (Tapper 2009, 65). When he is diagnosed with diabetes, it further adds to the protagonist's body 'reflecting the wellbeing of the modern nation state' (Peacock 2012, 42).

Mankell's first instalment in the *Wallander* series has promoted different – and contradictory – readings. McCorrestine views it as an expression of the author's political concern and as a locus where the author is able to 'highlight the alarming rise in racism, xenophobia and anti-immigration feeling in Sweden, which traditionally regarded itself as a tolerant and generally welcoming country' (2011, 78). Tapper, on the other hand, reads Wallander as a misogynist and xenophobic character, and asserts that *Faceless Killers,* 'rather than countering or even analysing the roots of paranoid and racist narrative, [...] confirms it in every detail' (2014, 170). Nestingen mediates between these two views by stressing the ambivalence and double vision in the novels, viewing these as characteristic of Wallander as protagonist, as well as 'an allegorical register that insists on the ambivalence of Swedish, and Western, global enmeshment with the Third-World Other' (2008, 244).

Conclusion

During the past decade, there has been an increased scholarly focus on crime fiction from the Nordic region, which has developed alongside the international commercial success of the genre. Scandinavian crime fiction is now the basis of a developed academic field, with scholars working in various areas and adopting interdisciplinary approaches. What remains for scholarship to do to a larger extent is to develop nuanced arguments for highlighting the distinction between two frequently and problematically elided terms of critical shorthand: Scandinavian crime fiction and Nordic Noir. The first of these – characterised by a reflection on and critique of the cultural, social and political environment in the region – has existed since long before the term Nordic Noir came into currency following the decline of the Scandinavian welfare state. However, the Nordic Noir construct – ultimately a marketing one – has taken the upper hand in both scholarship and popular culture. Nordic Noir can therefore be seen not only as a post-welfarist lens through which Nordic crime fiction is read, but also as a post-welfarist filter through which the Nordic region is mediated in the age of neoliberalism. Such critical refinement is especially important given the fact that recent Scandinavian crime fiction's precise subject is the uneasy transition between two socio-economic paradigms, a transition that is occluded by the retrospective application of a simplistic if appealing categorisation (Nordic Noir) to a genre characterised by diversity and discontinuity in its themes and in its contexts.

Notes

1. In this and all subsequent instances of quotations given in English from Scandinavian texts, the translations are my own, unless otherwise stated.
2. The BBC adaptation, featuring Kenneth Branagh as Wallander – just to take one example – offers a mediation of source culture through a particular focus on setting, especially landscape and architecture, which for Waade 'represents […] a "Swedishness" constructed according to a particular British point of view', a perspective 'used explicitly in the framing and marketing of this crime series' (2012, 47–8).
3. A *mise en abyme* ('placing into the abyss') is a device in art where a representation of a small copy of the image is placed in the image, suggesting a recursive appearance. In a broader understanding, the term is used to refer to self-reflexivity, when for example a novel appears within a novel, a film within a film or a play within a play (e.g. the play in Shakespeare's *Hamlet*). In the case of Wallander, the *mise en abyme* happens as a thematic recurrence at various levels.

References

Bergman, Kerstin. 2014a. *Swedish Crime Fiction: The Making of Nordic Noir*. Milan: Mimesis International.

Bergman, Kerstin. 2014b. 'The Captivating Chill: Why Readers Desire Nordic Noir', *Scandinavian-Canadian Studies* 22: 80–9.

Forshaw, Barry. 2012. *Death in a Cold Climate: A Guide to Scandinavian Crime Fiction*. Basingstoke: Palgrave Macmillan.

Fraser, Nancy. 1997. *Justice Interruptus: Critical Reflections on the 'Postsocialist' Condition*. New York: Routledge.

Gregersdotter, Katarina. 2013. 'The Body, Hopelessness, and Nostalgia: Representations of Rape and the Welfare State in Swedish Crime Fiction'. In *Rape in Stieg Larsson's Millennium Trilogy and Beyond: Contemporary Scandinavian and Anglophone Crime Fiction*, edited by Berit Åström, Katarina Gregersdotter and Tanya Horeck, 81–96. Basingstoke: Palgrave Macmillan.

Gregorek, Jean. 2017. 'The Man Who Refused to Smile: Henning Mankell's Wallander Series and Postmodern Cynicism', *Genre* 50 (2): 153–79.

Lundin, Bo. 1981. *The Swedish Crime Story = Svenska deckare*. Bromma: Jury.

Mankell, Henning. 2000. *Danslärarens återkomst*. Stockholm: Ordfront.

Mankell, Henning. 2002. *Faceless Killers*, translated by Steven T. Murray. London: Vintage.

Mankell, Henning. 2008. *One Step Behind*, translated by Ebba Segerberg. London: Vintage.

Mankell, Henning. 2009. *The Pyramid*, translated by Ebba Segerberg and Laurie Thompson. London: Vintage.

Maricourt, Thierry. 2010. *Dictionnaire du roman policier nordique*. Paris: Encrage.

McCabe, Janet. 2015. 'Appreciating *Wallander* at the BBC: Producing Culture and Performing the Glocal in the UK and Swedish *Wallanders* for British Public Service Television', *Continuum: Journal of Media and Cultural Studies* 29 (5): 755–68.

McCorristine, Shane. 2011. 'The Place of Pessimism in Henning Mankell's Kurt Wallander Series'. In *Scandinavian Crime Fiction*, edited by Andrew Nestingen and Paula Arvas, 77–88. Cardiff: University of Wales Press.

Nestingen, Andrew. 2008. *Crime and Fantasy in Scandinavia: Fiction, Film, and Social Change*. Seattle: University of Washington Press.

Nestingen, Andrew and Paula Arvas, eds. 2011. *Scandinavian Crime Fiction*. Cardiff: University of Wales Press.

Peacock, Steven. 2011. 'The Impossibility of Isolation in *Wallander*', *Critical Studies in Television* 6 (2): 37–46.

Peacock, Steven. 2014. *Swedish Crime Fiction: Novel, Film, Television*. Manchester: Manchester University Press.

Platten, David. 2011. *The Pleasures of Crime: Reading Modern French Crime Fiction*. Amsterdam: Rodopi.

Sjöwall, Maj and Per Wahlöö. 1971. 'Kriminalromanens fornyelse', *Politiken*, 30 July, p. 24.

Stougaard-Nielsen, Jakob. 2017. *Scandinavian Crime Fiction*. London: Bloomsbury Academic.

Sunesson, Sune, Staffan Blomberg, Per Gunnar Edebalk, Lars Harrysson, Jan Magnusson, Anna Meeuwisse, Jan Petersson and Tapio Salonen. 1998. 'The Flight from Universalism', *European Journal of Social Work* 1 (1): 19–29.

Tapper, Michael. 2009. 'More than ABBA and Skinny-Dipping in Mountain Lakes: Swedish Dystopia, Henning Mankell and the British Wallander Series', *Film International* 7 (2): 60–9.

Tapper, Michael. 2011. *Snuten i skymningslandet: Svenska polisberättelser i roman och på film 1965–2010*. Lund: Nordic Academic Press.

Tapper, Michael. 2014. *Swedish Cops: From Sjöwall and Wahlöö to Stieg Larsson*. Bristol: Intellect.

Toft Hansen, Kim and Anne Marit Waade. 2017. *Locating Nordic Noir: From Beck to The Bridge*. Cham: Palgrave Macmillan.

Waade, Anne Marit. 2011. 'BBC's *Wallander*: Sweden Seen through British Eyes', *Critical Studies in Television* 6 (2): 47–60.

Wahlöö, Per. 1967. 'Grisen är ett gåtfullt djur'. In *Tryckpunkter: 23 författare i egen sak*, 174–81. Stockholm: Norstedt.

Westerståhl Stenport, Anna. 2007. 'Bodies Under Assault: Nation and Immigration in Henning Mankell's *Faceless Killers*', *Scandinavian Studies* 79 (1): 1–24.

9

North Atlantic Drift: Contemporary Greenlandic and Sami Literatures

Kristin Lorentsen and Jakob Stougaard-Nielsen

To most readers in and outside the Nordic countries, a map of the region's literatures would arguably consist of a few *national* literatures from the Scandinavian 'mainland': Danish, Norwegian and Swedish. Most would likely also note the world-famous saga tradition of the Icelanders, and some would include Finnish-language literature as well. However, such 'maps' are necessarily incomplete in their representation of the languages and literatures of this linguistically and culturally diverse region.

Literary maps or historiographies are conceived, drawn and written, often implicitly, by institutions and various gatekeepers belonging to cultural and metropolitan centres: by universities, journals, theatres, publishing houses, state funders, explorers, translators, prize committees, literary festivals and the news media, and so on. The history of Nordic literature is intricately tied up with a long political and cultural history, with economic and colonial powers, in shifting constellations over time, situated in the capitals of Stockholm, Copenhagen and Oslo. From these centres, concentric circles of peripheral and marginalised literatures have been drawn relative to their geographical, political and cultural distance.

In a Nordic context, Sami, Greenlandic, Ålandic and also Faroese literatures have historically been relegated to the peripheries with the common misconceptions often bestowed on 'indigenous' cultures of being 'backward', traditional and of mere ethnographic interest – in much the same way that literatures from the colonies or rural areas have been perceived from European metropolitan centres for centuries. Just as literatures from former colonies have attracted much attention in literary criticism over the past decades for how they may be seen to 'write back' to the imperial and metropolitan centres, so the map of Nordic literatures is currently undergoing a revision of previously stable dichotomies of centres and peripheries. It is, in fact, no longer possible to merely perceive Nordic literature as 'mainland' Scandinavian literatures and then 'the rest' (see Moberg 2014; Thomsen 2007; Volquardsen 2014, 392–3).

According to the literary historian Pascale Casanova, the way national literatures are mapped is intricately tied to a belief system of 'literary prestige' or 'literary capital', which depends on 'the existence of a more or less extensive professional "milieu"' that legitimises certain literatures over others. According to Casanova, '[c]ountries of great literary tradition continually renew their literary patrimony, through the efforts of all those who participate in it and who consider themselves accountable for it' (2004, 15). In her seminal book *The World Republic of Letters* (2004), Casanova is concerned with how literatures circulate out of the location of their production, how they accrue value in a world of literature dominated by a regime of inequality ('the uneven distribution of resources among national literary spaces', 83) maintained by literary, cultural and economic 'centres' that demonstrate what she calls 'ethnocentric blindness' (23).

The Nordic countries constitute a small literary world-system unto itself, whose literatures travel across geographic and linguistic borders following the routes of existing hegemonies of power, before they may eventually travel further into the world. The map of Nordic literature may be viewed as a regional 'contact zone', according to Mary Louise Pratt's definition: 'social spaces where disparate cultures meet, clash, and grapple with each other, often in highly asymmetrical relations of domination and subordination – such as colonialism and slavery, or their aftermaths as they are lived out across the globe today (2008, 7).

The traditional cultural capitals of the Nordic 'literary world' may, of course, themselves be considered peripheral on a literary world map as belonging to 'small nations' and 'minor languages' (Casanova 2004, 277; Chitnis et al. 2019), in a system where Francophone and Anglophone literatures have accrued the most prestige over the past 200 years. However, the Nordic region has had its own unequal system of literary prestige, with a few centres that have to a large extent been 'blind' to their numerous peripheries. For instance, Denmark's two North Atlantic dependencies, Greenland and the Faroe Islands, and the indigenous Sami peoples whose traditional land spans northern regions of Norway, Sweden and Finland, have struggled to achieve what Casanova defines as, '*two forms of independence* simultaneously: political independence, in order to give existence to the nation as a state and share in its recognition on the international level; and a properly literary independence, by establishing a language that is both national and popular and then contributing, through their work, to the literary enrichment of their country' (2004, 193).

Today, academic research and educational institutions across and beyond the region have begun to confront inherited blind spots, to explore and draw more complex maps of what constitutes Nordic literature beyond the confines of mono-ethnic nations and identities and – more or less – colonial relations of power (see also chapter 10 in this volume). A good recent example of this new current in literary studies is evidenced by the anthology *Nordic Literature: A Comparative History*, which 'strives to examine the region's shared processes of literary production and communication without minimizing their diversity' (Sondrup and Sandberg 2017, 1; see also Volquardsen and Körber 2014b). Contemporary work on Nordic literature should not fail to include habitually ignored literary cultures of the Faroese, Greenlandic and Sami, to include genres formerly not deemed part of the literary canon, and to confront biases in gender and ethnicity that have remained unacknowledged in the past. A contemporary literary map of the Nordic region emphasises literary, linguistic and ethnic diversity and hybridity. It is a much more diffuse map of shifting centres and peripheries. These are intricately involved in the wider globalising world, with its cosmopolitan and hybrid identities that offer new perspectives on past literary traditions and their relation to colonised and peripheral 'others' elsewhere.

This chapter will explore examples of what we have called the 'North Atlantic Drift' in contemporary Nordic literature. Originally an oceanographic term for the north-eastward extension of the Gulf Stream, which brings warmer surface waters of the Atlantic to the North Atlantic seas between Greenland and Norway, we use the term figuratively to signify a reversal of the traditional centre-periphery paradigm within the Nordic region. With this term, we want to illustrate that the literary currents flowing back southwards to the old centres from the North Atlantic region are transported by global waves whose interference within the Nordic region may be seen as particularly intense at the region's fringes. This perspective is in line with Volquardsen and Körber's discussion of what they have called the 'Postcolonial North Atlantic': 'what seems like a loosely scattered collection of peripheral outposts from a London or Copenhagen perspective is suddenly transformed into a coherent transatlantic world region, a *center* in its own right' (Volquardsen and Körber 2014a, 9).

Particularly in the period following the Second World War, the nations and peoples of the North Atlantic have fashioned and negotiated their political and cultural identities against the political centres to the south, notably by using literary and other artistic expressions. The chapter will proceed to consider authors who have played a central part in 'writing back' to the centre; writers who have given voice to aspirations of what Casanova termed 'literary independence'.

Greenland: Gazing Inward, Gazing Outward

'Seen from an external perspective, the Nordic countries may themselves be very exotic, "the far North"', Kirsten Thisted suggests, 'but then again, viewed from within the Nordic countries, the Arctic North certainly constitutes a periphery!' (2007, 201). This peripheral geo-political construction of Greenland from the perspective of the colonial centre in Denmark, Thisted argues, shares traits with what postcolonial scholars call 'orientalism' (a term that captures the way the West has represented peoples and cultures in the East as stagnant, undeveloped and exotic 'others', thereby fabricating the idea that the West is conversely developed, superior and rational (see Said 2003)). Thisted designates the colonial and later postcolonial relationship between Greenland and Denmark a product of 'Arctic Orientalism': an 'othering' of the Arctic periphery that expresses a cultural, political and economic asymmetric relationship also characterising other geo-political and cultural 'contact zones'.

However, this colonial relationship between Greenland and Denmark went through gradual change from the 1953 constitutional law that changed Greenland's status from a colony to a county in the Kingdom of Denmark, up to 1979 when Greenland gained home rule. Since then, steps have been taken to expand Greenland's self-government with the implementation of self-rule in 2009, which meant a greater autonomy in administration and economy, and the introduction of Greenlandic as the country's official language (Körber 2011, 184–5), perhaps with the aim of one day achieving full economic and political independence from Denmark. An important contribution to the changing relationship between the Greenlandic periphery and the Danish centre, is the ability of Greenlandic writers to forge a sense of 'literary independence' through their own 'self-representations' and to make themselves known in the wider Nordic region and beyond.

Although Inuit cultures and Greenlanders have long oral storytelling traditions, and Greenlanders have published fiction in Greenlandic at least since the national awakening of the early 1900s (the first Greenlandic novel *Singnagtugaq* [The Dream], written by Mathias Storch [1883–1957], was published in 1914), no Greenlandic authors really made a name for themselves in Denmark until the bilingual writer Ole Korneliussen (1947–) wrote his novel *Tarrarsuummi tarraq* (1999, published in Korneliussen's own Danish version in 2000 as *Saltstøtten*; The Pillar of Salt). In 2002, Korneliussen was nominated for the Nordic Council Literature Prize, a year after Hans Anton Lynge (1945–), one of the few Greenlandic writers of the same generation to be translated into Danish, found praise for his novel *Allaqqitat* (Confessions). Neither Korneliussen nor Lynge (or any other Greenlandic writer since the prize was first awarded in 1962) won the prize and the wider Nordic circulation of their works in translation that it guarantees. However, as Thisted remarks, 'at least their names were mentioned and Scandinavia was reminded that modern Greenlandic literature does exist! Making Greenlandic literature known to the outside world is an important step in Greenland's drive towards self-representation' (2007, 203).

A new generation of Greenlandic women writers are today in different ways 'writing back' from the North Atlantic by simultaneously exploring the social and existential darkness of their native Greenland from within and gazing out onto a wider world beyond the Nordic region. Niviaq Korneliussen's (1990–) *Homo Sapienne* (2014) and Sørine Steenholdt's (1986–) *Zombieland* (2015) were both nominated for the Nordic Council Literature Prize. Though they did not win, their works have travelled well beyond Greenland and Denmark, with Korneliussen's debut novel attracting particular attention in multiple translations, published interviews with the author and reviews in publications such as *The Guardian*, *The New Yorker* and *The Economist*. *Homo Sapienne* has been translated into several languages and was published for the UK market as *Crimson* (Virago 2018) and the US market as *Last Night in Nuuk* (Grove Press 2019), both translated from the Danish version by Anna Halager.

Sørine Steenholdt's *Zombieland* is a collection of short stories and poems. They are all dream-like allegories that convey a sharp criticism of Greenlandic society, its traditions and institutions. This critique is especially visible in the story 'Mor er blot et ord' (Mother is just a word), which can be read as criticism of the older generation of Greenlanders and how many of them fell into alcohol abuse and left their children to fend for themselves. In this short story one of the neglected children has grown up and is attending her mother's funeral. She feels that the traditional Greenlandic costume – a metaphor for the country and its traditions – is suffocating her. She is disappointed in how her alcoholic mother led her life, and remembers an incident where one of her mother's drinking companions, a Danish man, tried to rape her. However, unlike her mother, who was drunk and sedated at the time, she recalls that she was able to raise her voice and resist the assailant. She refuses to let the Dane destroy her. This can be read as an allegory of how the younger generation of Greenlanders do not see themselves as subservient to the Danes anymore but as an independent people with their own, strong voice. Alcoholism has decreased, and sovereignty has been claimed, but the memories of the suffering and betrayal of the older generation remains. The traditional Greenlandic costume remains a heavy burden on the shoulders of the young.

All of Steenholdt's stories tell of this era. However, the emphasis is on the flaws in contemporary Greenland: poor journalism, untrustworthy leadership, ineffective social institutions and a dysfunctional legal system are but a few. Above all, as the collection title and title of the final story indicate, Steenholdt's Greenland is now a 'Zombieland' – a place where everyone seems to march to the same tune and where no original thinking is to be found. It is a place where people enjoy themselves too much – they party, dance, drink and eat beyond their means – and do not stop to consider their dazed existence. When news break that the prime minister has stolen 100,000 kroner from the national treasury, all the mob seems to care about is revenge and the entertainment value of the case, while the politicians fail to take action and blame the people for the turmoil. It is a country where no one is in control.

A similar tension between traditions, a stagnant society, and a new generation with different lifestyles, hopes and dreams is found in Korneliussen's *Homo Sapienne* (Figure 9.1). In this novel, we follow five young, queer Greenlanders. Each of them is trying to come to terms with their own sexual identity in a society where stereotypical gender roles are etched into everyone. The opening chapter is about Fia, who struggles in her relationship with her boyfriend, slowly realising that she is not into men – or 'sausage', as she has it – and that she prefers women. She finds it difficult to accept this and does not immediately admit to it. However, a traditional life with a man, with all its expectations, fills Fia with a feeling of emptiness and despair. This is aptly illustrated in the opening paragraph of the novel where Fia lists her plan for life in five bullet points, which equate to: 1. Buy a house, 2. Get married, 3. Have kids, 4. Do the same thing over and over every day until finally: 5. Death. But when she realises and accepts that she is lesbian her plan becomes delightfully simple: 'No more sausage' (Korneliussen, 2018, 5).

One of the other characters we follow is Inuk, Fia's brother, who flees to Denmark because word gets out that he has had an affair with a male, married member of the Greenlandic Parliament. A prison analogy is used to describe how he feels about staying in Greenland after the affair is made public. He is afraid that his fellow prisoners, who he compares to a pack of bloodthirsty dogs, will revel in his misery and bite him to death. The gossipy Greenlandic mob is presented as vile and uncontrollable, just like the zombies in *Zombieland*. But even though Inuk escapes to Copenhagen, a place where, according to him, people are 'wiser' (39), he soon discovers that he does not belong there: 'I am not a Dane. [...] Denmark is not my country' (61). On the other hand, Greenland is not a place he wants to return to either. When reflecting on what Greenlandic identity is, Inuk begins with the typical romantic, patriotic definition: 'You're a Greenlander when you respect your ancestors. You're a Greenlander when you love your country. You're a Greenlander when you're proud of your nationality' (58). But then his tone changes: 'What it really means to be a Greenlander: You're a Greenlander when you're an alcoholic. You're a Greenlander when you beat your partner [...] You're a Greenlander when you're evil. You're a Greenlander when you're queer' (58). This juxtaposition of evil and queer emphasises how much Inuk hates both his sexual and national identities. Stuck in this existential limbo, not belonging anywhere, Inuk realises that he needs to accept himself first to eventually find a home: 'Home is me. I am: home' (72).

Korneliussen originally published *Homo Sapienne* in Greenlandic before she translated it into Danish. Through the practice of self-translation, Korneliussen reaches a broader audience beyond her potential readership in Greenland, which has a population of only 56,000. Given that Danish has a strong presence alongside Greenlandic in Greenland (many are bilingual), Korneliussen might have considered publishing directly in Danish. But in an interview given to *The Economist*, Korneliussen states: 'I think [Greenlanders] have a unique voice because we're so small and our language is so different' (Ditum 2018). By prioritising Greenlandic over Danish, she ensures that in her literary work, her mother tongue is not marginalised within the postcolonial realm of Greenland, but, more importantly, Korneliussen suggests that when writing in an 'ultra-minor' language, she is able to provide a distinct accent to Nordic literature.

She keeps true to these perspectives on language even in the Danish version of the novel, where some Greenlandic words, such as *iggu* and *Inatsisartut,* are left untranslated and unexplained. The preservation of Greenlandic words in *Homo Sapienne* resembles so called 'hybrid languages' – for example those that developed in former British colonies where English was mixed with elements of their native tongue, creating their own 'culturally marked English' (Kehinde 2009, 80). The effect of this hybridisation in Korneliussen's novel – in addition to possibly sparking curiosity about the Greenlandic language – is to constantly remind the reader of where the book is from and who is telling the story. It is a literary self-presentation, one that does not essentialise a certain authentic mono-ethnic Greenlandicness, but one that is constantly in translation between several identities – not all of them national.

Homo Sapienne is not simply self-translated but 'born translated', a term for works to which translation 'is not secondary or incidental' but a 'condition of their production' (Walkowitz 2015, 4). Born translated texts challenge a sense of clear distinction between original and derived language. In Korneliussen's case, this is reinforced by the fact that the Greenlandic and Danish versions have identical cover design with a young, naked, Greenlandic woman eating a banana; they are published by the same Nuuk-based publisher Milik (the name of the publishing house is 'tattooed' onto the arm of the woman on the cover); and the two versions have the same title, *Homo Sapienne* (a foreign and made-up term to both languages, suggesting an ironic re-construction of Homo sapiens as a hybrid species). The only paratextual element (those textual and material aspects of a book that surround the text itself) of the two versions that is different is the genre ascription on the cover marking the linguistic difference: *Oqaluttualiaq/Roman* – the Greenlandic and Danish terms for a novel.

By leaving some Greenlandic words in the Danish-language version, the author not only provides a sense of exotic authenticity to the 'translated' Danish version, she also reminds the reader (both the bilingual Greenlander and the mostly non-Greenlandic-speaking Danish reader) that the novel is, although also authored/written in Danish, still in translation, embedding different reader communities. The two versions, therefore, highlight the unintelligibilities that haunt the 'contact zone' between translations and the 'original'; unintelligibilities that also, more symbolically, characterise the identities, genders and relations between the youths. Writing and identity as contact zones of struggles and hauntings are, to a bilingual writer and modern Greenlander like Korneliussen, an inescapable condition. Korneliussen's self-translation is, therefore, not only (though of course also) a ploy to reach a wider readership and preserve a minor language within the hegemonic language of the former

Figure 9.1   Cover for the Danish edition of Niviaq Korneliussen's novel *Homo Sapienne*. Published by Greenlandic publishing house Milik in Nuuk 2014. Cover photo featuring the actor Maria Mathiassen is by Jørgen Chemnitz in collaboration with Korneliussen. Cover design by Ivalu Risager. © Milik Publishing.

colonisers, but, perhaps more importantly, an embrace of the hybrid nature of being a young, queer, bi- or multilingual Greenlander today.

However, the book does not restrict itself to Danish and Greenlandic – global English is also thrown into the mix. English phrases are frequent elements in the dialogue, and each chapter is named after and contains lyrics from American songs, which mirror the characters' emotions and their struggles: 'Home' by Foo Fighters, for instance, illustrates Inuk's longing for belonging when he leaves Greenland for Denmark. Such references to American pop culture and the use of English reflect how Korneliussen's young Greenland is a part of the wider globalised world.

That the characters in *Homo Sapienne* are navigating a much wider, more intricately connected world than the generations that came before, is suggested by the novel's incorporation of illustrations that look like screenshots of text-message conversations. Korneliussen here joins a Greenlandic reality with a global literary trend that seeks to capture modern life through visual representations of social media and mobile multi-modal communication technologies. In *Homo Sapienne* Korneliussen not only turns her gaze inward to her own society but also outward to the world beyond.

Both Korneliussen and Steenholdt are part of the new generation of authors who contribute to the progress towards Greenlandic literary independence. Their works discussed in this chapter debate what it is to be a young Greenlander and the challenges modern-day Greenland faces, while they at the same time weave local Greenlandic issues into a global web through treatments of multiple languages and hybrid identities. Therefore, the 'North Atlantic drift' in contemporary Greenlandic literature, exemplified by Korneliussen and Steenholdt, involves literary works that take a stand against the 'othering' and marginalisation of Arctic Orientalism and instead bring into focus new hybrid, globalised Greenlandic identities.

Sami Literature: Language and Identity

Sami is the language and the name of the indigenous people who inhabit Sápmi – the northern territories of Norway, Sweden, Finland and Russia. The precise Sami population is unknown, due to the lack of a census, but it is roughly estimated to be between 80,000 and 100,000 people throughout the four countries ('Sami in Sweden'). There are ten different Sami languages – some mutually unintelligible. Of these ten, North Sami is spoken by 90 per cent of the Sami-speaking Sami population. The languages have historically constituted a dialect continuum; neighbouring varieties have differed slightly and the speakers have been able to understand each other. Today however, we cannot talk about a continuum, as many of the areas in which Sami is spoken do not border other Sami-speaking areas. In fact, many people who are registered as Sami do not speak Sami at all. The Sami people have historically been subject to discrimination and racism, and some have consequently turned their backs on their Sami heritage. They have experienced land dispossession from the sixteenth century onwards, as well as a missionary period in the seventeenth and eighteenth centuries that sought to eradicate the pre-Christian religion of the Sami (Dooner). Furthermore, the Sami have been subject to both segregation and assimilation, for instance in Norway between 1859 and 1980 where they were subjected to *fornorskningspolitikken* or Norwegianisation politics (Minde 2003), which attempted to unify the languages and cultures of Norway, partly by eradicating or restricting all other cultures and languages apart from Norwegian. The policies entailed restricting property rights for those who did not speak Norwegian or did not have a Norwegian name; it also involved sending Sami children to boarding schools, where they were forbidden to use their native languages (Weinstock 2013).

Due to these historical events, many Sami cannot read or speak Sami. Therefore, novels published in Sami have a small readership and usually attract little attention. However, since the 1980s incentives to increase the body of Sami literature have been implemented with, for instance, the establishment of Sami publishing houses with subsidies from the Norwegian state, which has led to an increase in the number of books published in Sami. The 1980s and 1990s also saw the emergence of several Sami authors writing in other Nordic languages (for example Ailo Gaup and Aagot Vinterbo-Hohr), and since 1985 the Nordic Council Literature Prize has reserved one spot annually for submissions from the Sami language area. In 1991, Nils-Aslak Valkeapää won the prestigious prize for his *Beaivi, áhčážan* (*The Sun, My Father*) – though he has so far been the only Sami author to win the coveted prize.

Today there are between ten and twenty titles of Sami literature published each year. Several young, prominent authors have contributed to this development since 2000, such as Sigbjørn Skåden, Maren Uthaug, Ann-Helén Laestadius, Simon Issát Marainen, Hege Siri, Niillas Holmberg, Rawdna Carita Eira, Jens Martin Mienna and Máret Ánne Sara (Gaski and Skåden 2017). These authors write in different genres for different audiences, and the two novels discussed in the following were originally written and published in languages other than Sami.

Sigbjørn Skåden decided to publish *Våke over dem som sover* (Watch over Those who Sleep, 2014) in Norwegian to reach a larger audience (Myhre, 2014). This appears to have worked, as the novel received generous reviews and wider publicity than is customary for Sami-language literature. Skåden even received *Havmannsprisen* for the best northern-Norwegian novel in 2014. *Våke over dem som sover* is centrally concerned with the mistreatment of the Sami, but it also touches on more generic themes of art, loss of innocence and abuse of power.

It is a 'generational novel' told through *Oldemor* (Great grand-mother), *Bestefar* (Grandfather), *Mor* (Mother) and *Sønn* (Son), all named in the book with their family titles to emphasise their Sami heritage. Their story begins in a turf hut where Oldemor desperately tries to provide a better life for her family. All she can do is trust in the educational system – a system that also instils a feeling of shame in Bestefar by its denigration of the Sami language and culture. As Bestefar too, however, wishes for a better life for his daughter, he refuses to teach her Sami. Sønn is the last link in this chain. He grows up speaking Norwegian but still suffers discrimination for being Sami by other Sami children who deny their own ancestry, and he is furthermore discriminated against for being Norwegian by other children because he cannot speak Sami. Therefore, he is stuck in an identity limbo due to the internalised shame and cultural marginalisation of the older generations. However, as he grows up, he learns Sami and becomes a renowned artist – and in art is power; Sønn now has a strong voice and a fierce determination to tell the stories of his people.

The novel is based on a series of sexual abuse cases that were uncovered in the little village of Kautokeino in the late 1980s and again in the early 2000s. A negative culture of young men in their twenties having sex with under-aged girls appears to have dominated the little village. As the people of Kautokeino do not want journalists from the south to come and lecture them about their own problems (drawing attention to the us/them dichotomy that exists between the north and the south of Norway, as well as between Sami and Norwegians), Sønn, an insider, considers himself the perfect man for the job. He wishes to expose and end this culture with a film project. However, in doing so he becomes complicit in the exploitation of the marginalised; he films himself taking advantage of a young girl to unveil the truth and make art. Once a victim himself, he has now become a perpetrator.

Like the Greenlandic novels previously discussed, Skåden's novel reaches outwards and crosses borders between the Nordic nations by including intertextual references to other Western and European works of art. For instance, Mor listens to Ricky Nelson's 'Hello, Mary Lou' when driving, illustrating that the times and the world are becoming more globally connected and influenced – perhaps opening up a world where Sami people do not have to deny their heritage. Another example is when Sønn watches *Swimming Pool* by François Ozon – a multilingual film that may suggest to him the possibility of two languages co-existing, even if only in a work of art. More revealing of Sønn's nature is his reference to Joseph Conrad's short story 'Secret Sharer', where a captain chooses to lodge a wanted criminal on his ship without anyone knowing about it. He deliberately chooses to do the 'wrong' thing and go against social norms. Sønn uses this story as an analogy to his own actions: 'It is what art is. I do not have to be like that myself, because I can make films that are like that' (Skåden 2015 [2014], 158). Sønn uses this analogy to see his art – and consequently his sexual abuse – as something separate from himself. He justifies the doubleness of his personality, being both a victim and a perpetrator, as necessary for his art. And with this, *Våke over dem som sover* problematises both the complex role of art and the agency the Sami have today. How should a people that has been marginalised for so long behave?

Another writer exploring Sami identity is Maren Uthaug. She is herself half Sami, half Norwegian, though raised in Denmark. She does not speak Sami, and neither does the protagonist of her 2013 novel *Og sådan blev det*. Written in Danish, it has been translated into Sami, but not into English. If it were, the title might be 'And So it Was', which is the guiding mantra that echoes through the pages of the book. We follow Risten, a young girl born in Sápmi, and learn how a series of events outside her control cut her off from her roots and force her to take on a different identity. Her Norwegian father leaves her mother to follow the Danish woman Grethe to her home country. They bring Risten with them to Denmark, but her looks and her language make her an outsider in the new country. Only when she grows up can she return to the place and the mother she was once taken away from, to try to reconnect with her lost past.

Uthaug's novel thematises culture clash, prejudice and identity. These issues are most notably illustrated by language. No matter where Risten goes, to the north of Norway or to Denmark, her language is always criticised and corrected, illustrating a sense of non-belonging. It begins with Risten's grandmother, Áhkku, who greatly disapproves of having a Norwegian as her son-in-law. He speaks Sami fluently, but Áhkku turns a deaf ear when he talks. She does her very best to prevent Risten from becoming too Norwegian, most notably by pressuring her to use Sami instead of Norwegian. She even tells her that Norwegian is the language of the Devil and that Sami is the language of the heart. Later, Risten is forced to leave the Sami language behind, as she is ridiculed and misunderstood every time she tries to speak to someone in Denmark. This loss of identity is further illustrated by the fact that Grethe gives her a new, Danish name: Kirsten. This small but significant change causes confusion when Risten calls her mother to revive their relationship: 'It's me. Who? Kirsten. Who?' (Uthaug, 2015, 66). Risten cannot even remember her original name when she calls her mother – the attempts to eradicate her Sami identity have been forceful and invasive.

Risten, however, is not the only one Grethe has renamed. Risten's best friend and later boyfriend, a Vietnamese boat refugee, is given the common Danish name Niels. He is the second outcast of the book, even more so than Risten. At first, he is forced to live in Grethe's basement, because she does not want him on the upper floors, and later he is banished from the premises entirely. Overt racism adds an extra layer to the novel, and it is a jab at present day Nordic debates about immigration policies. Sami people still experience prejudice, but refugees from Asia and Africa are lower still on the social ladder – at least Risten is welcome to live on the same floor as Grethe.

Even though Skåden and Uthaug's novels were not originally published in Sami, they both thematise topics dealing with Sami culture and identities. The protagonists of both stories find themselves in an existential identity crisis, not knowing if they are Sami, Norwegian or Danish. Language plays a major part in their ability to identify or not identify with Sami heritage and identity. Being denied access to their heritage language may force them to deny their Sami identity, which instils in them a fear of alienation. However, Risten eventually accepts that she has forgotten the Sami language, her Sami heritage and belonging, and she finds peace elsewhere. Her past is still part of her identity, but it is not where she belongs anymore. Her name is Kirsten, not Risten. But in the end Kirsten is not that different from Risten – with only one letter differentiating the two, Kirsten always carries Risten with her. Sønn, on the other hand, chooses to speak Sami instead of Norwegian as an adult to emphasise his Sami heritage, even though Sami is not his mother tongue. And so the two novels seem to come to different yet related conclusions: the feeling of being Sami is intimately linked to speaking Sami; however, Sami identity cannot be rooted out by forcibly supressing the Sami language alone.

Drifting into the wider realm of contemporary Nordic literatures from the previously peripheral North Atlantic and marginalised Sápmi cultures, then, is a more intensely felt experience of living in a constantly shifting, globalising world. It is a world where previously hierarchical identities still impose a heavy burden; yet a new generation of writers, such as the Greenlandic and Sami writers explored in this chapter, are finding powerful voices with which to claim literary independence for their cultures. They claim it through an embrace and acceptance of hybrid identities, as well as new individualised notions of home and belonging, and linguistic plurality.

References

Casanova, Pascale. 2004. *The World Republic of Letters*, translated by M.B. DeBevoise. Cambridge, MA: Harvard University Press.

Chitnis, Rajendra, Jakob Stougaard-Nielsen, Rhian Atkin and Zoran Milutinović, eds. 2019. *Translating the Literatures of Small European Nations*. Liverpool: Liverpool University Press.

Ditum, Sarah. 2018. 'Breaking the Ice: Greenland's New Literary Star', *1843 Magazine*, October/November. Accessed 13 February 2019. https://www.1843magazine.com/culture/breaking-the-ice-greenlands-new-literary-star.

Dooner, Erin. 'Sweden's Saami Policy 1550–Present: Racist?'. Accessed 5 May 2019. https://www.laits.utexas.edu/sami/dieda/hist/race.htm.

Fredriksen, Lill Tove, Sigbjørn Skåden and Harald Gaski. 2019. 'Samisk litteratur'. Accessed 6 October 2019. https://snl.no/samisk_litteratur.

Kehinde, Ayo. 2009. 'English and the Postcolonial Writer's Burden: Linguistic Innovations in Femi Fatoba's *My "Older" Father and Other Stories*', *Journal of African Cultural Studies* 21 (1): 75–89.

Körber, Lill-Ann. 2011. 'Figurations of the Hybrid: Julie Edel Hardenberg's Visions for a Post-Postcolonial Greenland'. In *Globalizing Art: Negotiating Place, Identity and Nation in Contemporary Nordic Art*, edited by Bodil Marie Stavning Thomsen and Kristin Ørjasæter, 183–203. Aarhus: Aarhus University Press.

Körber, Lill-Ann and Ebbe Volquardsen, eds. 2014. *The Postcolonial North Atlantic: Iceland, Greenland and the Faroe Islands*. Berlin: Nordeuropa-Institut der Humboldt-Universität.

Korneliussen, Niviaq. 2015. *Homo Sapienne: Oqaluttualiaq*. Nuuk: Milik Publishing.

Korneliussen, Niviaq. 2018. *Crimson*, translated by Anna Halager. London: Virago.

Minde, Henry. 2003. 'Assimilation of the Sami – Implementation and Consequences', *Acta Borealia* 20 (2): 121–46.

Moberg, Bergur Rønne. 2014. *Resten i Vesten: Verdenslitteratur i modernismens margin*. Hellerup: Forlaget Spring.

Myhre, Tove. 2014. 'Skam og seksualitet', *Nordlys*, 29 April. Accessed 10 March 2019. https://www.nordlys.no/kultur/skam-og-seksualitet/s/1-79-7324832.

Pratt, Mary Louise. 2008. *Imperial Eyes: Travel Writing and Transculturation*. 2nd ed. London: Routledge.

Said, Edward W. 2003. *Orientalism*. London: Penguin.

Skåden, Sigbjørn. 2015. *Våke over dem som sover*. Oslo: Cappelen Damm.

Sondrup, Steven P. and Mark B. Sandberg. 2017. 'General Project Introduction'. In *Nordic Literature: A Comparative History, Volume I: Spatial Nodes*, edited by Thomas A. DuBois and Dan Ringgaard, 1–18. Amsterdam: John Benjamins Publishing Company.

Steenholdt, Sørine. 2015. *Zombieland*. Nuuk: Milik Publishing.

Swedish Institute. 2019. 'Sami in Sweden'. Accessed 9 March 2019. https://sweden.se/society/sami-in-sweden/.

Thisted, Kirsten. 2007. 'Stepping off the Map? Greenlandic Literature between Nation and Globalisation'. In *Centring on the Peripheries: Studies in Scandinavian, Scottish, Gaelic and Greenlandic Literature*, edited by Bjarne Thorup Thomsen, 201–10. Norwich: Norvik Press.

Thomsen, Bjarne Thorup, ed. 2007. *Centring on the Peripheries: Studies in Scandinavian, Scottish, Gaelic and Greenlandic Literature*. Norwich: Norvik Press.

Uthaug, Maren. 2013. *Og sådan blev det*. Copenhagen: Lindhardt og Ringhof.

Uthaug, Maren. 2014. *Sånn ble det*, translated by Eivind Lilleskjæret. Oslo: Bastion.

Volquardsen, Ebbe. 2014. 'Pathological Escapists, Passing and the Perpetual Ice: Old and New Trends in Danish-Greenlandic Migration Literature'. In *The Postcolonial North Atlantic: Iceland, Greenland and the Faroe Islands*, edited by Lill-Ann Körber and Ebba Volquardsen, 391–417. Berlin: Nordeuropa-Institut der Humboldt-Universität.

Volquardsen, Ebbe and Lill-Ann Körber. 2014. 'The Postcolonial North Atlantic: An Introduction'. In *The Postcolonial North Atlantic: Iceland, Greenland and the Faroe Islands*, edited by Lill-Ann Körber and Ebba Volquardsen, 7–29. Berlin: Nordeuropa-Institut der Humboldt-Universität.

Walkowitz, Rebecca L. 2015. *Born Translated: The Contemporary Novel in an Age of World Literature*. New York: Columbia University Press.

Weinstock, John. 2013. 'Assimilation of the Sámi: Its Unforeseen Effects on the Majority Populations of Scandinavia', *Scandinavian Studies* 85 (4): 411–30.

10
New Scandinavians, New Narratives

Anne Grydehøj

A range of terms – *kebabnorsk*, *Rinkebysvenska* and *perkerdansk* – has been deployed to describe speech varieties mixing standard language, slang and minority languages, employed by young people in Scandinavian suburbs with demographic concentrations of immigrants. In recent decades, fictional texts have emerged from these spaces – often considered marginal in relation to a perceived homogeneous and normative culture – which creatively use hybrid languages to explore issues of identity, relationships between majority and minority cultures, and cultural diversity.

This chapter discusses three such texts, each from one Scandinavian country: Jonas Hassen Khemiri's *Ett öga rött* (One Red Eye, 2003) from Sweden, Yahya Hassan's *Yahya Hassan* (2013) from Denmark, and Maria Navarro Skaranger's *Alle utlendinger har lukka gardiner* (All Foreigners have their Curtains Closed, 2015) from Norway. The chosen texts prompt comparative analysis because they deal with themes of identity, issues of national and cultural belonging, and youth experiences in ethnically heterogeneous urban spaces on the periphery of cities (respectively: Stockholm, Aarhus, Oslo). Formally, they also share a number of features such as their use of constructed, non-standard sociolects and their focus on an adolescent first-person narrator/lyrical voice in intimate genres: the diary form (Khemiri and Skaranger) and autofictional poetry (Hassan).[1]

Another common feature of these works is their pigeonholing by media and academics in the ostensibly self-evident yet problematic category 'indvandrerlitteratur' (immigrant literature) and its Norwegian and Swedish equivalents – a category where questions of authenticity, supposedly accurate accounts of life in the 'ghettos', and authors' biographical backgrounds have been blended with literary appreciation. To this extent, the works have also generated broader debates – in which the writers themselves have participated – on issues of immigration, integration, multiculturalism and multilingualism.

This chapter, following a summary of the texts' reception and of terminological issues concerning how they are situated by commentators in the cultural landscape, will focus on their employment of speech styles which are seemingly characteristic of multi-ethnic youths, and function as a means for them to record the experience of suburban environments and to engage with issues of identity.

Categorisation and Terminology

One preoccupation of literary criticism when it engages with texts which deal with issues of identity in intercultural contexts, has been that of labelling and categorisation. Multicultural literature (Leonard 2008), minority literature (Gröndahl 2007), immigrant literature (Hauge 2014), transnational literature (Walkowitz 2007), migration literature (Frank 2013) are but a few of the designations applied to these texts, of which some deserve further comment.

The media attention generated around writers with immigrant backgrounds has prompted scholarly talk of an 'ethnic breakthrough' (from the Danish: 'Det etniske gennembrud') in Scandinavian literature (Leonard 2008), implicitly alluding to the late-nineteenth-century literary and social movement 'Det moderne gennembrud' ('The Modern Breakthrough'; see chapter 7 in this volume). Leonard highlights a competition organised by the publisher Gyldendal and the newspaper *Berlingske Tidende*, aiming to attract Danish authors with other-ethnic backgrounds in order to bring Denmark up to speed with the other Scandinavian countries in terms of the 'important metric' of modernity constituted by 'an internal ethnic literature' (Leonard 2008, 32).[2] The ethnic background of the writer is perceived as a selling point at a time when Scandinavian societies are experiencing demographic change: 'The iconic images of "immigrant writers" can be seen as a marketable commodity [...] profitable for both domestic and international consumption and reflect[ing] many levels of power struggle of superiority and inferiority, center and periphery' (Gokieli 2015, 212).

Another way of approaching these texts is to see them as part of a wider literary trend reflecting an age of migration. Khemiri, Hassan and Skaranger are not the first authors to record experiences of migration and navigation of multiple cultural spaces in literature. Rather, publications like theirs can be seen in terms of a twentieth-century trend, which Frank (2008) coins as 'migration literature'. Reflective of cultural shifts relating to demographic, ethnic and social changes, this category also includes works by modernist and late-modernist writers from James Joyce and Henrik Ibsen to Doris Lessing and Salman Rushdie, all exiled either by force or by choice and thus living between two or more languages and cultures (Frank 2013, 200–3). In a similar vein, Walkowitz (2007) employs a broad and inclusive definition and specifies that 'the political and social processes of immigration shape the whole literary system [...], and not simply the part of that system that involves books generated by immigrant populations' (533).

The term 'immigrant literature' is thus far from helpful, yet it has been a persistent feature of discussion of works of the kind outlined above. A typical example can be found in a 2014 article by Hans Hauge, the title of which – echoing postcolonial theorist Gayatri Spivak's famous enquiry 'Can the Subaltern Speak?' (1985) – asks: 'Kan indvandrere skrive litteratur?' (Can immigrants write literature?). Unlike Spivak's complex reading of subalterity, however, the framing of the discussion following this question presents 'immigrant literature' in very narrow terms:

> [I]mmigrant literature in the Nordic countries is literature written by Arabs, who are more or less culturally Muslim. [...] [P]articular about migrant literature is that it is a closed category for the majority. I cannot as a native Dane write it. I cannot choose to be a Palestinian-Danish author.
>
> (Hauge 2014)

Hauge, defining his label solely in terms of the writer's (Muslim, Arab) background, links it to a notion of authenticity: 'Suddenly, place of birth, biography and nationality have become defining categories [making] the texts authentic' (Hauge 2014). A position on 'immigrant literature' such as Hauge presents has been criticised by scholars and writers alike. The author Astrid Trotzig (2005) has mounted a far-reaching critique of the term's use in the Swedish context, where ethnicity has become the 'lens' through which all works written by writers of foreign background are mediated. This view, for Trotzig, risks 'homogenizing' and 'discriminating', in that it overlooks authors' or narrators' highly individual perspectives (2005, 107–10). Literary scholar Magnus Nilsson takes this point further in *Den förestallda mångkulturen* (The Imagined Multi-Culture), shifting the focus of critical attention from the biography of the authors to one of discursive context:

The key to understanding the relationship between ethnicity and literature is the insight that ethnicities are *culturally constructed identities*. And this insight implies in turn that literary texts can never be considered as an *expression* of any ethnic culture or identity. The fact that ethnicities are cultural constructions implies that they are *constituted* in cultural practices. And given that fiction is one of these practices it must be regarded as a phenomenon contributing to the *construction* of ethnic identities.

(2010, 220)

Bounced against readers' expectations, ethnic identity in Khemiri, Hassan and Skaranger's works is therefore manifestly a construct in dialogue with prior constructs, in the same way as the supposedly mimetic representations of 'ethnic' youth language in these works are constructs, subverting expectations of linguistic 'authenticity'. This subversive quality can be seen in all the respective examples, which we will now examine in turn.

Jonas Hassen Khemiri: *Ett öga rött* (2003)

Jonas Hassen Khemiri's *Ett öga rött* (2003) was marketed by publisher Norstedts as 'den första romanen skriven på tvättäkta Rinkebysvenska' (The first novel written in real Rinkebysvenska) (Khemiri 2006, 28).[3] Media responses followed suit, hailing Khemiri's debut novel as 'a breakthrough for Swedish immigrant literature' in which the readers can get 'to know how the "other side" lives' (Gunnarson 2003). These narrated 'experiences of the ethnically-defined underclass' depend 'not least on the fact that the sociolect – Rinkeby Swedish or whatever you choose to call it – gives an expressive contemporary colour' (Gunnarson 2003). Another characteristic of journalistic engagement with the novel is the inclination to merge Khemiri and his protagonist: '*Ett öga rött* is not characterized by subtle distinctions between the author and the written [...]. [Khemiri] stands for every word, every assertion about the order of things' (Strömberg 2003). Khemiri himself, however, rebuts the reception's reductive classification of *Ett öga rött* regarding his protagonist Halim's use of language:

I would probably call it innovative Swedish or Halim-Swedish. The worst word is Rinkeby Swedish, that's such a simple box to close the language into. It would be great if the book wasn't seen as a 'Rinkeby book' or a 'ghetto book'.

(cited in Leonard 2005, 24)

In fact, the starting point for the novel's narrative is precisely a departure from the 'ghetto'. After his mother's death, Halim moves to a less ethnically diverse part of Stockholm with his father, who makes concerted attempts to assimilate to Swedish culture. The novel, written from Halim's point of view in diary form, tells of the complex relationship between the Moroccan-born father trying to escape his cultural background and his Swedish-born son, rebelliously refusing to 'svennefieras' ('be Swedified') and seeking his Arab roots (31). Convinced that the government has designed an integration plan for the purpose of suppressing the Arab identity he aims to (re)discover, he sets out to assert it through the element of it with which he has familiarity: language. Dalanda – the elderly Libyan woman who shares her Islamic-world perspectives with Halim – introduces him to a pithy aphorism (in the form of an invented Arabic proverb) implicitly linking language with individual identity and worth, and demonstratively deploying a stereotype associated with the cultural identity Halim aims to inhabit: 'A man without language is like a camel without humps – worthless' (12). Having internalised the importance of language, Halim singles out writing as its most significant vehicle. The notion of language as recorded in text is something stable and liberating, established as a theme in the novel from the outset: Dalanda gives Halim a notebook, an action she accompanies with a speech about prominent Arab writers and how Arabs invented letters. Dalanda, asserting that 'texts are not like people who change and forget', advocates Halim's use of the book (a star and crescent on its cover) as a means of preserving his Arab identity. This is doubtless also reflected in the red and gold 'Oriental' rug motif on the cover of the novel in the Norstedts edition.

Halim's conscious choice to break the grammatical rules of Swedish when writing his diary therefore forms part of his rebellion against the pressure placed upon him to become Swedish and forget his Arab roots. Halim's creative use of broken syntax and invented vocabulary is an example of a subversive productivity arising from imposed cultural constraints, and yet sits at odds with his utterances to his father in Arabic, which are rendered in grammatically perfect Swedish.

Language is closely connected to Halim's physical and mental well-being. When Dalanda moves away at the end of the first part of the novel, his language collapses at the same time as he falls ill. In a stream of consciousness with fragmented syntax and scarce punctuation, he describes a feverish bath focusing on each of his body parts. Fragmentation of the body into discrete and disconnected components no longer forming a coherent whole is mirrored in the incoherent sentence structure. This breakdown of bodily and textual stability leads to Halim's deliberations at the beginning of the novel's second part, where he considers abandoning his diary. These thoughts are closely related to the young teen's grief at the loss of Dalanda, which further mirrors the loss of his mother. The physical loss of loved ones projects itself into agonising thoughts about the text, concluding with it being regarded as a force that prevents memory from fading away, significantly when Halim consciously chooses his Arab voice:

> It's been like two voices fighting in the brain. One says it's time to put the writing on the shelf [...] For why keep writing philosophies and thoughts when people like Dalanda say they will always be there, and then leave town? The other voice has spoken with a Libyan accent and reminded me that the text is the best way of keeping the memory and at the same time keeping the balance. Plus, words are the hardest weapon, never going blunt or running out of bullets.[4]

Halim refers to himself as 'not a complete Swede'. The notion of incompleteness is reinforced further by a motif of fragmentation: in particular, a fragmentation of the self. This fragmentation is also played out on a narrative level where Halim, who is writing his diary in the first person, frequently removes the *I* from the text and adopts third-person description. This often happens when Halim finds himself in an insecure position – he steps away from the first-person narrative voice and observes himself from the outside: 'It's not often that Halim speaks, but when he does, people understand that it's serious. Despite this he sometimes gets the feeling that they are laughing when he's not looking' (38–9).

Just as Halim inhabits different narrative personae, he also inhabits different varieties of language, between which he can switch to suit a given situation. It bears reiteration that the language in Khemiri's novels is above all literary, and not to be mistaken for a faithful reproduction of Rinkebysvenska (Myhr 2018, 84). Khemiri's description of the language Halim employs focuses similarly on the youth's cognisant manipulation of the language: 'What Halim does is to try to dissect the Swedish language on purpose – he can speak the language perfectly, but tries to give the impression of the opposite' (Thompson 2005, 3). This linguistic dissection, which can be seen as another form of fragmentation, is essential to Halim's assertion of his own individuality. For Khemiri, again: 'he purposely gets expressions and constructions "wrong" in order to create an identity for himself, in order to express himself in a language he doesn't regard as being his own' (Thompson 2005, 3).

Halim, then, who feels he does not belong in Sweden, longs for a homeland, but the 'homeland' for which he longs is not geographically located in Morocco, where his parents originate, but is rather an imaginary dreamland constructed across the Arabic-speaking Muslim world of North Africa and the Middle East. This imaginary setting is at odds with the notion of imposed assimilation in Sweden, represented by the authorities' integration plan that Halim is convinced is real and designed to make all Arabic-speaking people assimilate and abandon their own identity. His proof for this sinister agenda is an article he finds, which asserts that multiple housing associations have threatened to give notice to 'all *blattar* [≈'pakis'] who have a satellite dish on their balcony' (55).

In defiance of this imagined threat, Halim undertakes precisely to obtain a satellite dish as a birthday present for his father, Otman, whose assimilation to Swedish culture is linked with watching TV programmes such as *Who Wants to be a Millionaire? Expedition Robinson* and *Jeopardy*.[5] The satellite dish, Halim assumes, can enhance the signal and provide them with authentic Arab culture, countering what he sees as an unthinking and unquestioning assimilation. However, when his father finally installs the antenna, they are presented with the same range of programmes dominating the television entertainment industry worldwide. Within globalising geopolitical structures, the novel suggests that the hope for a single cultural identity is futile.

Maria Navarro Skaranger: *Alle utlendinge har lukka gardiner* (2015)

Like Khemiri's *Ett öga rött,* Norwegian-Chilean author Maria Navarro Skaranger's debut novel depicting the fringes of society and challenging contemporary Norwegian literature – 'full of narratives from the academic middle class' (Prinos 2015) – is written in a fictional diary form. The novel's reflections on life in the ethnically heterogeneous and multicultural Romsås in suburban Oslo, written in the teenage narrator's own composite, hybrid language, immediately attracted attention upon publication. Not surprisingly, familiar tropes were used to describe the book, here summed up from excerpts from newspaper reviews chosen for the back cover of the novel's second edition: 'Bullseye in Kebab Norwegian', 'a rare experience of authenticity' and 'everybody who wants to know more about the society in which we live, ought to have a look at this novel'.

Skaranger, brought up in Romsås, intends her book to counter a public discourse on immigrants and where they live: 'You get tired of the way Romsås is stigmatised' (Petersen 2015). Questioned about the novel's prejudicial titular claim, she says: 'This is how the media depicts places like Romsås [...]. My book shows the opposite: that it is a diverse and open place' (NRK 2015). The leopard skin on the front cover of the novel, which has been seen as an allusion to kitsch hip-hop music videos (Jagne-Soreau 2018, 10), likewise plays with people's preconceptions of the Romsås environment.

Mariana, the main character, has a Norwegian mother and a Chilean father, and she captures this bicultural background in her email address Chica_chile_norge@hotmail.com. Linguistically, her Spanish-speaking background is barely identifiable. She adopts a variety of Arabic, Turkish, Persian, Urdu and English-American words and phrases. Mariana's constructed suburban language is therefore decisively a multi-ethnolect, which in sociolinguistic terms can be outlined as 'a variety or style which has developed in multi-ethnic urban communities and which is associated with speakers of mixed ethnic groups' (Quist 2008, 44).

Another important dimension of the multi-ethnolect is the users' conscious linguistic choice to establish a common expression of identity: 'several minority groups use it collectively to express their minority status and/or as a reaction to that status to upgrade it' (Clyne 2000, 87). Whereas Khemiri's text deploys the distinct speech style as an expression of the narrator's assertion of an individual identity in his navigation of two cultures, Mariana's language is a manifestation of a multicultural collective identity where age and place (being young in Romsås) are more significant markers of identity than individual ethnic and cultural origins. However, it is also clear that Mariana's language is a literary manipulation of the variation of Norwegian spoken in Romsås, and Skaranger emphasises herself that the novel's language is 'exaggerated and constructed' (NRK 2015).

Similarly to what we have seen in Khemiri, language is also for Mariana a means of searching for and expressing an identity. On the one hand, Mariana subverts normative linguistic strictures within society; on the other, she challenges familial authority by asserting the very same linguistic norms she elsewhere subverts. In an exchange with her father, this irony is articulated in a linguistic assertion that reveals linguistic gaps typically existing between first- and second-generation immigrants:

Mariana, why have you put your 'sminsker' in the middle of the corridor, and I'm like: it's 'smykker' [jewelry] and not 'sminsker', and dad's like: what do you mean, and I'm like: learn Norwegian before you get you to Norway, so daddy goes mental and that's why I'm now sitting in my room.[6]

Mariana counters the paternal authority to which she is subjected by in turn subjecting her father to integrationist authority, reminding him of the need to speak the host language.

In Khemiri's *Ett öga rött*, Halim, desperately trying to separate Swedish culture from his self-imagined homogenous Arabic culture, discovers that in a globalised world different cultures have merged. For Mariana, however, cultural plurality and mixing is an integral and unproblematic part of the cosmopolitan community where she lives. The fact that she has a mixed background is nothing unique in Romsås, where there are only a few 'poteter' (potatoes), i.e. ethnic Norwegians, in her class. In a lesson on Norwegian emigration to the United States, the discussion touches upon questions of nationality, on which the narrator comments:

> In class we are all Norwegian, but everybody, except Ruben, Nora, Johnny and Marius, also considers themselves foreigners, either halfway or fully, and Johnny wants always to discuss if can you say that everybody who is half-Norwegian and half-foreigner also can count as genuine foreigners (22).[7]

It is clear here that the notion of a 'true' identity – whether foreign, or, as is implicit, Norwegian – does not make sense. Hybridity has become, paradoxically, a norm, which is reiterated throughout the text, such as when Hispanophone and South-Asian identities are unproblematically juxtaposed during an international week at the school: 'Til slutt punjabigruppa kom på scenen som er alle pakkisgutta pluss Anders som også er blitt pakkis på sin egen måte og hadde tatt på seg sånne hvite pakkisklær, og Anders også er latino og derfor de kaller gruppa El Punjabi' (At the end the Punjabi group came on stage which is all the paki guys plus Anders who has also become a paki in his own way and had put on these like white paki clothes, and Anders also is Latino and therefore they call the group El Punjabi) (41).

Yahya Hassan: *Yahya Hassan* (2013)

Danish literary scholars at the beginning of the twenty-first century had been concerned with the dearth – by Scandinavian standards – of Danish writers from immigrant backgrounds on the literary scene (Hauge 2014, Leonard 2008, Frank 2013). Yahya Hassan's volume of poems therefore stirred considerable debate in the Danish media on publication in 2013: 'When Yahya Hassan's poetry collection finally came out, it was a moment of release. Finally, many people sighed. They can write', Hans Hauge wrote in his review of the book (2014). The book, which sold over 100,000 copies within a couple of weeks, also tapped into ongoing debates in Denmark, prompting remarks on literature as a potential vehicle for societal critique:

> In this tribal country, we have for decades shouted about the need for 'coherence', while in reality we have treated refugees and immigrants as second-class people in asylum centres and special areas of towns, which have been put on the government's official ghetto list, but we needed an 18-year-old poet from the ghetto to talk, before the elite would listen.
>
> (Pedersen 2014)

The publication was subsequently employed by people on different sides of the political spectrum to argue their case for/against immigrants and integration in Danish society, and was deemed equivalent in its provocation of debate on freedom of speech to the publication of the Mohammed drawings in 2005 (Søndergaard 2013).

In addition to the political readings, *Yahya Hassan* also prompted discussion because of its autofictional character, blurring the already ambiguous space between fiction and biography. The biographical content of the self-titled collection of poems centres around the reflections of a young poet raised in a Muslim-Palestinian family in the housing estate Trillegården in a suburb of Aarhus – which the speaker refers to as 'GHETTOEN'. The back cover of the collection carries the brief statement 'Yahya Hassan, født 1995. Statløs palæstinenser med dansk pas' (Yahya Hassan, born 1995. Stateless Palestinian with a Danish passport), conflating the author's biography with the collection's textual substance. As a contrast to the Oriental(ist) paratextual wrapping of Khemiri's *Ett öga rött,* the cover of *Yahya Hassan* is streamlined and monochrome, suitable for any coffee table in a setting surrounded by minimalist Scandinavian interior design. However, the contrasts can also be seen as a comment on the binary and rigidly deadlocked schemes dominating the discourse on cultural cohabitation: 'The colours mime the dichotomous categories of the "self" and "other" in the debates on "immigrant literature", the black and white of the ethnicized world view, the alleged insurmountability of cultural differences' (Gokieli 2015, 217).

The poems shout. Entirely written in uppercase, the exclamatory and angry typography matches the content, which mounts a fierce and aggressive attack on authorities (the father, Islam, the Muslim community, drugs, the police, etc.) and their physical and mental abuse. The poems have as such been seen as 'a breaker of taboo of political correctness' (Hoffmann 2018, 143). The author's controversial public interventions, featuring angry critiques of his parents, the Muslim community, religion and Danish authorities – alongside his criminal history – added considerably to the media hype surrounding the publication, further blurring the borders between text and context: '[t]he iconicity of an "immigrant writer" makes an immediate assumption between the signifier and the signified, the migrant experience inscribed in the foreign body and the textual story of the same' (Gokieli 2015, 218). As a literary phenomenon, the publication has therefore also been seen as a catalyst for revising literary methodology and theory, as well as renewing literary reading practices by including extra-textual elements.

Hassan's poetic playfulness runs through a spectrum of rhetorical registers from a linguistically complex and vocabulary-rich version of Danish pertaining to a formal, standard variant of the language to a rudimentary and grammatically 'incorrect' suburban youth version. The chronological order of the poems runs from early childhood, where the speaker narrates criminality, brutality and violence (both at home and in the housing estate), the lack of understanding of the welfare institutions, break-ins, assaults, police chases, Yahya's arrest (making up the first 75 poems), to adulthood, where Yahya is a sought-after poet (the last poem).

Curiously, the descriptions in the first part are written in standard Danish, whereas the last and longest poem, 'LANGDIGT' [Long-poem], is written entirely in what has been characterised as 'a stylised perkerdansk' (Andersen Nexø 2013). 'LANGDIGT' functions as an epilogue that rewinds time to past childhood events, to which is added a fierce critique, from the perspective of the adult writer, of parental, religious and societal authorities. In this 34-page poem, 'Yahya' having been accepted at the prestigious *Forfatterskolen* and about to have his poems published, starts off with the self-assessment: JEG ER EN SUND OG VELINTEGRERET DIGTER (I am a healthy and well-integrated poet; 135). The following description of the performance of the 'well-integrated poet', however, mocks a perceived view of the 'immigrant writer' as someone who ought to behave in engaged and productive dialogue with the establishment on unproblematic issues:

OG MIG JEG INSPIRERER TIL ARTIKEL
OG MIG JEG SIGER DET TIL GYMNASIEELEVER
OG TIL UNIVERSITETSSTUDERENDE
OG TIL KUNSTNERNE OGSÅ
MIG JEG SIGER DET TIL INTERVIEWER
FRA DANMARKS RADIO
MIG JEG TALER OM MARKEN OM TRÆERNE
MIG JEG SIGER
DET ER EN SMUK LAND! (136).[8]

Writing poetry about the beauty of nature is decisively not the errand of the speaker. This initial ironic staging of the writer as a nature-loving poet in a classic pastoral tradition is denounced by the contrasting story of life in the 'ghetto', which is laid out for discussion:

HER ER MIN HISTORIE! DISKUTER DEN
MED SUKKERKNALD OG KAFFE I JERES MÆLK
NU DER ER OPKALD FRA MELLEMØSTEN IGEN (137).[9]

There follows an aggressive litany of incoherent biographical flashbacks in random order, reiterating many episodes already described in the first part of the collection, all spiced with abundant profanities, sexual explicitness and inserted Arabic words.

The double referent MIG JEG (Me I), which is a typical linguistic feature of speakers of Danish from Arabic-speaking backgrounds, appears more than 150 times in the poem. This rhythmic recurrence of MIG JEG enforces the sense of centrality of the speaker's navigation of a hyphenated identity:

MIG JEG SIGER HEJ DEM DE SIGER SALAM
MIG JEG SMILER JEG KIGGER PÅ MIN SELV I SPEJLEN
JEGEN I SPEJLEN KIGGER PÅ MIN SELV (151).[10]

However, the significant split of the speaker into both an object (MIG) and a subject (JEG) pronoun can also be regarded as a poetic device alluding to the construction of the immigrant voice from both internal and external positions.

Language is an explicit theme in the poem, in which the alternation between different linguistic registers forms part of the subject's navigation of different environments (the intellectual and literary scene versus the 'ghetto'). A well-crafted sentence such as JEG SIGER AT JEG I DET

MINDSTE TALER MANIPULERENDE GODT DANSK (I say that at least I speak Danish manipulatively well; 139), in which form corresponds to content, contrasts with the following sentence, characterised by oral speech markers, informal contractions, swearing and grammatical incorrectness: MIG JEG SIGER HAN SKA HOLD HANS FUCKING KÆFT (Me I say he should keep his fucking mouth shut; 139). Pointing to the linguistic markers characterising 'perkerdansk', the MIG JEG speaker is conscious of the characteristics of the speech style: MIG JEG KOKSER I MIN ORDSTILLING/OG JEG SIGER WALLAH (Me I mess up the word order/ and I say Wallah; 149). At various points in the poem, the pulsing MIG JEG is interrupted and replaced by an equally ambiguous second person pronominal addressee: the hypocritical religious criminal, who is linguistically incompetent in both languages:

> DIG DU BLIVER HIP HOP OG KRIMINEL OG MUSLIM
> DIG DU TALER EN GEBROKKEN DANSK
> OG EN GEBROKKEN ARABISK (147).[11]

The enunciation (*about* broken language) and the way the enunciation is performed (*in* broken Danish) thus correspond to and are further refracted from the MIG JEG to the DIG DU.[12] Rather than just being a mimetic rendition of language spoken in multicultural suburban Aarhus, the 'perkerdansk' employed in 'LANGDIGT' is a poetic device which retains both issues of identity and meta-literary commentary on the stigmatisation and stereotyping of the 'immigrant (writer)' in a re-appropriation of language:

> MIG JEG LAVER BARE EN KLICHÈ
> SÅ VÆRSGO/EN KLICHÈ
> TIL DIN LILLE KLICHÈHOVED (163).[13]

To this effect, the poem, after its tirades of fierce attacks and obscene language, points to its own poetic fictionality in the concluding sentence by having the JEG retreat to the initial classic vision of the poet in harmony with nature: 'OG OVENPÅ UGERNINGEN JEG DØSER HEN I FORÅRS-SOLEN' (And following the misdeed I doze off in the spring sun; 169).

Conclusion

On the one hand, texts such as those discussed here have been sold precisely on the basis of their authors' and protagonists' non-normative identities, giving rise to suspicions of a commercialisation of ethnicity and a fetishisation of otherness. However, the texts explicitly engage with these questions: self-consciously and ironically, they reflect critically on expectations relating to literary categories such as 'immigrant literature'. While the reception of these authors suggests that a binary us/them mentality is flourishing in Scandinavian media and on the cultural-criticism scene, the works themselves contrarily accentuate their subjects' multi-positionality. Rather than constituting stable categories, individual, cultural and national identities are negotiated from a plurality of positions and narrative perspectives, rendering them a process, rather than a state of being. Language, as a signifier of identity, likewise undergoes a manipulation, making the notions of authenticity and reality ambiguous. While the categories of *Rinkebysvenska*, *kebab-norsk* and *perkerdansk* assume one single homogenous language entity of 'young people with immigrant background', these speech varieties and the identities associated with them become literary devices functioning within their own literary framework to different ends.

Notes

1. A sociolect is a term used in sociolinguistics to designate a language variation pertaining to a particular social group, defined by, for instance, age, ethnicity, gender or class. The sociolects employed by the works discussed in this chapter are intersectional, used in speech communities characterised by youth, non-normative ethnicity and lower socio-economic standing.
2. In this and all subsequent instances of quotations given in English from Scandinavian texts, the translations are my own, unless otherwise noted.
3. Rinkebysvenska – named after the Stockholm suburb of Rinkeby, which has a high demographic proportion of immigrants – has come to refer to any language variety spoken by youths mixing slang, loanwords mainly from English and Arabic, and a simplified Swedish grammar. The Swedish Language Council recommends the term 'förortssvenska'. The quotation is a statement by the protagonist Khemiri in Jonas Hassen Khemiri's second novel, *Montecore: en unik tiger* (2006), in which the boundaries are blurred between fictional and authorial personae – perhaps as a meta-literary commentary on the conflation in the reception of these two otherwise separate categories.
4. '[D]et har varit som två bråkande röster i hjärnan. Den ena har sagt det är dags lägga upp skrivandet [...] För varför man ska fortsätta skriva filosofier och tankar när såna som Dalanda säger dom kommer alltid finnas nära och sen flyttar från stan? Den andra rösten har pratat med Libyendialekt och påmint texter är bästa sättet att behålla minnet och samtidigt hålla balansen. Plus ord är som mäktigaste vapnet som aldrig blir oslipat eller får slut på kulor' (Khemiri 2003, 89).
5. *Expedition Robinson* (1997–) is a Swedish reality TV programme set on a tropical island where the contestants compete in various survival disciplines.
6. 'Mariana, hvorfor du har legget sminskene dine midt på gangen, og jeg bare: det heter smykker og ikke sminsker, og pappa bare: hva mener du, og jeg bare: lær deg norsk før du kommer du til Norge, så pappa klikka mentalt og derfor jeg nå sitter i rommet mit.'
7. '[I] klassen vi er alle norske, men alle utenom Ruben, Nora, Johnny og Marius også regner seg som utlendinger enten halvt eller helt, og Johnny alltid skal diskutere om kan man si alle som er halvt norsk og halvt utlending også kan regnes som ekte utlendinger' (Skaranger 2015, 9).

8. 'And me, I inspire an article/and me, I say it to A-level students/and to university students/ to artists too/me, I say it to interviewer/from Denmark's Radio/Me, I talk about the field the trees/me, I say/it is beautiful country.'

9. 'Here is my story! Discuss it/with sugar lump and coffee in your milk/now is there a call from the Middle East again.'

10. 'Me I say hi them they say salam/Me I smile I look at my self in the mirror/ the I in the mirror looks at my self.'

11. 'You [object] you [subject] become hip hop and criminal and Muslim/you you speak broken Danish and broken Arabic.'

12. The noun phrase incorrectly uses common gender instead of neuter, and it should have read 'du taler et gebrokkent dansk og et gebrokkent arabisk'.

13. 'Me I just make a cliché/so there/a cliché/for your little cliché head.'

References

Andersen Nexø, Tue. 2013. 'Et forfærdeligt stærkt ærinde', *Information*, 18 October. Accessed 6 October 2019. https://www.information.dk/kultur/anmeldelse/2013/10/forfaerdeligt-staerkt-aerinde.

Björklund, Jenny and Ursula Lindqvist, eds. 2016. *New Dimensions of Diversity in Nordic Culture and Society*. Newcastle upon Tyne: Cambridge Scholars Publishing.

Clyne, Michael. 2000. 'Lingua Franca and Ethnolects in Europe and Beyond', *Sociolinguistica* 14: 83–9.

Frank, Søren. 2008. *Migration and Literature: Günter Grass, Milan Kundera, Salman Rushdie, and Jan Kjærstad*. New York: Palgrave Macmillan.

Frank, Søren. 2013. 'Is There or is There Not a Literature of Migration in Denmark?'. In *Literature, Language, and Multiculturalism in Scandinavia and the Low Countries*, edited by Wolfgang Behschnitt, Sarah De Mul and Liesbeth Minnaard, 197–223. Amsterdam: Rodopi.

Gokieli, Natia. 2015. 'The Iconicity of the "Immigrant Writer": Jonas Hassen Khemiri and Yahya Hassan', *Akademisk Kvarter* 10: 208–21.

Gröndahl, Satu 2007. 'Identity Politics and Construction of "Minor" Literatures: Multicultural Swedish Literature at the Turn of the Millennium', *Multiethnica* 30: 21–9.

Gunnarson, Björn. 2003. 'Den unge Halims lidanden', *Göteborgs Posten*, 4 August.

Hassan, Yahya. 2013. *Yahya Hassan: Digte*. Copenhagen: Gyldendal.

Hauge, Hans. 2013. 'Sættes indvandrerproblemer under debat i dansk samtidslitteratur?'. In *Indvandreren i dansk film og litteratur*, edited by Søren Frank and Mehmet Ümit Necef, 12–45. Hellerup: Spring.

Hauge, Hans. 2014. 'Kan indvandrere skrive litteratur?', *Berlingske*, 22 February. Accessed 6 October 2019. https://www.berlingske.dk/kronikker/kan-indvandrere-skrive-litteratur.

Jagne-Soreau, Maïmouna. 2018. 'Halvt norsk, äkta utlänning', *Edda* 105 (1): 9–28.

Khemiri, Jonas Hassen. 2003. *Ett öga rött*. Stockholm: Norstedt.

Khemiri, Jonas Hassen. 2005. 'From *An Eye Red*', translated by Laurie Thompson, *Swedish Book Review* 1: 3–14.

Khemiri, Jonas Hassen. 2006. *Montecore: En unik tiger*. Stockholm: Norstedt.

Kongslien, Ingeborg. 2007. 'New Voices, New Themes, New Perspectives: Contemporary Scandinavian Multicultural Literature', *Scandinavian Studies* 79 (2): 197–226.

Leonard, Peter. 2005. 'Imagining Themselves: Voice, Text, and Reception in Anyuru, Khemiri and Wenger'. Master's thesis, University of Washington.

Leonard, Peter. 2008. 'Det Etniske Gennembrud – Multicultural Literature in Denmark', *Multiethnica* 31: 32–34.

Lönngren, Ann-Sofie, Heidi Grönstrand, Dag Heede and Anne Heith, eds. 2015. *Rethinking National Literatures and the Literary Canon in Scandinavia*. Newcastle upon Tyne: Cambridge Scholars Publishing.

Nilsson, Magnus. 2010. *Den föreställda mångkulturen: Klass och etnicitet i svensk samtidsprosa*. Hedemora: Gidlund.

Nilsson, Magnus. 2012. 'Swedish "Immigrant Literature" and the Ethnic Lens: The Representation of Cultural Diversity in Jonas Hassen Khemiri's *Ett öga rött* and Marjaneh Bakhtiari's *Kalla det vad fan du vill*', *Scandianvian Studies* 84 (1): 27–58.

NRK. 2015. *Dagsrevyen*, 29 January, 27'55"–34'50".

Olaru, Ovio. 2017. 'Norwegian *innvandrerlitteratur* and the Spell of Transnationalism', *Metacritic Journal for Comparative Studies and Theory* 3 (2): 132–53.

Opsahl, Toril. 2009. '*Wolla I Swear* This is Typical for the Conversational Style of Adolescents in Multiethnic Areas in Oslo', *Nordic Journal of Linguistics* 32 (2): 221–44.

Pedersen, Jes Stein. 2014. 'Litteraturredaktør: Litteraturprisvinderen har allerede forandret verden', *Politiken*, 26 January. Accessed 6 October 2019. https://politiken.dk/kultur/boger/litteraturpris/art5499277/Litteraturredakt%C3%B8r-Litteraturprisvinderen-har-allerede-forandret-verden.

Quist, Pia. 2008. 'Sociolinguistic Approaches to Multiethnolect: Language Variety and Stylistic Practice', *International Journal of Bilingualism* 12 (1/2): 43–61.

Skaranger, Maria Navarro. 2015. *Alle utlendinger har lukka gardiner*. Oslo: Forlaget Oktober.

Spivak, Gayatri Chakravorty. 1985. 'Can the Subaltern Speak? Speculations on Widow-Sacrifice', *Wedge* 7/8: 120–30.

Strömberg, Ragnar. 2003. 'Räkna med bråk', *Aftonbladet*, 4 August. Accessed 6 October 2019. https://www.aftonbladet.se/kultur/a/4doELq/rakna-med-brak.

Trotzig, Astrid. 2005. 'Makten över prefixen'. In *Orientalism på svenska*, edited by Moa Matthis, 104–27. Stockholm: Ordfront.

Walkowitz, Rebecca L. 2007. 'The Location of Literature: The Transnational Book and the Migrant Writer'. In *Immigrant Fictions: Contemporary Literature in an Age of Globalization*, edited by Rebecca L. Walkowitz, 527–45. Madison: University of Wisconsin Press.

Part III
Images

11
Nordic Nature: From Romantic Nationalism to the Anthropocene

Jakob Stougaard-Nielsen

Designed by the architects Todd Saunders and Tommie Wilhelmsen, the dramatic Stegastein observation deck, perched 650 metres above the spectacular Aurlandsfjord in the Sogn og Fjordane region of Norway, was conceived as part of a nationwide project to promote nature tourism (see this book's cover image). It is no coincidence that the British art historian and broadcaster, Andrew Graham-Dixon, chose this backdrop of Norwegian mountains and fjords to introduce his three-part television series *Art of Scandinavia* (BBC 2016). In this series, Graham-Dixon contemplates how the spectacular Nordic natural environment, these 'landscapes of forbidding beauty', has shaped not only the art of Scandinavia, but the cultures, societies and the inhabitants of these 'dark lands' themselves:

> You could say the Scandinavian mind itself has been shaped by nature, like a landscape formed by a glacier. Despite their remoteness, the Nordic peoples have managed to fashion one of the most remarkable civilisations. And the art of Scandinavia shares many of the characteristics of the Scandinavian landscape – hardness, sharpness, clarity. I think the north has also given it some of its most distinctive moral and psychological characteristics. Pride, tempered by a sense of living at the margins – anxiety, loneliness, melancholy. And blowing through it all, like a cold, piercing wind, an absolute determination to endure, come what may.
>
> (Graham-Dixon 2016)

Despite the varied geography and cultures of the Scandinavian countries, from the sparsely populated high mountains of Norway to the flat and densely populated island-nation of Denmark, Graham-Dixon's essentialist notion that a particular 'Scandinavian mind' has been shaped by a particular Nordic nature has deep roots in a tradition, going back to at least the early nineteenth century, of perceiving the North as a homogeneous whole.

According to the cultural historian Joep Leerssen, the outside image or the xenostereotype of the Nordic countries has been deeply influenced by a 'North-South schematization of temperamental oppositions', where the North is considered cool, frugal, cerebral, morally inclined and the South warm, sensual, opulent and immoral (Leerssen 2009, 16). This kind of environmental determinism is nowadays generally regarded as defunct, but it has exerted a powerful hold on the imagination. Leerssen describes it thus: '[c]limate is associatively correlated with landscape, with human habitation patterns, with social and political organization, and in turn rationalized by reference to the inhabitants' purported "character"' (16).

Graham-Dixon's sense of a Nordic mentality shaped by the region's geography is by no means a unique example; it has long been a dominant trope in how the Nordic countries have been perceived abroad and how, in turn, the Nordic countries have moulded their own self-image, their own autostereotype:

> [C]limatic and geographic characteristics of the Nordic countries – such as the light spectacle of the midnight sun – are combined with stereotyped ideas of naturalness, authenticity, and purity and are mythically or even magically charged. Idealizing topoi of longing serve as a kind of branding specific to the region [...]. They are functionalized as self-images or public images to create a region-spanning identity of the North.
>
> (Alsen and Landmann 2016, 14–15)

While environmental determinism is a disputed theory of what makes a nation, a region and its inhabitants, this chapter explores how natural environments, and the pictorial and poetic invention of certain 'Nordic' landscapes, have contributed to the formation of deep-seated identifications with places that are deemed recognisably Danish, Finnish, Icelandic, Norwegian, Swedish or, indeed, Nordic (Olwig and Jones 2008, xi). When Graham-Dixon contemplates the scenery in Norway he is not, in fact, looking at a natural environment, but is instead taking part in a long tradition of creating landscapes, defined by Denis Cosgrove and Stephen Daniels as 'a cultural image, a pictorial way of representing, structuring or symbolising surroundings' (1988, 1) (see also chapter 2 in this volume).

Landscapes have played a central role in the formation of national identities, including from within the Nordic region, through the power of images to create cultural memories. According to Simon Schama:

> [I]nherited landscape myths and memories share two common characteristics: their surprising endurance through the centuries and their power to shape institutions that we still live with. National identity [...] would lose much of its ferocious enchantment without the mystique of a particular landscape tradition: its topography mapped, elaborated, and enriched as a homeland (1995, 15–16).

The first part of this chapter will explore how painters and poets in the first part of the nineteenth century, often referred to as the Romantic period, began to re-imagine the natural world and Nordic spaces as particular landscapes in order to forge national identities and belonging in an age of European political upheavals. The second part will explore how such inherited relations between humans and the environment are being re-examined in an age of global environmental crisis, in the age of the Anthropocene, where natural environments have become, at the same time, fragile and threatening places.

The Invention of Nordic Landscapes

The invention of national landscapes in the Nordic countries was intricately tied to the rapid development of geology as a science in the first part of the nineteenth century. In this period, natural philosophers and geologists fundamentally revised the history of the earth, partly by including ourselves within nature as taking part in an interrelated organic whole. This had a profound impact on how artists and poets would rethink the relationship between nature and culture, where the natural world was no longer imagined as external and subordinated to a human will and rational mind. In the age of the Anthropocene – our current geological age, so named to signify the profound effects of human activities on the earth's crust, the atmosphere and the environment – we continue to ponder how human activities may be better attuned to environmental coexistence (see Gremaud and Hedin 2018; Körber, MacKenzie and Westerståhl Stenport 2017).

In the Nordic countries, the impact of geology and natural philosophy on the arts can be traced back to a series of events beginning in the summer of 1802, when the Danish-Norwegian geologist and natural philosopher Henrich Steffens (1773–1845) returned to Copenhagen from four years of study in Germany. In Jena, a few years previously, he had studied the natural philosophy (*Naturphilosophie)* of Friedrich Schelling (1775–1854), and then mineralogy under the influential geologist Abraham Gottlob Werner (1749–1817) in Freiberg, where he also published his main scientific work *Beyträge zur innern Naturgeschichte der Erde* (Contributions to the internal natural history of the earth) in 1801.

In Copenhagen the following year, he gave a series of nine lectures at Elers Kollegium where he introduced German Romanticism to several central figures in what became known as the Danish Golden Age. Among the listeners were the pastor, poet, historian and ideological father of the Danish folk high school N.F.S. Grundtvig (1783–1872), and the Danish 'national' poet and playwright Adam Oehlenschläger (1779–1850), who was to be crowned with a laurel wreath as the king of Nordic poetry in the cathedral of Lund in 1829.

Steffens' lectures were influenced by Schelling's organicist thought that every part exists for the whole and the whole for each part, that everything from minerals and plants to animals and humans, the historical progress of culture, the geological layers of the earth and the heavens, are connected by a common spirit. A special place was reserved for the poet, who could harmonise conflicts and express the connections between the material world and the immaterial spirit in poetic language by recording the evocation of sensations.

Oehlenschläger was in 1802 an aspiring poet who heeded Steffens' call. Following one of the lectures, according to his memoirs, he spent sixteen hours in conversation with Steffens and the next morning wrote down the poem 'Guldhornene' (The Golden Horns), which would come to stand as the breakthrough of Romantic poetry in Denmark when published in *Digte 1803* (Poems 1803). In this famous poem, Oehlenschläger gives poetic form to Steffens' organicist thinking, lending a voice to nature in his frequent use of anthropomorphism, and providing his own age with a sense of deep connection to a glorious past only waiting to emerge out of the soil to those few who:

ane det Høie
i Naturens Øie,
som tilbedende bæve
for Guddommens Straaler, – i Sole, i Violer,

i det Mindste, i det Største,
som brændende tørste
efter Livets Liv,
som – o store Aand
for de svundne Tider!
(sense what is high / in Nature's eye / who adoringly learn / divine
rays to find, / in suns, violets – in all, / the great and the small /
who thirsting still burn / for the Life of Life, who – oh great spirit /
of ancient times!)

(Danish original and translation by John Irons
in Bredsdorff and Mai 2011, 142–3)

The poem centres on the discovery of the fifth-century Golden Horns of
Gallehus in a field in Southern Jutland in 1639 and 1734 and the theft of
the horns in 1802. Yet it is also a larger drama of history where the Norse
gods allow the horns from an ancient golden age to reappear at the feet of
a young infatuated girl in the present. Steffens' spirit of conjoined nature
reveals itself in 'En sagte Torden / dundrer! / Hele Norden / undrer!
('A peal of / distant thunder! / The North's / in total wonder!' (140–1)
as the horns emerge from 'earth's black hold'. Oehlenschläger's poem
exemplifies the confluence of two significant 'discoveries' associated with
Romantic nationalism: on the one hand, a 'new' scientific understanding
of an interdependent natural environment and, on the other, the realisation that art and poetry could be used to shape national identities by
assuaging and connecting a turbulent, modern present to a deep cultural,
mythic and geological past.

Mountain Envy in Danish Romantic Landscapes

The preoccupation in the Romantic age with the natural world and,
especially, the ability of art and literature to create a sense of authentic
connectedness between a gradually more urbanised modern experience
and an idealised landscape beyond the city gates, would grow into a
Romantic nationalist movement. Understood as 'the celebration of the
nation (defined by its language, history, and cultural character) as an
inspiring ideal for artistic expression; and the instrumentalization of
that expression in ways of raising the political consciousness', Romantic
nationalism in Scandinavia grew out of German Natural Philosophy and
responded to a wider European configuration of nation states in the wake
of the French Revolution and Napoleonic Wars (Leersen 2013, 9).

Particularly in Denmark, the Golden Age of the early nineteenth century and its soon dominating Romantic nationalism was directly tied to external political pressures and subsequent internal fractions. Denmark lost its sizable fleet to the British in 'Slaget på Reden' (the Battle of Copenhagen) in 1801 and in the Bombardment of Copenhagen in 1807, as a result of Denmark siding with France in the Napoleonic Wars. Denmark's subsequent participation in the wars became a costly affair leading in 1813 to uncontrollable inflation and state bankruptcy. Following Napoleon's defeat in 1814, the Treaty of Kiel forced Denmark to hand over Norway, which had been in union with Denmark since 1380, to Sweden. Denmark, once a North Atlantic power, had lost around two thirds of its territory, and now had to rebuild a small-nation identity, as Norway embarked on a path towards full independence.

In both Denmark and Norway, poets and artists used their art to celebrate aspects of their nations by providing an imagined conflation of national, historical and geographical belonging. While not previously considered the preeminent genre of painting, landscape painting became the preferred instrument in Scandinavia to capture a Romantic notion of national identity. Christopher Wilhelm Eckersberg (1783–1853) was one of the first Danish painters to explore the link between geology and a Romantic aesthetic sensibility with his 'Udsigt af Møns Klint og Sommerspiret' (The Cliffs at Møn. View to Sommerspiret, 1809). The painting is one of many from the first decades of the century to centre on one of the most distinctive features of the six-kilometre stretch of chalk cliffs along the eastern coast of the Danish island of Møn in the Baltic Sea: the chalk formation called Sommerspiret. These cliffs 'became an important site for the development of geology in Denmark during its heroic age – the years between 1790 and 1840 when geology was consolidated as a science internationally' (Hedin 2013, 77). In the same period, the site became frequented by painters, who sought landscapes where the natural environment would have its most authentic and powerful impact on human emotions. The spectacular, towering coastal chalk formations were the closest the mostly Copenhagen-based artists could get to experiencing the sublime *in situ*: 'The passion caused by the great and sublime in *nature* [...] is astonishment: and astonishment is that state of the soul in which all its motions are suspended, with some degree of horror,' according to Edmund Burke in his *A Philosophical Inquiry into the Origin of Our Ideas of the Sublime and the Beautiful* ([1757] 1887, Part II, sect. 1).

In Eckersberg's painting, the sublime sensation is captured in a female figure who turns away from the view as if horrified by its height and scale. She is held gently by a male figure, who appears to be trying to convince her of its beauty when viewed from a safe distance behind the wooden railing of the viewpoint. Less interested in a realistic depiction of the chalk formations and the surrounding vegetation, Eckersberg turns nature into a landscape (see Cosgrove and Daniels' previously quoted definition of landscape) pre-prepared to stimulate particular human desires as a tourist site, thereby pointing to the connectedness, the distractions and attractions, between an idealised natural environment, human bodies and emotions.

Perhaps it was the loss of Norway with its sublime mountainous wilderness that inspired a degree of mountain envy in Danish painters in the nineteenth century. Johan Thomas Lundbye's (1818–48), 'En Dansk Kyst. Motiv fra Kitnæs ved Roskilde Fjord' (A Danish Coast. View from Kitnæs on Roskilde Fjord, Zealand, 1843), picks up the fascination for geological formations and majestic cliffs in a monumental painting that seeks out a more common Danish motif from the island nation's long stretches of coast line (see Figure 11.1). While Lundbye attends to the smallest details of vegetation in the foreground, the two life-like figures on the beach with a horse-driven cart that has lost a wheel, and the iconic

Figure 11.1   The Danish painter Johan Thomas Lundbye's (1818–48) 'En Dansk Kyst. Motiv fra Kitnæs ved Roskilde Fjord' (A Danish Coast. View from Kitnæs on Roskilde Fjord. Zealand, 1843). Oil on canvas. 188.5 × 255.5 cm. Source: Statens Museum for Kunst.

Danish beech trees crowning the cliff, he has made the cliff appear dramatically higher than it was, as if emphasising the reach of the roots that connect the Danish cultural landscape above to its foundation below through layers of sedimented rock and geological deep-time.

Lundbye's landscape painting was part of the heated contemporary debates about national identity in the 1840s – debates that would reach their zenith with the end of absolute monarchy and the adoption of Danmarks Riges Grundlov, the democratic constitution that made Denmark a constitutional monarchy governed under a parliamentary system in 1849. In the arts it was particularly the art historian N.L. Høyen (1798–1870) who influenced artists to place their work in the service of the nation. In his 1844 lecture, 'Om betingelserne for en skandinavisk nationalkunsts udvikling' (On the preconditions for the development of a Scandinavian national art), he said:

> The history of Scandinavia, based on the fundamental characteristics of the country and its people, is the raw material from which the art that we have received fully formed from abroad must be reborn among us [...] Only then will the people recognize in it bones of their bones and flesh of their flesh, and only then will it be dear to them, like a child to its mother, when its features arouse holy, deeply entrenched memories [...] The Scandinavian must first be perceived in his complete uniqueness, our sense must first be sharpened to awareness of the grandiose and the familiar in the nature that surrounds us, before we can hope to have a national, historical art.
>
> (cited in Vammen 2002, 252–3)

Danish painters like Lundbye sought out the 'grandiose and the familiar' in nature, and painted landscapes deemed characteristic and particular to the nation, which not only promised to connect the present to a deep national history, but also to produce new cultural memories for a future more self-conscious nation. Although very little was left of a wild or 'authentic' Danish natural environment in the nineteenth century, as agriculture and deforestation had all but cleared the woodlands and coniferous trees were being introduced from Germany, the Danish painters found the tall light-green beech forest to be 'authentically' Danish.

Paintings of beech forests would proliferate throughout the century, most famously in Peter Christian Skovgaard's (1817–75) idyllic 'Bøgeskov i maj. Motiv fra Iselingen' (Beech Forest in May, 1857). The long sandy coasts, flat lands and open sky became preferred subjects of Lundbye, who, like several of his contemporaries, would dot his landscapes with ancient stone barrows to illustrate the 'entrenched memories' linking the Danes to a deep heroic past – as in 'En gravhøj fra oldtiden ved Raklev på Refsnæs' (An ancient burial mound by Raklev on Refsnæs, 1839). With the Romantic nationalist movement, the organicist ideal of a spirit connecting the material and immaterial world, geology and history, became a programme for a renewed national 'spirit' connecting the people, their history and future, to an idealised, imagined landscape through a stock of national icons.

Such 'landscaping' of national identity had already found its way into poetry. In Oehlenschläger's 'Der er et yndigt land' (There is a lovely country, 1819), today known as Denmark's national anthem, the country is described as 'et yndigt Land, / Det staaer med brede Bøge / Nær salten Østerstrand' (a lovely land / with spreading, shady beech-trees, / Near a salty eastern shore), an always sunny, pastoral and mythic landscape ('Og det er Freias Sal' [and it is Freya's hall]) where, in ancient days, 'harniskklædte Kæmper, / Udhvilede fra Strid; [...] Nu hvile deres Bene / Bag høiens Bautasteen' (armoured giants rested / between their bloody frays [...] now found in stone-set barrows, / Their final resting place) (Oehlenschläger 1823, 102). While founded on a heroic past, when Danes were brave and victorious, Oehlenschläger's Romantic nationalist landscape is serene, the Danes inward-looking, and content to inhabit their small nation of picturesque 'Danish islands' surrounded by calm blue seas and lush green beech trees.

Like the British art historian Graham-Dixon, whom we met at the beginning of this chapter, with his sense of a deep connection between the natural environment and the peoples who inhabit it, Danish Romantic poets such as Oehlenschläger, the art historian Høyen and painters such as Lundbye and Skovgaard seek not merely to understand and depict nature in its own right. Instead, from their very different perspectives, they turn the natural environment into a projection of human experiences, longing, a sense of destiny and belonging often conflated, in the nineteenth century, with the rise of European nationalisms and modern urbanisation (see chapter 4 in this volume).

Transnational Landscapes and Local Idylls

By contemplating the geographic or environmental origins of a particular Nordic character from a culturally and physically elevated distance, Graham-Dixon and his Nordic nineteenth-century forebears step into the shadow of the iconic Romantic painting 'Der Wanderer über dem

Nebelmeer' (Wanderer above the Sea of Fog, *c.*1818) by Caspar David Friedrich (1774–1840). Friedrich's wanderer is not an art critic, but instead a contemplative mountaineer leisurely posed upon a rocky precipice with his back to the viewer, gazing out on a sea of fog inclosing the mountain peaks below, demonstrating the sublime natural environment and the detached mastery of the human within it. This quintessential Romantic landscape is an imagined, idealised landscape cobbled together in the artist's studio from detailed sketches of rock formations he had recorded from nature when travelling through the Elbe Sandstone Mountains southeast of Dresden.

Friedrich was born in Greifswald in Swedish Pomerania, a Dominion under the Swedish Crown from 1630 to 1815, situated on what is now the Baltic coast of Germany and Poland. He studied under the Danish portrait painter Jens Juel, who was one of the first landscape painters in the Nordic countries, at the renowned Copenhagen Academy of Art in 1794, before moving to Dresden. There, in 1818, he was joined by the Norwegian artist J.C. Dahl (Johan Christian Dahl, 1788–1857), often referred to as the father of Norwegian painting, who would find in Friedrich a mentor and a friend, and in Dresden a new home away from home.

Dahl's best-known work, his monumental 'Fra Stalheim' (View from Stalheim, 1842), has become a Norwegian national icon for its dramatic mountain view, Dahl's eye for realistic botanical detail and its knowledgeable depiction of Norwegian rural architecture. Painted from sketches in Dresden decades after he had last been to the village of Stalheim in Hordaland county (only about 26 km from Stegastein view point), the scenery has become grander than it already was: the mountains are higher, the valley narrower, the light more dramatic and the whole view crowned by a double rainbow (see Figure 11.2). The painting is a representative of German Romanticism and a testament to its ideal that the artist does not simply record or copy nature but paints instead his own feelings – as a kind of self-portrait (Gunnarsson 1998, 94). At the same time, Dahl's landscape painting is a central example of Nordic Romantic nationalism, as it records an idyllic, perhaps nostalgic, mood of longing for a specific landscape and the life and work of the inhabitants within it.

Paradoxically, Danish and Norwegian landscape painters, who were central to the invention of a unique national spirit connecting the people to their lands, were deeply indebted to German Romantic philosophers and painters. In Denmark the indebtedness to German culture for the fashioning of renewed national pride following defeat in the Napoleonic Wars was to take a particularly ironic turn when Denmark shrank even

Figure 11.2 Johan Christian Dahl's (1788–1857) painting 'Fra Stalheim' (View from Stalheim, 1842). Oil on canvas. 190 × 246 cm. Source: National Gallery of Norway.

further in the latter part of the century following the Schleswig wars against Prussia and the Austrian Empire in 1848–52 and 1864: following the 1864 Treaty of Vienna, Denmark was forced to concede the Duchies of Schleswig, Holstein and Saxe-Lauenburg to Prussia and Austria.

However, while the political storms raged over Europe, artists and poets turned their attention inwards, to idyllic landscapes and homely peasant life – a motif that had always been part of the Romantic nationalist landscape tradition; we recall the two diminutive figures on the beach with their broken cart on Lundbye's Danish coast and the small homesteads in Dahl's Stalheim. A preoccupation with rural life was also central to popular Swedish painters around the turn of the century. In Anders Zorn's (1860–1920) 'Midsommardans' (Midsummer Dance, 1897), rural life and customs are depicted in the shape of dancers celebrating the evening light of a Midsummer's Eve celebration. A desire for a simple, domestic life is also noticeable in Carl Larsson's (1853–1919) much loved idyllic watercolours of family life in his home and garden in Sundborn in Dalarna, Sweden. When published as an internationally bestselling book with the title *Ett Hem* (A Home, 1899), these artworks by Carl Larsson and his wife Karin, who created much of the interior design for their home, co-created a vision of rustic, idyllic country living that came to have a great influence on twentieth-century Scandinavian design, not least on the home furnishing style of Ingvar Kamprad's global 'flat-pack empire' IKEA.

It was also around 1900 that a national spirit contributed to the flourishing of art in Finland leading up to its independence from Russia in 1917. A distinct national school of painting employed motifs, well-known from their Nordic neighbours and predecessors, to create a particular Finnish landscape. One of the most renowned Finnish artists, the cosmopolitan Akseli Gallén-Kallela (1865–1931), painted expressive, unspoilt landscapes with scenes from everyday life, drawing heavily on national myth and the epic *Kalevala* (see chapter 3 in this volume).

Some painters, like Dahl and Gallén-Kallela, would travel far beyond the Nordic region to discover their longing for landscapes they had left behind. Some were called by the raging nationalist sentiments of the long nineteenth century to distil in shapes and paint the imagined connections between Nordic peoples and their changing national geographies and societies for political purposes. Paradoxically, 'nature' had to be left behind (e.g. due to urbanisation) in order to become the object of our desires and our imagination. The genre of landscape painting itself presupposes, therefore, a sense of distance between the human observer and the natural environment.

As Graham-Dixon, Friedrich, Dahl, Høyen, Oehlenschläger and Lundbye do, we are historically conditioned to perceive nature as spectators looking onto a stage, where human conflicts between sublime experiences of terror and homely comfort, between the fractures of a modern war-torn world and a Romantic nationalist promise of a healing sense of belonging, are enacted. It would, therefore, not be entirely correct to say that 'the Scandinavian mind itself has been shaped by nature'. Instead, we could say that today's multiple notions (foreign and domestic) of what it means to be Nordic are intricately entangled with the diverse landscapes Nordic peoples have imagined and fashioned for themselves, with significant inspiration from abroad, over the past two and a half centuries.

Nordic Nature in the Anthropocene

The nature philosopher and geologist Steffens had preached an organicist understanding of human dwelling among minerals, plants and animals, but the natural world remained (not only in industry but also in the arts) the expression of a superior human will and imagination. However, the sense that only when we appear to have removed ourselves entirely from nature does it become an object for our longing and desire provokes a growing sense of apprehension in the twentieth century. As scientists sounded the alarm for the unsustainable human misuse of natural resources and the pollution of ecosystems, Nordic politicians, philosophers, artists and poets began to reimagine how humans could find their place among animals, stones, trees and seas on more equal organicist terms.

The Nordic countries have been successful in creating an international brand of environmental exceptionalism. In other words, the now defunct assumption that the inhabitants of the Nordic lands were deeply, and perhaps authentically, connected to their natural environments has returned in our day as a neo-Romantic xeno and autostereotype (see chapter 14 in this volume) that holds Scandinavians as somehow predisposed to mitigate climate change and instinctively driven towards appropriate environmental legislation. Despite their advanced, and by no means carbon-neutral, industrial economies, the Nordic countries are today associated with sustainable development, authentic natural environments, ecological awareness and 'green' energy.

This Nordic environmental brand has its own internationally renowned philosopher, mountaineer and environmental activist in the Norwegian Arne Næss (1912–2009). He was the progenitor of ecosophy (a philosophy of ecological equilibrium he introduced in the early 1970s) and 'deep ecology', which shares some characteristics with Romantic nature philosophy, as it sees the human as part of a wider ecosystem, but insists that all life forms have value in themselves and not simply for the value they represent to humans. In writings drawing on years spent in his cabin at Tvergastein high in the Norwegian mountains, such as those collected in *The Ecology of Wisdom* (2009), Næss opposed a hierarchical view of the relationship between humans and other forms of nature and presented a critique of anthropocentrism (preferring a biocentric view) as a central tenet of deep-ecological thinking.

In literature, an environmentalist critique of anthropocentric thinking and behaviour for its role in the unfolding climate crisis has taken many forms since the 1960s. In the Nordic tradition of ecopoetry, biocentric views have been given poetic form in Inger Christensen's (1935–2009) *Sommerfugledalen: Et requiem* (1991, *Butterfly Valley: A Requiem*) with its invocation of 'the planet's butterflies' soaring like 'pigments from the warm body of the earth, / cinnabar, ochre, phosphor yellow, gold / a swarm of basic elements aloft' (Christensen 2004, 3). In the 'wooded' poetic world of the poet-lumberjack Hans Børli (1918–89), the true owners of the Norwegian forest are not the exploitative timber companies, but instead *his* own 'people', who 'have never owned a tree', who live in biospheric symbiosis like a 'child owns its mother' (Børli 2007, 39–41). In Tomas Tranströmer's (1931–2015) poem 'Några minuter' ('A Few Moments', 1970), the poetic human consciousness finds itself deeply intertwined with 'another creature', enmeshed in an ecosystem of trees and roots: 'The dwarf pine on marsh grounds holds its head up: a dark rag. / But what you see is nothing compared to the roots, / the widening, secretly groping, deathless or half- / deathless root system. // I you she he also put roots out. / Outside our common will. / Outside the City. [...]' (Tranströmer 2018, n.p.).

The poetic pursuit of a biocentric rather than an anthropocentric standpoint, where nature is not understood as a mere projection of human experiences and activities but on its own non-human terms, has continued into the twenty-first century with the emergence of the notion of the Anthropocene. Aase Berg (1967–) is a Swedish poet who explores the boundaries between the human and the non-human. Her poetry is characterised by an eerie forewarning of how the Anthropocene human is enmeshed in natural processes of regeneration and destruction beyond our control, as in the poem 'Moloss' ('Mastiff') from her first collection *Hos rådjur* (1997, *With Deer* 2009): 'Det jäser i substanserna, det fräser och bubblar i svalgen det dånar och det bryter sammam bakom oss' ('The substances are fermenting, throats are corroding and bubbling, things are rumbling and crumbling behind us') (Berg 2009, 38–9).

The contemporary landscapes described in *Digte 2014* (Poems 2014) by Danish poet Theis Ørntoft (1984–) may, as its title suggests, lead us back to Oehlenschläger's similarly titled collection from 1803, but Ørntoft's is not a Golden Age about to break through the soil into the present. Like Berg, Ørntoft presents a post-apocalyptic world with a much 'darker ecology' than the harmonic dreamscape of the deep ecologists (Morton 2016). His is a vision of a landscape where the climate catastrophe has already happened and where the human will and body, digital and capitalist networks, have been painfully swamped and consumed by an avenging geological and natural environment:

> der vokser planter op gennem mine underboers halse / der vokser planter op gennem min etages gulve / men hvad vil du have jeg skal gøre ved det, siger jeg / og kigger forvirret ud gennem mine øjne / ud til askelandskaber der snart skal smeltes om / [...] mens verden vælter ind gennem mine fem tsunamisanser / og ødelægger alt på sin vej / så skriger en stemme i min hals. (Ørntoft 2014, 15)

(plants grow up through my downstairs neighbours's throats / plants grow through the floor boards of my flat / but what do you want me to do about it, I ask / and glare confused out of my eyes / out into ashen landscapes soon to be melted down / […] while the world submerges my five tsunami senses / and destroys everything in its wake / a voice screams in my throat.)

Not merely a source for utopian narratives of a new exceptionalist Nordic identity, deep history, belonging and continuity, today's Nordic landscapes are beset with the fear, guilt and traumas that follow anthropogenic climate change and the degradation of ecosystems.

The Golden Age Romantic nationalist landscapes are, however, not simply a distant memory. Their instrumentalisation of the natural environment emerges as a complex precondition for contemporary landscape painting as a genre in its own right, and can, arguably, be seen as implicated in idealising anthropocentric appropriations of nature, which have taught us to gloss over destructive human interventions in the planet's ecology and geology.

The early history of National Romantic painting in Denmark featured painters who set out to re-imagine their sense of belonging as layered in the ancient geology of mountains and chalk cliffs. In 2007, the Danish painter Allan Otte painted the chalk cliffs at Stevns in 'Indgreb' (2007, Interference), on a canvas where the chalk factory has relegated the cliffs (the emblem of a deep authentic national history) to the periphery as mere industrial material. In a similar critical dialogue with the Golden Age, Otte recalls Lundbye's always sunny Romantic nationalist landscapes in 'Lundbye Remake' (2011), where industrialised agriculture now takes centre stage with windmills in the background and plastic-wrapped straw bales dotted over the fields. The Golden Age landscapes are ripe for ecological critique and in multiple, often contradicting, ways are a constant presence in contemporary understandings, idealisations and depictions of Nordic landscapes and national identities – even in a globalised age of the Anthropocene.

References

Alsen, Katharina and Annika Landmann. 2016. *Nordic Painting: The Rise of Modernity*. Munich: Prestel.

Berg, Aase. 2009. *With Deer = Hos rådjur*, translated by Johannes Göransson. Boston: Black Ocean.

Børli, Hans. 2007. *We Own the Forests and Other Poems*, translated by Louis Muinzer. Norwich: Norvik Press.

Bredsdorff, Thomas and Anne-Marie Mai, eds. 2011. *100 Danish Poems: From the Medieval Period to the Present Day*, translated by John Irons. Copenhagen: Museum Tusculanum Press.

Burke, Edmund. 2005. 'A Philosophical Inquiry into the Origin of Our Ideas of the Sublime and Beautiful'. In *The Works of the Right Honourable Edmund Burke, Volume I*. Project Gutenberg. Accessed 13 October 2019. http://www.gutenberg.org/files/15043/15043-h/15043-h.htm#A_PHILOSOPHICAL_INQUIRY.

Christensen, Inger. 2004. *Butterfly Valley: A Requiem*, translated by Susanna Nied. New York: New Directions.

Cosgrove, Denis and Stephen Daniels, eds. 1988. *The Iconography of Landscape: Essays on the Symbolic Representation, Design and Use of Past Environments*. Cambridge: Cambridge University Press.

Graham-Dixon, Andrew. 2016. 'Dark Night of the Soul'. *Art of Scandinavia*. BBC Four. http://www.bbc.co.uk/programmes/b073mp87

Gunnarsson, Torsten. 1998. *Nordic Landscape Painting in the Nineteenth Century*, translated by Nancy Adler. New Haven: Yale University Press.

Hedin, Gry. 2013. 'Seeing the History of the Earth in the Cliffs at Møn: The Interaction between Landscape Painting and Geology in Denmark in the First Half of the 19th Century', *Romantik* 2: 77–101.

Hedin, Gry and Ann-Sofie N. Gremaud, eds. 2018. *Artistic Visions of the Anthropocene North: Climate Change and Nature in Art*. New York: Routledge.

Körber, Lill-Ann, Scott MacKenzie and Anna Westerståhl Stenport, eds. 2017. *Arctic Environmental Modernities: From the Age of Polar Exploration to the Era of the Anthropocene*. London: Palgrave Macmillan.

Leerssen, Joep. 2009. 'Foreword'. In *Images of the North: Histories, Identities, Ideas*, edited by Sverrir Jakobsson, 15–17. Amsterdam: Rodopi.

Leerssen, Joep. 2013. 'Notes towards a Definition of Romantic Nationalism', *Romantik* 2: 9–35.

Morton, Timothy. 2016. *Dark Ecology: For a Logic of Future Coexistence*. New York: Columbia University Press.

Naess, Arne. 2016. *Ecology of Wisdom*, edited by Alan Drengson and Bill Devall. London: Penguin.

Oehlenschläger, Adam. 1926. 'Fædrelands-Sang'. In *Poetiske Skrifter I*, 102–4. Copenhagen: Holbergselskabet.

Olwig, Kenneth R. and Michael Jones. 2008. 'Introduction: Thinking Landscape and Regional Belonging on the Northern Edge of Europe'. In *Nordic Landscapes: Region and Belonging on the Northern Edge of Europe*, edited by Michael Jones and Kenneth R. Olwig, ix–xxix. Minneapolis: University of Minnesota Press.

Ørntoft, Theis. 2014. *Digte 2014*. Copenhagen: Gyldendal.

Schama, Simon. 1995. *Landscape and Memory*. New York: Alfred A. Knopf.

Tranströmer, Tomas. 2018. *The Half-Finished Heaven: Selected Poems*, translated by Robert Bly. London: Penguin.

Vammen, Hans. 2000. '"Schouw is Wonderful …": A Professor and His Golden Age Network'. In *Intersections: Art and Science in the Golden Age*, edited by Mogens Bencard, 246–57. Copenhagen: Gyldendal.

12
Emigration and Scandinavian Identity

Mart Kuldkepp

Contemporary perspectives on the Nordic countries often frame the region as a destination of immigration, focusing on the various challenges that increased cross-border mobility might pose to the Nordic political landscape, ethnic and cultural composition, or the resilience of the Nordic welfare states. However, it is worth keeping in mind that throughout centuries, the Nordic region has much more commonly been a place that people have wanted to leave – not least during times of economic depression or political turmoil.

Examples of significant emigration from the three Scandinavian countries – Denmark, Norway and Sweden – reach back at least to the times of Germanic tribes invading the West-Roman Empire in the Migration Period of the fourth to the sixth century CE (see chapter 1 in this volume); and, famously, Scandinavian seafarers becoming a Europe-wide nuisance in the Viking Age from the eighth to the eleventh century, when Scandinavian settlements were established in both Western and Eastern Europe. Even more recently, during the era of industrialisation and political change in the nineteenth century, there was major Scandinavian emigration, especially to the USA. This direction of movement was substantially reversed only after the Second World War, when the Social Democratic states in Scandinavia experienced a period of prolonged economic growth and thus received and even encouraged labour migration from other, less advantaged countries. Their humanitarian refugee policies, first formulated in Sweden in the 1960s and 1970s under the influence of new radical human-rights thinking, and subsequently also applied in Norway and Denmark, soon led to the arrival of increased numbers of asylum seekers (see Brochmann 2017, 230).

The first purpose of this chapter is to consider nineteenth-century emigration from Scandinavia – particularly from Sweden – as a complex and multifaceted phenomenon, and engage with questions such as why the Scandinavian emigrants wanted to leave, the forms their emigration took, and how well they became integrated into the societies of their destination countries. Secondly, we will consider official and semi-official Swedish responses to the emigration question in the late nineteenth and early twentieth century, both in terms of trying to understand the causes of emigration and how it might be prevented, as well as attempting to preserve and strengthen the Swedish identity of those already living abroad.

As we will see, attitudes towards emigration in the modern era were closely connected to reactions to broader, often deeply disruptive contemporary processes of nation building, modernisation and societal change. Engagement with 'the emigration question' could therefore become a point of departure for a reformist, optimistic vision of modernity, but it could also serve as an outlet for a national-romantic yearning for the supposedly simpler times of the past (see chapters 4 and 11 in this volume). Furthermore, if emigration were to be embraced rather than shunned, it could be accepted either from a liberal point of view as a much-needed safety valve against overpopulation, or from a radical nationalist perspective as a praiseworthy example of daring colonialism.

In the interests of cohesiveness and brevity, the story presented here will primarily focus on Sweden, the most populous of the Scandinavian countries. This is not to say that the Swedish case is particularly unique. Similar studies could be done on other Nordic nations, and other European states, even though they would naturally differ in their specifics. But the intention here is to be representative, rather than comprehensive; and Sweden, in its attempts to take a markedly managerial approach to its 'emigration problem', is a good example of tendencies that became expressed with perhaps less clarity elsewhere.

Emigration in the Nineteenth Century

Between the years 1800 and 1914, the populations of Denmark, Norway and Sweden tripled in number. The reasons behind this population growth were famously summed up by the Swedish poet Esaias Tegnér in 1833 as 'peace, vaccines and potatoes' ('freden, vaccinet och potäterna') (Jansson 2016, 685). Indeed, with the exception of the two Schleswig-Holstein wars in 1848–51 and 1864, the century after the end of the Napoleonic Wars in 1814 was remarkably peaceful for the Scandinavian kingdoms. Perhaps because young men did not die in wars, more children were being born. The early nineteenth century also saw the widespread adoption of a vaccine against smallpox, which Denmark made legally mandatory in 1810 – one of the first countries in Europe to do so (Orfield 1953, 57). Also important for longer lifespans were better medical education, hospitals, hygiene and an emerging understanding of the causes of certain diseases.

Moreover, while crop failure was still a possibility – as shown by the great Swedish famine of 1867–9 – the increasingly widespread cultivation of potatoes and decreased dependence on grain greatly reduced the threat of hunger. Better agricultural practices were also facilitated by private ownership of land replacing the obsolete open-field system, and, towards the end of the period, the introduction of the first examples of horse-drawn mechanical agricultural machinery. Thanks to improved methods of transport and food preservation, the menu of even lower-class people was becoming more varied and nutritious. Consequently, while nativity rates remained high, the mortality rates – especially of infant mortality – dropped significantly (Gjerde 1995, 86; Gustafsson 1997, 160–1; Ljungmark 2008, 9).

The population of Scandinavia (in millions of people):				
	1800	1850	1900	1910
Denmark	0.93	1.42	2.43	2.74
Sweden	2.35	3.48	5.14	5.52
Norway	0.88	1.39	2.24	2.39

(Martinsson 2018)

The population growth had significant social and economic consequences, the aggregate effect of which was not unequivocally positive. First, both economic prosperity and social cohesion were threatened by rural destitution as agricultural expansion was limited by the availability of arable land. By mid-century, increasing numbers of people were forced into poverty in the countryside, unable to feed their families from their own fields. Second, an increase in the numbers of surviving children drove up the number of potential heirs, which often led to ancestral farmlands being divided up and individual farms ending up smaller and less efficient in food production. For this reason, Sweden had already in 1827 officially forbidden the further sub-division of farmsteads unless the resulting farms could feed their occupants and pay the requisite taxes. This ban was abolished in 1881, meaning a renewed increase in the numbers of rural poor (Barton 1975, 10; Söderberg 1981, 37).

At the same time, nineteenth-century Scandinavians had more opportunities to migrate and settle elsewhere than ever before since the end of the Viking Age. Movement from the countryside to the towns (urbanisation) was one major facet of it, but significant population movements also took place between rural areas, motivated by overpopulation, unemployment, and a desire for better living conditions. A degree of inter-Nordic migration also occurred: for example, from Finland to Northern Norway, and from Sweden across Öresund to Copenhagen. Emigration overseas was fundamentally yet another aspect of the same mobility, which remained a major feature of life in Scandinavia up until the beginning of the next century when industrialisation as a new source of economic growth began to alleviate unemployment (Gustafsson 1997, 187, 96).

Between about 1825 and 1930 (when American policies started severely restricting further immigration), *c*.3 million Scandinavians moved abroad, including 300,000 Danes, 850,000 Norwegians and 1.2 million Swedes (Gjerde 1995, 85). Norway had the highest proportion of its population emigrate, while Sweden, where emigration without royal permission was officially decriminalised in 1840, led in absolute numbers. Again, this did not make Scandinavia exceptional. Between the Napoleonic Wars and the Great Depression of the 1930s, more than 50 million Europeans emigrated and settled abroad (Baines 1994, 525), most of them in the USA, but also in Canada, South America, South Africa and Australia. This list of destinations was shared across Europe. In the case of the three Scandinavian kingdoms, well over 95 per cent of emigrants moved to the USA and, to a lesser extent, Canada (Gjerde 1995, 85).

The immediate causes of emigration, sometimes called the 'push factors', were often connected to the economic and social problems that had ensued from overpopulation. Many Swedish emigrants came from poor rural areas, such as Småland in the south. However, there could also be other reasons. Indeed, the first émigré groups from Scandinavia had a religious rationale: in 1832, 52 Norwegian Quakers travelled from Stavanger to the state of New York and from there to Illinois where they settled (Nordstrom 2000, 232). In 1846, the Swedish sectarian preacher Erik Jansson and his pietist followers established the Bishop Hill colony in the same state (see Ljungmark 2008, 18–21). Members of these and other religious minority groups (especially the American-inspired ones: Methodists, Baptists, Mormons etc.) left because of the oppressive Lutheran state churches at home, with Swedish laws against religious dissenters remaining in force up until 1860 (Barton 1975, 12–13). Causes of emigration could also be political or semi-political, such as the rigid social hierarchies and the undemocratic nature of political life in Scandinavia.

The attractive features of the destination country, the so-called 'pull factors', included better chances at economic and social mobility – such as lower land prices or better-paid jobs – freedom of religion, more democratic and open societal structures, and, for many émigrés, a badly-needed chance to start afresh lives that for one or another reason had taken a wrong turn. Furthermore, the choice of destination was heavily influenced by the pre-existence of immigrant communities from the same country: at least initially, emigrants tended to travel together with other countrymen, and in many cases also to settle with them after arrival. Among the most important immediate pull factors were probably letters from relatives who had already settled abroad, often tending to downplay the endured hardships and encouraging family members to follow. The 1860s and 70s also saw a dramatic increase in print propaganda in the form of booklets and newspaper articles, often disseminated by agents of steamship companies looking to sell tickets, or even visiting Swedish Americans who were granted rebates if they took countrymen back with them (Barton 1975, 16–17, 109–10).

In the first half of the nineteenth century, whole families had tended to emigrate together and settle in rural areas. By the 1880s, this had changed, and most emigrants were young, unmarried men and women travelling alone. They tended to settle in towns and cities, rather than in the countryside, and seek work in factories (the men) or as maids (the women). Having established themselves, they would often be able to pay the ship fare for their family members and bring them over as well. There was also an increasing amount of return migration, and many emigrants travelled several times back and forth over the Atlantic as their circumstances changed (Barton 1975, 111–12; Nordstrom 2000, 233).

Some emigrants were assimilated rapidly in their new country of residence, but for others, it was a process that could take several generations – especially if they retained a strong connection to the emigrant community. Community leaders, especially pastors, would often play a significant role in preserving the national heritage. Emigrant communities quickly established their own ethnic churches (Scandinavian Lutheran, but also Baptist, Methodist etc.) with services in the heritage language. They would also educate children in the language of their parents, which in some areas, such as in Porter, Indiana, lasted well into the interwar period. In more urban settings, such as in the major Swedish community in Chicago, a significant role was played by secular organisations: sport, music, theatre and temperance societies, ethnic trade unions, clubs and local history societies. As a rule, however, pre-emigration ethnicity was better preserved in the countryside. Some communities in rural USA were homogenous to the extent of being inhabited by families who had all come together from the same parish or village (Nordstrom 2000, 233–4).

Also important for preserving ethnic identity was access to journalism and literature in the heritage language. Starting with just one newspaper published in New York in 1851–3 – entitled *Skandinavien* and meant for all Nordic immigrants – hundreds of newspapers in the USA eventually came to be published in Scandinavian languages for immigrants from different parts of Scandinavia, but also with different political and religious views. The majority of these did not switch to English before the 1920s, but many eventually came to find readers also in communities with speakers of other Scandinavian languages, highlighting the extent to which many Swedes, Danes and Norwegians came to adopt a more 'Scandinavian' identity in their new country of residence (Barton 1975, 19; Ljungmark 2008, 108–15). There were many reprints of Scandinavian authors and an émigré literature made an appearance, often dealing with the emigration experience (Nordstrom 2000, 235). Examples of the latter include novels by the Swede Ernst Skarstedt (1857–1929), the Norwegian Ole Edvart Rølvaag (1876–1931) and the Dane Sophus Keith Winter (1898–1983).

Nevertheless, over generations, Scandinavian identity tended to fade away. Partially, this tendency was reversed in the post-Second World War decades when many people again discovered and embraced their ethnic roots in the form of hybrid identities such as Danish-American or Swedish-American. Even if they no longer speak the heritage language, the heritage ethnicity has been important to many descendants of emigrants, particularly in the USA. Examples of heritage institutions in the USA include the American Swedish Institute in Minneapolis (founded in 1929), the Nordic Museum in Seattle (founded in 1980) and many others. There are also whole communities that are strongly dedicated to their Scandinavian heritage, such as the originally Danish town of Solvang in Santa Barbara County, California, and the old Janssonist settlement Bishop Hill in Henry County, Illinois.

Emigration and Opposition to Emigration

It is probably fair to say that emigration was a largely positive phenomenon for nineteenth-century Scandinavia. If overpopulation had not had a safety valve of this kind, it might have led to even stronger social and economic tensions in Scandinavia itself. According to one estimate, emigration reduced the growth of the Norwegian population by half, likely making it more sustainable at a time when the country's economy had not yet industrialised enough to provide for a larger population (Nordstrom 2000, 236). Many emigrants also ended up sending home substantial sums of money and some eventually returned with new ideas and money to invest in their native land. Finally, another arguable benefit of emigration routes was that they could be used to exile troublemakers, such as the Danish socialist Louis Pio (1841–94), founder of the organised workers' movement in Denmark, and in the realm of fiction, the mischievous Emil i Lönneberga, who had the whole village collect money to send him off to America, as depicted by the Swedish children's author Astrid Lindgren (Hult 2008, 576).

Contemporary attitudes towards emigration were mixed. There was some early recognition of its value for dealing with overpopulation – in 1840, Swedish liberals even founded a short-lived and controversial Émigré Society (Emigrantföreningen) to publicise opportunities in the New World. However, it was also true that most emigrants were young and potentially productive members of society, not necessarily the poorest and the most desperate. Indeed, it seems that it was often fear of destitution that drove emigration, rather than destitution itself (Barton 1975, 11, 16). Starting in the 1840s, at a time when the Scandinavian economies finally experienced a period of growth, the danger of workers moving abroad prompted the first movement of public opposition to emigration. Critical voices condemned emigrants as criminals and layabouts, content to abandon their native land and look for a better life abroad. Warnings were also issued about the various dangers awaiting on the other side of the ocean, especially during the American Civil War of 1861–5, when many in Europe predicted a total collapse of the young republic (Barton 1990, 13–14).

The recession that began in Scandinavia in the mid-1860s provided a further impetus for emigration, especially since it now coincided with economic growth in post-Civil War USA. The famine caused by three successive crop failures in Sweden in 1867–9, and later the import of cheap American grain towards the end of the 1870s also made the numbers go up as local conditions worsened (Barton 1975, 107–8; Ljungmark 2008, 31).

The importance of religious push factors decreased, but more emigrants now had a political motivation, especially after the 1866 Swedish parliamentary reform was found insufficient by many liberally-minded people. Liberal Swedish journalists also visited their compatriots living in the USA, encouraging more people to emigrate with their positive depictions of life in the New World. Emigration was further facilitated by regular Trans-Atlantic steamship services becoming available in the 1870s, which made travel both cheaper and faster. A journey from Stockholm to Chicago which in 1846 had taken 93 days, including 74 days at sea, could thanks to railways and steamships now be completed in merely 20 days (Barton 1975, 108; 1990, 14; Ljungmark 2008, 69–72).

In Sweden, not least in academic circles, these developments led to widespread resignation to emigration as a necessary evil. The historian Wilhelm Erik Svedelius argued in 1875 that since some of Sweden's population could not provide for themselves in their native land, emigration was unavoidable and best thought of as a form of development assistance to the USA. In another approach, the political economist Knut Wicksell suggested in 1882 that the core of the problem was overpopulation and recommended the use of contraceptives, rather than measures against emigration per se (Barton 1990, 14–15).

The émigrés themselves would naturally also defend their choice, sometimes by appealing to a nationalist sentiment. Johan A. Enander, editor of the Chicago newspaper *Hemlandet* and a leading proponent of 'Swedish-Americanism' (Ljungmark 2008, viii) described the modern Swedish emigrants as the spiritual descendants of both the Viking discoverers of Vinland and the small group of seventeenth-century Swedish colonists in Delaware. According to Enander, the latter had embodied American moral values better than the 'egoistic Anglo-Saxons'. Now, when ships full of Swedes were again landing on American shores, they were to be regarded as once more peacefully conquering 'Vinland the Good' which was rightfully theirs. Similar idealisation of emigrants also made inroads into the Swedish debate, for example in the writings of the priest and publicist Carl Sundbeck, who had been awarded grants by the state to study Swedish emigrants in the USA and Canada. Sundbeck went even further than Enander, arguing that the émigrés were the most exemplary Swedes of all, daringly spreading the Swedish language and culture to the wild American prairies in a kind of 'national imperialism'. It was now the duty of the emigrants to inspire a similar resoluteness for national action back home, so that other Swedes would set to work with the same enthusiasm and sense of purpose, even without having to travel abroad (Barton 1990, 15–17).

In the 1890s, the USA turned less welcoming again. The frontier of settlement evaporated, as most available land resources had been exhausted. At the same time, competition in industry grew fiercer and working conditions worsened. Scandinavia was now also going through its belated industrialisation: from 1870 to 1914, the rural population in Sweden sank from 72.4 per cent to 48.4 per cent of the total. Travelogues from the USA became more critical and opposition to emigration grew in conservative nationalist circles. As a result, the numbers of emigrants dropped substantially between 1894 and 1900 (Barton 1975, 203–6; Ljungmark 2008, 5, 29).

Around the turn of the century, however, the numbers picked up again, culminating in 1903 with more than 35,000 people leaving Sweden. In response, emigration became yet again an object of intense public debate, not least because Sweden's worries were also piling up in other ways. The Russification policies enacted in Finland, and Norwegian separatism (the latter ending in secession in 1905), were putting Swedish foreign policy on the defensive, while sharpening class tensions and the emergence of the labour movement undermined the domestic power of traditional political elites. In 1901, the period of compulsory military service was extended from 90 days to either eight or twelve months. This was strongly resented by the poor who had to bear the financial burden of interrupted employment and lost income. From the perspective of the state, emigration therefore became perceived as a security issue, since the outflow of young men reduced the pool of available conscripts (Barton 1975, 204; 1990, 16; Ljungmark 2008, 39–43).

Emigration and Swedishness Abroad

The staunchest early opponents of emigration had been large landowners, worried about the lack of farm workers and the rising wages emigration would cause. Instead, they proposed the creation of 'a new America in Sweden' through adoption of modern, large-scale agriculture. After 1900, they were also joined in their criticism by the burgeoning Social Democratic movement, adamant to condemn the lack of labour rights in the USA, which they considered 'the workers' hell'. Yet other critics had a radical nationalist point of view which regarded emigration as basically unwelcome and unpatriotic – a part of the state of 'slumber' of the Swedish nation that had begun with the defeat of Sweden in the Great Northern War of 1721, which had ended its Great Power Era (*Stormaktstiden*). A new national awakening was now needed, and ending emigration was to be an important part of it (Barton 1990, 14–16).

Meanwhile, academic and parliamentary circles presented more rationally oriented proposals to investigate the causes and effects of emigration in detail. In 1907, a state-funded research group headed by Gustav Sundbärg began its work on a full review of the emigration issue feeding into policy proposals, the so-called *Emigrationsutredningen*. Their work resulted in a thick volume with twenty appendices, published over 1908–13, which attempted to cover all the issues related to emigration – from the social to the psychological – and amounted to nothing less than a broad socioeconomic survey of Sweden as a whole. The authors' policy suggestions recognised industrial growth and social reforms as the means to reduce emigration, but Sundbärg also allowed himself an appendix on the 'Swedish national character' (titled *Det svenska folklynnet*), where he accused his fellow Swedes of a fondness for fanciful ideas, a weak sense of national identity, envy, a weakness for everything foreign, and lacking psychological sense, all of which he thought were the fundamental causes of emigration beyond the statistics (Barton 1990, 16–18, 21; Scott 1965, 314–16).

In political groups with less faith in officially sanctioned solutions, voluntary organisations sprang up with the purpose of either limiting emigration or preserving the 'Swedishness' of those already settled abroad. The year 1907 saw the establishment of *Nationalföreningen mot emigrationen* (the national union against emigration), dominated by Conservative landowners, businessmen and academics, and headed by the young radical conservative Adrian Molin. *Nationalföreningen* tried to convince people contemplating emigration to abandon the idea either by providing them with cheap loans to build a family home in a less-populated part of Sweden – what came to be known as *Egnahemsrörelsen* (the home ownership movement) – or by mediating work placements. They also attempted to convince people who had already emigrated to return to Sweden (Lindkvist 2007, 35–57). H. Arnold Barton argues that this was an opposite approach to the one taken by *Emigrationsutredningen*: instead of modernisation and industrialisation, the solution was seen to lie in the reinvigoration of the Swedish countryside according to a national romantic vision of rural life. Thanks to its good financial resources, *Nationalföreningen* was able to organise several large-scale propaganda campaigns which probably had some effect (see Figure 12.1). However, it quickly lost its purpose as emigration streams dried up. In 1917, the organisation had 16,000 members, but in 1925 only 2,500, indicating how substantially the issue had dropped in importance (Barton 1990, 18–19, 21).

In 1908, the year after the establishment of *Nationalföreningen*, *Riksföreningen för svenskhetens bevarande i utlandet* (the State Union for the Preservation of Swedishness Abroad) was founded. It was an

Figure 12.1 *Res icke till Amerika* (Do not travel to America). Poster from *Nationalföreningen mot Emigrationen* (the National Union Against Emigration). Source: Riksantikvarieämbetet. CC BY.

organisation of mainly civil servants and academics headed by Vilhelm Lundström, professor of classics at the University of Gothenburg. The task of *Riksföreningen* was to 'morally and economically support the preservation of the Swedish language and culture by Swedes abroad, to further the feelings of unity between Swedes abroad and at home, and to generally promote knowledge of the Swedish language and culture abroad' (Kummel 1994, 77). Modern mass emigration, which Lundström agreed was a tragedy, had in his opinion nevertheless resulted in something of value: the existence of Swedish communities abroad. *Riksföreningen* was keen to make the point that out of the nine million Swedes in the world, a whole third was living outside Sweden itself. Since the state was not doing anything to ensure that these diaspora Swedes would not lose their Swedishness, private organisations had to step in (Barton 1990, 19–20).

Although the intention of *Riksföreningen* had mainly been to work with recent émigrés, most of its activities ended up being concerned with the Swedish minorities in Finland and Estonia (then parts of the Russian Empire), which dated back to the Middle Ages. There, *Riksföreningen* attempted to consolidate Finnish-Swedish and Estonian-Swedish identities as 'Eastern Swedes' (*östsvenskar*). Its efforts in Finland were largely unsuccessful, although it did make some substantial contributions, for example by facilitating the reopening of the Swedish-speaking university Åbo Akademi in Turku in 1918. It had more success in Estonia, where the Swedish community was much smaller and poorer, and thus had reason to be more grateful for help and recognition from Sweden (Kummel 1994, 247–51).

Riksföreningen's efforts to promote what Lundström called the pan-Swedish idea (*den allsvenska idén*) can be considered an example of the so-called pan-movements or a macronationalism aiming to unite members of a particular ethnicity over state borders to 'another, larger fatherland' (Barton 1990, 20). In this sense, its role was not limited to the emigration question alone, and, unlike *Nationalföreningen*, *Riksföreningen* still exists today, having in 1979 changed its name to *Riksföreningen Sverigekontakt*.

The Aftermath and Reverberations

By the 1920s, emigration from Scandinavia to the USA had reduced to a trickle, and during the Great Depression of 1929–34 it ended almost entirely. On top of widespread unemployment in the USA that discouraged further emigration, in 1930 the American authorities introduced restrictive immigration laws which, in spite of favouritism shown to immigrants from Northern Europe, made the country a less attractive destination. At the same time, the 1930 census showed 1,562,703 persons born in Sweden or of Swedish-born parents living in the USA, out of a population of almost 123 million (Barton 1975, 3; Ljungmark 2008, 8) – the largest diaspora of ethnic Swedes (or half-Swedes) that has ever existed.

In Sweden itself, memories of emigration persisted, as did many personal and family contacts with relatives who had settled abroad. Fictionalised and romanticised versions of the emigrant experience would now find a fertile ground there, as the importance of emigration as a burning societal problem had ceased. More than anyone else, it was the novelist Vilhelm Moberg (1898–1973) who helped to shape a Swedish popular imagination of emigration with his monumental tetralogy: *The Emigrants* (1949, *Utvandrarna*), *Unto a Good Land* (1952, *Invandrarna*), *The Settlers* (1952, *Nybyggarna*) and *The Last Letter Home* (1959, *Sista brevet till Sverige*). The series of novels depicts the fate of a family from Småland: Karl-Oskar Nilsson and Kristina Johannesdotter, their three surviving children and a number of relatives and neighbours who decide to emigrate to Minnesota in 1850. Settled in the New World, they gradually adapt to the local conditions and live through a number of formative events in American history, including the California Gold Rush (1849–55) and the American Civil War.

Considered some of the greatest works of modern Swedish literature, Moberg's novels also became the basis for two major feature film adaptions by director Jan Troell: *The Emigrants* (1971, *Utvandrarna*) and *The New Land* (1972, *Nybyggarna*), starring Max von Sydow, Liv Ullmann and Eddie Axberg. Both films were nominated for several Academy Awards and *The New Land* won the Golden Globe Award in 1973 for the best foreign language film. In 1995, Benny Andersson and Björn Ulvaeus (of ABBA) further premiered a musical based on the novels, which received instant acclaim and widespread popularity. Dealing with 'the great questions of our time', according to the critics, it ran for nearly four years in Sweden, generated guest performances and concert versions abroad, and both the recorded album and a single held considerable positions in the national charts throughout the late 1990s.

Conclusion: Emigration and the Nation

Emigration from Sweden – and from the rest of Scandinavia – in the nineteenth and early twentieth century was a complex phenomenon with a number of causes and a multifaceted impact on the countries of both its origin and destination. Peaking in the late 1860s, early 1880s and around the turn of the century, emigration changed in volume over time. However, beyond the concrete material and ideational circumstances that encouraged people to emigrate – hopes for employment and social advancement, fear of material destitution or religious and political persecution – the 'emigration question' also had a wide societal resonance as a focal point in public debates around which various fears and hopes would congregate, often reaching far beyond the question of emigration per se.

It is somewhat ironic that *Emigrationsutredningen*, the impressive study of the causes and effects of emigration from Sweden, became obsolete almost as soon as it was concluded – the beginning of the First World War and subsequent closure of international borders made it nearly impossible to emigrate. Nevertheless, it remains an important milestone in the history of Swedish statistics and exemplifies more generally its culture of state-commissioned research projects (*statliga utredningar*). The widely felt need to 'do something' about emigration in the decade around the turn of the century was an important impetus in the development of the rational and scientific ways of solving perceived societal problems that subsequently became a hallmark of the Swedish Social Democratic welfare state and the 'Nordic model' more generally (Hall 2000, 241).

But whether presenting an emotive and nostalgic vision of rural Swedishness, or seeking social science 'solutions' to emigration as a societal 'problem', arguments in opposition to emigration (and in some cases in support of it) ultimately tended to be about Sweden's future as a state and a nation. This became visible in how modernity – the great divisive issue in nation building in the age of industrialisation – was alternatively embraced or rejected in the emigration debate as various commentators attempted to secure the unreachable ideal of a unitary and well-governed, materially prosperous nation state. Perhaps more than anything else, it was this strongly idealistic, but at the same time also pragmatic and hands-on, approach to public policy that came to define Sweden and the rest of Scandinavia in the century that followed.

References

Baines, Dudley. 1994. 'European Emigration, 1815–1930: Looking at the Emigration Decision Again', *Economic History Review* 47 (3): 525–44.

Barton, H. Arnold, ed. 1975. *Letters from the Promised Land: Swedes in America, 1840–1914*. Minneapolis: University of Minnesota Press for the Swedish Pioneer Historical Society.

Barton, H. Arnold. 1990. 'Svenska reaktioner till utvandringsfrågan kring sekelskiftet'. In *Studier i modern historia: Tillägnade Jarl Torbacke den 18 augusti 1990*, 13–25. Stockholm: Militärhistoriska Förlaget.

Brochmann, Grete. 2018. 'Immigration Policies of the Scandinavian Countries'. In *The Routledge Handbook of Scandinavian Politics*, edited by Peter Nedergaard and Anders Wivel, 229–39. London: Routledge.

Gjerde, Jon. 1995. 'The Scandinavian Migrants'. In *The Cambridge Survey of World Migration*, edited by Robin Cohen, 85–90. Cambridge: Cambridge University Press.

Gustafsson, Harald. 1997. *Nordens historia: En europeisk region under 1200 år*. Lund: Studentlitteratur.

Hall, Patrik. 2000. *Den svenskaste historien: Nationalism i Sverige under sex sekler*. Stockholm: Carlsson.

Hult, Marte. 2008. 'Lindgren, Astrid (1907–2002)'. In *The Greenwood Encyclopedia of Folktales and Fairy Tales, Volume 2: G–P*, edited by Donald Haase, 575–7. Westport, CT: Greenwood Press.

Jansson, Torkel. 2016. 'Scandinavia between the Congress of Vienna and the Paris Commune'. In *The Cambridge History of Scandinavia, Volume II: 1520–1870*, edited by E.I. Kouri and Jens E. Olesen, 685–90. Cambridge: Cambridge University Press.

Kummel, Bengt. 1994. *Svenskar i all världen förenen eder! Vilhelm Lundström och den allsvenska rörelsen*. Åbo: Åbo Akademis Förlag.

Lindkvist, Anna. 2007. *Jorden åt folket: Nationalföreningen mot emigrationen 1907–1925*. Umeå: Umeå Universitet.

Ljungmark, Lars. 2008. *Swedish Exodus*, translated by Kermit B. Westerberg. Carbondale: Southern Illinois University Press.

Martinsson, Örjan. n.d. 'Population of Scandinavia'. Accessed 11 July 2018. http://www.tacitus.nu/historical-atlas/population/scandinavia.htm.

Nordstrom, Byron J. 2000. *Scandinavia since 1500*. Minneapolis: University of Minnesota Press.

Orfield, Lester Bernhardt. 1953. *The Growth of Scandinavian Law*. Philadelphia: University of Pennsylvania Press.

Scott, Franklin D. 1965. 'Sweden's Constructive Opposition to Emigration', *Journal of Modern History* 37 (3): 307–35.

Söderberg, Kjell. 1981. *Den första massutvandringen: En studie av befolkningsrörlighet och emigration utgående från Alfta socken i Hälsingland 1846–1895*. Umeå: Umeå Universitet.

13
Film and the Welfare State: Three Informational Films about Healthcare

C. Claire Thomson

The decade following the Second World War was a period of consolidation of the Scandinavian welfare states. While the notion of *folkhemmet* or 'The People's Home' was popularised by Swedish Prime Minister Per Albin Hansson in 1928, the occupation of Denmark and Norway by Nazi Germany from 1940 to 1945 slowed progress in the social sphere. From the late 1940s onwards, a decade of new legislation, social organisation and increasing productivity and prosperity paved the way for the 'Golden Age' of the welfare state in the 1960s (see Hilson 2008 and chapter 5 in this volume). This period coincided with an international 'golden age' of informational cinema: film in the service of the state, industries and non-governmental organisations. Such films were made to educate, inform and persuade rather than primarily to entertain, and in Scandinavia they were a crucial tool for government efforts to explain social, technological and legislative change to domestic and foreign audiences.

This chapter examines three examples of short informational films made between 1947 and 1963 for a range of audiences, all of which focus on a specific aspect of the welfare state: healthcare and sickness insurance. The first film, *Health for Denmark* (Torben Anton Svendsen, Denmark, 1947) was produced as part of a series of short films presenting aspects of Danish social policy to the English-speaking world in the immediate post-war period. The second, *Marianne på sykehus* (Marianne in Hospital, Titus Vibe Müller, Norway, 1950), was primarily intended to reassure Norwegian children about potential hospital treatment, but also promoted Norway's sickness insurance scheme to parents. Finally, *The Riddle of Sweden* (Gösta Werner, Sweden, 1963) was made to inform international viewers about what was often referred to as 'the Swedish Model' of a welfare state underpinned by industrial productivity.

Before considering these films in detail, however, the chapter first provides an overview of lines of enquiry into the relationship between cinema, the state and national identity. It then introduces the particular kind of cinema of which our case studies are examples: informational film, or 'useful cinema', and suggests various points of focus for the analysis of such films.

Cinema and the State

From its earliest days in the mid-1890s, moving image technology was developed for the purposes of commercial entertainment (see for example Grieveson and Krämer 2004). However, precisely because of cinema's potential to generate revenue, and its perceived power to affect collective and individual behaviours and beliefs, governments and other institutions have sought to intervene in or harness the influence of cinema in different ways at different times. The relations between cinema and the state thus present a wide range of potential perspectives for analysis.

In the Nordic context, film scholars have investigated a number of distinctive features of the national cinema industries. For example, the decade up to 1916 is generally regarded as a 'golden age' for Danish cinema, when genre films such as mysteries, science fiction and erotic melodrama were exported worldwide (see for example Schepelern 2010). From the late 1910s, Swedish cinema blossomed, with emphasis on sophisticated literary adaptations (see for example Larsson and Marklund 2010). In both cases, national censorship bureaux were established early on, and cinema tickets were subject to an entertainment tax (Hedling 2016; Schepelern 2010). Through the mechanism of film censorship, governments intervene to police social and moral norms, such as gender roles, sexual behaviours and depiction of violence. The entertainment tax functioned to re-route income from commercial entertainment into other policy areas, such as enlightening public information films. Similarly, in newly-independent Norway, the government enacted legislation in 1913 which would mitigate the potentially corrupting effects of cinema through censorship and through the provision of enlightening films, and also generate income for the public purse to support cultural life more broadly. A distinctive feature of the Norwegian system was its organisation at municipal level: film distribution and programming, ownership of cinemas, and, later, filmmaking, fell under the aegis of local authorities (see Solum 2016). The monopoly of municipal authorities over cinema in Norway lasted until the 2010s.

A key concept in the study of Nordic film cultures has been 'small-nation cinema' (Hjort 2005; Thomson 2018). This approach to film history posits that countries around the size of the Nordic states display a range of distinctive tendencies in film policy, filmmaker education, film production and distribution which can be attributed to their scale. In recent decades, Denmark and Iceland in particular can be seen to have leveraged the notion of 'small-nation' cinema, in two distinct ways. On the one hand, the Danish government, especially under the auspices of the Danish Film Institute, has sought to use cinema as an element in nation branding, and has operated a range of subsidy schemes for filmmakers producing films in both Danish and English (Hjort 2005, 9). On the other hand, Iceland has adopted the strategy of attracting international film productions to the country, promoting its spectacular scenery as a shooting location, offering tax breaks to filmmakers and fostering a national talent pool by ensuring a regular stream of overseas cinema practitioners to work in Iceland (Norðfjörð 2007). Overall, a wide variety of state support strategies for cinema can be observed across the Nordic region, encompassing, for example, subsidies for national productions and international co-productions, language-specific subsidies, publicly-funded filmmaker education, investment in technologies and expertise to ensure the preservation, restoration and digitisation of national film heritage, and inventive modes of mediating that heritage to domestic and overseas audiences (for a range of case studies, see Hjort and Lindqvist 2016).

Cinema and National Identity

Although films have always been produced, funded and circulated on an international scale, questions of national identity haunt cinema, in comparable ways to national literature or painting. Three factors in particular make the relationship between cinema and nation rather complex. First, filmmaking is an expensive and collective enterprise, so cast, crew and funding are often drawn from a number of countries. Second, as cinema has been an audio-visual technology since the advent of sound film around 1927, the language(s) spoken in a film imbue it with a cultural identity and can necessitate the use of subtitles, complicating its reception abroad. A third aspect of the relationship between cinema and nation is that films both tell stories about, and share images of, defined places. While novels, for example, have an important role in shaping how people understand themselves as belonging to 'imagined communities'

(Anderson 1991), by its very nature as an audio-visual medium, cinema photographically 'images' communities. As they travel, films are thus often understood to both document and represent the nation from which they emanate. And some films become emblematic of a national identity for the domestic population. Films are just one thread in the broader tapestry of the ever-shifting cultural identity of a nation or region (for a range of case studies and approaches, see Hjort and MacKenzie 2000).

Such networks of images have been a focus for research in Scandinavian cultural history over the last decade. One influential model that can be used as a tool to identify and analyse meaning-making about national identity was proposed by Kazimierz Musiał (2002). The key concepts are xenostereotypes and autostereotypes: ideas about a country that originate outside and inside the nation respectively (see also chapters 11 and 14 in this volume). For example, the idea that modern-day Scandinavians are descended from Vikings found expression in the marketing of the then newly-established Scandinavian Airline Systems (SAS) in the 1940s. The aircraft were given call names such as Dan Viking, and notepaper on board was emblazoned with 'On board the flying Viking ships'; the (fictional) voice of Dan Viking was used to narrate an English-language informational film called *They Guide You Across* (Ingolf Boisen 1949), which detailed the safety systems and navigation technologies which undergirded the then new route across the Atlantic to New York (Thomson 2018, 88–100). Such imagery was calculated to appeal both to Scandinavian and international passengers, and leveraged associations such as hardiness, navigational skill and regional (as opposed to national) cultural specificities. An important point is that both kinds of stereotype can be seen to interact and can be hard to disentangle.

State-Sponsored Informational Film

The example of *They Guide You Across* brings us to a very specific kind of state-sponsored filmmaking: the informational short. While film was used in educational settings from very early on in its history, and documentary film began to blossom from the late 1920s onwards (see Nichols 2017), it was in the two decades after the Second World War that short informational films proliferated worldwide as a means of informing and persuading populations about any number of subjects, from agriculture to sculpture, and from medicine to sport. Before television sets became common in European and North American homes from around 1960, and more than half a century before the advent of YouTube, short films were produced by governments, businesses, charities, trade unions and many other kinds of organisations, and circulated to audiences on the national and international scales. Such films were mobile thanks to the development of narrow-gauge film (especially the 16 mm format), and portable projectors which could be borrowed and set up anywhere: schools, libraries, churches, community halls, cafes. The films themselves were exchanged via networks of local and national film libraries, embassies, film festivals and trade fairs. This kind of filmmaking has been dubbed 'useful cinema', because its primary purpose is not to entertain (though the most impactful films were often the entertaining ones), but to inform, to educate and to persuade (for a range of case studies, see Acland and Wasson 2011).

The Scandinavian countries were prolific producers of this kind of film. In Denmark, the agency Dansk Kulturfilm was established in 1932 to act as a clearing-house for film projects requested by associations and ministries. From the early 1940s (that is, during the German occupation of Denmark) to the mid-1960s, Dansk Kulturfilm worked in tandem with Ministeriernes Filmudvalg, the Danish Government Film Committee. The twin committees oversaw the production, by various companies, of a stream of films for domestic and international consumption on topics ranging from home economics to traffic safety, and from architecture to science. The distribution of the films to schools, libraries and associations at home and abroad was coordinated by Statens Filmcentral (the State Film Centre), which later took on a production role as well (Thomson 2018, 47–63). In Norway, Statens Filmsentral (the State Film Centre) was established in 1948 by government statute to oversee the production of informational films required to support the work of the Ministry of Social Affairs (Diesen 1998, 48). In Sweden, the bulk of informational filmmaking was undertaken under the auspices of film studios such as Svensk Filmindustri and Sandrew (Hedling 2016; Jönsson 2016).

Because they were commissioned or facilitated by the state, industry or other organisations, in many cases it is possible to trace the production histories of such films. We can shed light on political and cultural priorities of the time by investigating why the films were commissioned and funded, by whom, and whether the commissioning bodies mandated particular criteria regarding the films' content. What do the films assume the viewer already knows, and what does s/he still have to learn? Just as revealing is the style of the films: how did they conform to, borrow from or re-work contemporary cinematic norms in an effort to capture and hold the attention of viewers? For example, how do they use music, costume or editing? What kind of voices can be heard in the voiceover and, where relevant, the dialogue? How the films were received and reviewed can also be revealing: how audiences understood the films did not always correspond to the intended message. In all these senses, informational films are snapshots of their time: they tell us something about the technological and legal novelties of the day, and about collective anxieties and beliefs.

Hundreds, if not thousands, of informational films from the twentieth century survive in the archives of companies, organisations and national film institutes. Increasingly, these films are digitised and made available online, primarily for national audiences. For example, the Danish Film Institute has created the streaming site danmarkpaafilm.dk, which associates informational, amateur and orphan films (films whose director, rights holder etc. are unknown) with geographic areas, and allows site visitors to contribute comments and information about the places and events depicted. At oslofilmer.no, Oslo City Archive has digitised many short films about the Norwegian capital, ranging from informational films about transport, sanitation and hospitals to tourist films promoting the capital as a cultural destination. And the Swedish Film Institute is developing filmarkivet.se, which gathers industrial, informational and advertising films under a range of themes. The majority of such films were made in the Scandinavian languages for domestic audiences, and today's streaming sites reflect this. However, a significant proportion of informational films were made in English and other languages for overseas audiences, promoting Scandinavia as a tourist destination, and sharing information about traditions, handicrafts, industrial products and social welfare.

We can thus study informational films as symptomatic of their time and, often, as documents produced with the intention of intervening in culture. They show us the images that Scandinavian societies nurtured about themselves, and the images that cultural institutions wished to project to the outside world. We need also to bear in mind that the actual viewers of the films might not have corresponded to the intended audiences, and that there was always scope for films to be misconstrued. In the case studies below, we can trace how the films play, narratively and visually, with auto- and xenostereotypes in order to communicate their messages to a range of audiences.

Health for Denmark (1947)

In April 1947, a package of five informational films premiered in Copenhagen under the rubric *Social Denmark*. The English title for the series was deliberate: the five films had been commissioned with a British audience in mind, and were made under the supervision of Arthur Elton, a leading figure in the British Documentary Movement. Around twenty copies of each film were sent to the UK (Thomson 2018, 82), introducing Danish social policy in the areas of healthcare, childcare, holiday pay, services for pensioners and support for single mothers. *Social Denmark* was thus a canny act of 'cultural propaganda' (Glover 2009), which kick-started two decades of filmmaking for foreign audiences alongside the production of informational film for Danes.

One of the *Social Denmark* films was *Health for Denmark*, which sketches the Danish sickness insurance scheme as it existed in the late 1940s: locally organised and government-subsidised 'sick clubs'. This system was identified by the Ministry of Labour and Social Affairs and by Arthur Elton as a particularly resonant topic, not least because the UK was in the process of establishing its own National Health Service (Thomson 2018, 74). Typically for the genre, *Health for Denmark* uses local, fictional characters as metonyms for a complex, abstract system that existed on a national scale. The film begins with a long shot of the town square of the fictional Nordkøbing. (The cathedral spires of the real-life town of Roskilde are clearly visible.) We are introduced to the local cobbler, postman and tobacconist as they exchange cigars for shoe repairs, establishing community-level cooperation. The three men are on the committee of the local sick club, and we see both a committee meeting and the club office, a gathering place for all classes and occupations. The voiceover introduces Mrs Ipsen, who is described as 'pretty typical'. She is asked to tell us about her use of the sick club, and so her voice forms part of the voiceover. When her husband Mr Ipsen is taken ill with flu, the action shifts to the local hospital and to a more straightforwardly documentary mode, showcasing the hospital's modern facilities in a montage of the latest medical treatments: x-rays, tests for tuberculosis, heat and light treatments featuring suspiciously glamorous women patients in bathrobes, isolation wards, nurses' quarters, and so on. The 'facts' of Denmark's sickness insurance system thus emerge in the film from a blend of narrative and visual strategies, including metonymy (fictional characters standing in for a national system), and the visual juxtaposition of traditional (the town's cathedral spires, the tobacconist shop) and modern (the gleaming hospital facilities).

Another notable strategy in *Health for Denmark* is the innovative use of voiceover. Arthur Elton had insisted that the films should be narrated through English-language voiceover, rather than shot with a Danish script and then dubbed or subtitled (Thomson 2019). The film's voiceover is ostensibly a typical example of mid-twentieth-century 'voice-of-God' (Nichols 2017, 53–5), an authoritative perspective on the action. In this case, the dominant voice is a clipped, male, upper-class English accent, which is spoken by Ralph Elton, brother of the above-mentioned producer Arthur Elton. However, the voiceover subverts expectations in two ways. First, Elton observes and explains, but leaves room for the locals, such as Mrs Ipsen, to recount their experience in their own voice. Second, the film plays with viewer expectations and knowledge about voiceover conventions in cinema. Twelve minutes into the film, during a meeting of the local hospital's Board of Governors, the voiceover suddenly intervenes in the meeting: 'Before they get down to business, I'd like to interrupt', he says. He asks the chairman to say something about the hospital. In Danish, the Chair asks the other Board members for permission, then switches to English to give an overview of the hospital's architecture, facilities and plans. This shift in the voiceover to a thickly-accented 'we' quite literally gives the local Danes a voice in the description of their achievements and future plans as regards social security and healthcare. But this is also a sophisticated strategy which compliments the viewer by assuming that s/he understands that the logic of cinema normally precludes direct interaction between voiceover and characters. This is a variant on the practice of 'breaking the fourth wall', the imaginary barrier between the world of the film and the world of the viewers. The effect is both gently amusing, and a comment on the artificiality of the informational film; both comedy and self-referentiality can be effective strategies for maximising the memorability and the impact of an informational film. This play with levels of narration serves as a surprising change of pace in the narrative; retaining audience engagement is the holy grail for informational filmmaking.

Health for Denmark and the other *Social Denmark* films presented Denmark as a socially progressive and culturally sophisticated nation, but also as a cosy, humble and pragmatic one. A 1948 catalogue of Danish informational films for export describes the ambition of the films as 'an experiment in post-war help and inspiration' to help the world get 'back to normal' after the war; 'perhaps there are things to be found in Denmark which may be useful in other countries', suggests the blurb for *Social Denmark* (Statens Filmcentral 1948, 69). Picking up on this stance, the British filmmaker Basil Wright wrote of the *Social Denmark* series that the films showed 'a healthy attitude of discontent with the status quo and an atmosphere of self-criticism which gives them a real validity for social students in all other countries' (Wright 1947, 24). Here we see an example of the intertwining of auto- and xenostereotypes in the production and reception of the films: the notion of Denmark as a small, modest, but socially and technologically advanced nation.

Marianne på sykehus (1950)

In Norway, government ministries also used film to inform the populace about healthcare. A particularly interesting example from 1950 is the 45-minute film *Marianne på sykehus* (Marianne in Hospital). While this film is narrated in Norwegian and not available with English subtitles, its voiceover and most of the dialogue is slow and clear, as befits a narrative aimed at children; the film should be relatively easy to understand for learners of Norwegian. The film was commissioned by Rikstrygdeverket, Norway's national social security agency, in collaboration with Rikshospitalet, the national hospital. Based on a popular children's book by Odd Brochmann, and directed by Titus Vibe Müller, the film's premiere in December 1950 was a national event attended by King Haakon, and the film was seen by 31,000 people in its first two weeks (Weium 2003, 3585). The film's purpose was to explain to children what goes on in a hospital, and what would happen to them should they need to have an operation.

Bearing in mind the primary target audience, it is not surprising that *Marianne på sykehus* begins with a 'spoiler': Marianne is about to leave hospital, healthy and smiling. The rest of the plot is then organised chronologically: she accidentally swallows a brooch which has fallen into her breakfast porridge, is found crying in pain by the local doctor, is sent by seaplane to hospital in Oslo, and has an operation to remove the brooch. The detail with which all the stages of the story are related panders to the curiosity and anxiety of children watching the film. We see the interiors of the medical seaplane, the ambulance, the x-ray room and the operating theatre, and are brought face to face with anaesthetic and surgical equipment. *Marianne på sykehus* is also infused with a sense of security. Despite the momentary lapse of attention which results in the brooch falling into the porridge pot, Marianne's mother and father are kind and attentive. The local doctor is introduced as a man so beloved in the small town of Lillesund that he cannot walk down the street without having to greet every passer-by. There is a recurring trope of kind nurses taking Marianne's hand to comfort her. The musical score is generally jolly and uplifting, except for a few moments of drama. And the film is held together by the voiceover, a narrating voice which is kind and expressive in tone, and also sustains a degree of solidarity with the viewer by occasionally stumbling over the pronunciation of difficult words like 'anestesi' (anaesthesia).

An example of the balance between drama, security and technical detail achieved by *Marianne på sykehus* is the sequence in which Marianne is being x-rayed. The sequence is dominated by a series of two-shots, in which Marianne stands behind the x-ray machine to the left, and the radiographer sits to the right of the screen, operating the machine. We cross-cut to a nurse in a nearby room who is operating the controls. The medics' curious code of communicating in whistles adds levity, while the radiographer speaks calmly and quietly to the 'little miss' whose stomach pain he has been asked to diagnose. Here the iconography of x-ray technology is used to increase suspense: the film cross-cuts between the eyes of the radiographer studying the glow from the screen, and Marianne's eyes watching him, until, with an ominous musical flourish, the camera pans upwards from the patient's hips and spine on the x-ray screen to reveal the sharp black outline of the brooch sitting under her ribs. Though the viewer has known for some time that Marianne swallowed the brooch, the cause of her malady is now confirmed by a modern visual technology.

The dialogue establishes that children whose parents are members of Trygdekassen, the national health insurance scheme, get free healthcare, including transportation across the country for specialist care. Here, again, we see progressiveness as a national autostereotype, co-existing with tradition and community, and harnessed in the service of perfecting that same progressive society by persuading its members to participate. As Frode Weium points out, *Marianne på sykehus* was also designed to function as a kind of propaganda film directed at parents: it paints an unrealistically positive picture of the efficiency with which Marianne is admitted and diagnosed, and it lingers on plans for the modern renovation and expansion of *Rikshospitalet* which were ongoing at the time (Weium 2003, 3587). Like *Health for Denmark*, this film is a snapshot of a welfare state under construction.

The Riddle of Sweden (1963)

A decade later, the very title of *The Riddle of Sweden* (directed by Gösta Werner, 1963) acknowledges that the projected audience – primarily North American – was both fascinated and puzzled by the Swedish model. The film opens with a drumroll and trumpet flourish, and a montage of aerial shots of lakes and mountains. A male American voice-over introduces Sweden:

> Let's take a look at a country which is off the beaten track. A small but much talked of country: Sweden. Admittedly Sweden lies a long way north, but she is by no means as cold as she is reputed to be. We've heard tell of this country, of the riddle that is Sweden. But the keys to this riddle are not easy to find.

One immediately obvious feature of the voiceover text is the pronoun 'we'. The 'voice-of-God' narrator thus aligns himself with the viewers, who are observing what is presumed to be a foreign country. These opening comments acknowledge both the existence of prevailing xenostereotypes and the difficulty of understanding the other culture.

During this introductory monologue, the opening montage of mountains is revealed to be the point-of-view of the passengers on a modern SAS aircraft. The plane glides to a halt on the runway, and businessmen spill out. Within the first minute of the film, then, the viewer's attention has been arrested by the spectacular scenery which is one xenostereotype associated with Sweden and other small, northern countries. The juxtaposition through montage of the landscape with another kind of spectacle – the impressively modern, gleaming plane – connects nature and technology for the viewer, framing the combination as both Swedish and a 'riddle'. This idea of contrasts as a riddle continues to underpin the film's narrative. After historical footage of the Nobel ceremony establishes Sweden as both a monarchy and a democracy, the voiceover asks what it is about Swedes that has enabled them to attain the highest standard of living in Europe. A montage of old wooden houses is juxtaposed with tower blocks, parks and fountains and the functionalist Slussen traffic complex. High levels of car ownership, compulsory comprehensive education with free lunches and care for the elderly are all mentioned before the film turns to the healthcare system.

The cost of healthcare is negligible, we learn, and it is 'the best possible medical care that modern research can give, with Swedish-designed equipment, like the artificial kidney, and the revolutionary heart-lung machine for cardiac operations'. The images in this sequence cross-cut between close-ups of technological detail – liquid bubbling through one gleaming machine, blood through another – and long shots of operations in progress. The climax to the healthcare segment of the film is the proton ray knife, used for brain surgery. A dramatic zoom and a close-up of a finger pointing to the machine are followed by a shot of a patient under-going proton ray treatment, and more recognisable x-ray images of brain lesions. Modern orchestral music punctuates the sequence, with wood-wind flourishes drawing attention to details such as the flow of blood through equipment. The film then turns its attention to a range of aspects of industry, but the first few minutes of *The Riddle of Sweden* have estab-lished that the welfare system, democracy, prosperity, national culture, science and technology are all inextricably linked with Swedish business and industry.

The Riddle of Sweden was commissioned and funded by what at the time was called *Sveriges Allmänna Exportförening*, The Swedish Export Association, and produced by the company AB Filmkontakt. It was used by the Association's network of international offices as part of its broader promotional strategy for Swedish business (Stjernholm 2018, 275). Typically for the kind of films discussed in this chapter, the 16 mm and black and white format facilitated screenings in a range of settings, for example, for specific interest groups and companies, and at trade fairs, and the film was available in five language versions for use by members of the Export Association. In another sense, though, *The Riddle of Sweden* is different to the Danish and Norwegian films discussed above: it was commissioned by business interests as opposed to a government agency. In fact, there was no Swedish equivalent to Dansk Kulturfilm or Statens Filmsentral, and much of the production and development of nonfiction film in mid-century Sweden was undertaken by commercial companies, especially Svensk Filmindustri, or SF (Jönsson 2016, 126). However, this does not mean that film was less important in the service of the state in Sweden; quite the contrary. Mats Jönsson, for example, has examined how a range of film genres, including advertising, newsreels and political films were part of the same project of affirming and propagating the 'unu-sually successful social engineering project' that constituted the Swedish 'People's Home'; film production was 'meticulously supervised by the state and its official representatives', so that the population was 'visually and audiovisually disciplined' by film and other media (Jönsson 2016, 125). In much the same way, the Swedish Export Association strategi-cally eschewed explicit advertising of products in *The Riddle of Sweden*, instead employing images of technological modernity and social progres-siveness to 'sell' Sweden itself. The Association recognised that industry could only benefit from the crystallisation of these xenostereotypes of a modern, productive and prosperous Sweden. In *The Riddle of Sweden*, the framing metaphor of the 'riddle' gives expression to the awareness of agencies charged with promoting Sweden in trade circles that Sweden's economic, political and cultural exceptionalism could itself be an oblique advertising strategy (Stjernholm 2018, 274-5).

The Riddle of Sweden can also be usefully contextualised in the broader frame of strategies meant to promote Sweden abroad in the post-war period. Nikolas Glover (2009, 248–56) discusses how The Swedish Institute was established after the Second World War in order to safeguard the positive international reputation of the country in the wake of a conflict in which it had, controversially, remained unaligned. The Institute's founders were aware that Sweden had been known overseas since at least the 1930s as a socially progressive nation, a conception which chimed with domestic beliefs about the fundamental nature of Sweden, and they moved to leverage that stereotype in publications such as the 300-page tome of 1949, *Introduction to Sweden* (Glover 2009, 252). Glover traces how Sweden's international reputation as progressive, internationalist and democratic came to be prioritised over more traditionally cultural aspects of Swedishness such as literature and music, not just in the country's cultural diplomacy aimed at overseas markets, but also in domestic popular self-understanding. In other words, the xenostereotype of the Swedish politico-economic model came to influence the prevailing autostereotypes.

On the other hand, these images of Sweden co-existed and competed with other images whose value for industry and cultural diplomacy is harder to parse. The international success of Swedish cinematic auteurs such as Ingmar Bergman during the 1950s had established the popular notion of Sweden as a land of nude bathing beauties, as one of the officials involved in the commissioning of *The Riddle of Sweden* observed (Stjernholm 2018, 275). In this particular case, then, we see an interesting example of so-called 'useful cinema' being strategically deployed to mitigate the more mercurial impact of art-house cinema in mediating images of Sweden.

Conclusion

This chapter has focused on three examples of informational film which engage with developments in healthcare in mid-century Denmark, Norway and Sweden, but for different purposes. By zooming in on sequences which visualise hospital treatment, we have been able to examine how the films address distinctive audiences. *Health for Denmark* provides a snapshot of an ambitious healthcare system under construction, expressly aimed at a British audience on the brink of establishing its own National

Health Service. *Marianne på sykehus* is designed to reassure nervous children and persuade their parents of the benefits of signing up to the new national sickness insurance scheme. And, aiming at an international business audience, *The Riddle of Sweden* frames Swedish healthcare as an iteration of the country's advanced social organisation and technological innovation.

The hospital imagery in all three films is surprisingly comparable, in that each film aims to connect treatment to modernity and national community. We can observe similarities in the oscillation between parts of machines and the teams of staff, in the use of x-ray images as popularly recognisable products of medical technology, and in the juxtaposition of old and new (through montage or within the frame) to construct a sense of modernity. Some of the interesting differences between the films lie in the voiceovers, from which we can glean a clear idea of the projected audience. As films made for foreign viewers, *Health for Denmark* and *The Riddle of Sweden* self-consciously exploit xenostereotypes to communicate their message. All three films address healthcare as a concrete expression of the rather abstract autostereotype of the modern, progressive welfare state.

While we can draw some conclusions about patterns and priorities in informational filmmaking from this kind of comparative analysis, it is important to bear in mind that the films which have been digitised and/ or subtitled may have been made available to us for a variety of financial, cultural, technological or political reasons which have little to do with their representativity. As with any archival resource, we need to be careful not to assume that the materials available to us are entirely representative of output. Many analogue film formats were delicate and have not survived into the digital age to be digitised, and archives are limited in their activities by economic restrictions and political priorities. These films are available to us because of state investment in the preservation and restoration of older analogue film, and investment in digital platforms that mediate the films to today's viewers. In fact, the selection of film case studies for this chapter was made on the basis of their availability online. At the time of writing (autumn 2018), the digitisation of informational films and their mediation via streaming sites is gaining pace in all three Scandinavian countries. By the time you read this chapter, an even wider variety of this kind of film will be available to viewers who want to explore the stories that mid-twentieth-century Scandinavians told about their culture to themselves and to the world.

Films

Health for Denmark (Torben Anton Svendsen, Denmark, 1947), https://filmcentralen.dk/museum/danmark-paa-film/film/health-denmark

Marianne på sykehus (Marianne in Hospital, Titus Vibe Müller, Norway, 1950), https://www.nb.no/nbsok/nb/a529de62bfaa33cba2b4a8c31be85147?index=1

The Riddle of Sweden (Gösta Werner, Sweden, 1963), http://www.filmarkivet.se/movies/the-riddle-of-sweden/

References

Acland, Charles R. and Haidee Wasson, eds. 2011. *Useful Cinema*. Durham, NC: Duke University Press.

Anderson, Benedict. 1991. *Imagined Communities: Reflections on the Origin and Spread of Nationalism*. Rev. ed. London: Verso.

Diesen, Jan Anders. 1998. *Film som statlig folkeopplyser: Statens Filmsentral 50 år* (Norsk Filminstitutts Skriftserie 9). Oslo: Norsk Filminstitutt.

Glover, Nikolas. 2009. 'Imaging Community: Sweden in "Cultural Propaganda" Then and Now', *Scandinavian Journal of History* 34 (3): 246–63.

Grieveson, Lee and Peter Krämer, eds. 2004. *The Silent Cinema Reader*. London: Routledge.

Hedling, Olof. 2016. 'Cinema in the Welfare State: Notes on Public Support, Regional Film Funds, and Swedish Film Policy'. In *A Companion to Nordic Cinema*, edited by Mette Hjort and Ursula Lindqvist, 60–77. Chichester: Wiley Blackwell.

Hilson, Mary. 2008. *The Nordic Model: Scandinavia since 1945*. London: Reaktion Books.

Hjort, Mette. 2005. *Small Nation, Global Cinema: The New Danish Cinema*. Minneapolis: University of Minnesota Press.

Hjort, Mette and Ursula Lindqvist, eds. 2016. *A Companion to Nordic Cinema*. Chichester: Wiley Blackwell.

Hjort, Mette and Scott MacKenzie, eds. 2000. *Cinema and Nation*. London: Routledge.

Jönsson, Mats. 2016. 'Non-Fiction Film Culture in Sweden circa 1920–1960: Pragmatic Governance and Consensual Solidarity in a Welfare State'. In *A Companion to Nordic Cinema*, edited by Mette Hjort and Ursula Lindqvist, 125–47. Chichester: Wiley Blackwell.

Larsson, Mariah and Anders Marklund, eds. 2010. *Swedish Film: An Introduction and Reader*. Lund: Nordic Academic Press.

Musiał, Kazimierz. 2002. *Roots of the Scandinavian Model: Images of Progress in the Era of Modernisation*. Baden-Baden: Nomos Verlagsgesellschaft.

Nichols, Bill. 2017. *Introduction to Documentary*. 3rd ed. Bloomington: Indiana University Press.

Norðfjörð, Björn. 2007. 'Iceland'. In *The Cinema of Small Nations*, edited by Mette Hjort and Duncan Petrie, 43–59. Edinburgh: Edinburgh University Press.

Schepelern, Peter. 2010. 'Danish Film History: 1896–2009'. Accessed 30 September 2018. https://www.dfi.dk/en/english/danish-film-history/danish-film-history-1896-2009.

Solum, Ove. 2016. 'The Rise and Fall of Norwegian Municipal Cinemas'. In *A Companion to Nordic Cinema*, edited by Mette Hjort and Ursula Lindqvist, 179–98. Chichester: Wiley Blackwell.

Statens Filmcentral. 1948. *Documentary in Denmark 1940-1948: 100 Films of Facts in War, Occupation, Liberation, Peace*. Copenhagen.

Stjernholm, Emil. 2018. *Gösta Werner och filmen som konst och propaganda* (Mediehistoriskt Arkiv 38). Lund: Mediehistoria, Lunds Universitet.

Thomson, C. Claire. 2018. *Short Films from a Small Nation: Danish Informational Cinema, 1935–1965*. Edinburgh: Edinburgh University Press.

Thomson, C. Claire. 2019. '"Here is My Home": Voiceover and Foreign-Language Versions in Post-War Danish Informational Film'. In *Nordic Film Cultures and Cinemas of Elsewhere*, edited by Arne Lunde and Anna Westerståhl Stenport, 141–56. Edinburgh: Edinburgh University Press.

Weium, Frode. 2003. 'Marianne på sykehus', *Tidsskrift for Den norske lægeforening* 24 (123): 3585–87.

Wright, Basil. 1947. 'Danish Documentary', *Documentary* (Journal of the Edinburgh International Film Festival) 47: 24.

14
Stereotypes in and of Scandinavia

Ellen Kythor

Rough-chiselled icy-white block capitals proclaiming 'Nordic Countries' adorned a sea-blue circular hanging banner above an array of uncluttered book display shelves, Arne Jacobsen chairs, and stylishly turned-out representatives of national arts councils in the Olympia exhibition hall for 2015's London Book Fair (LBF). Nordic arts councils have had a unified presence for many years now at international trade book fairs, representing Nordic authors and publishers together at one large stand, rather than as separate countries, as part of their *NordLit* project within the Nordic Council. This is a contemporary example of Nordic exceptionalism: an agreement by the Nordic nations that because there is brand commonality between all Nordic nations in relation to the rest of the world, it is worth both managing and embracing this 'brand'. Indeed, the regions of Scandinavia and Norden are often perceived synonymously from outside the region, and the brand colours at LBF 2015 invoked cold northerly imagery for all the Nordic countries conjointly. This shared branding is complicated not only by the multifaceted differences between the nations and inhabitants that make up the region, but also by the differences in perception of the region from within and outside. These different perceptions can be analysed via the concept of stereotypes. This chapter will first define different categories of stereotypes, and then present a number of examples of stereotypes of Scandinavia, paying particular attention to how these have been used by Scandinavians and outsiders.

Defining and Analysing Stereotypes

In the Oxford English Dictionary, a stereotype is defined as: 'a preconceived and oversimplified idea of the characteristics which typify a person, situation, etc.' (OED 2019b). Much like the word's etymology from the French adjective *stéréotype*, the solid metal copy of the mould used in letterpress printing (Oxford Dictionaries 2017); a stereotype is a fixed image that once formed is resistant to change (Beller 2007, 429).

Imagology, a concept developed by Beller and Leerssen (2007b), is a seminal approach to exploring these fixed images and national stereotypes in literature and other forms of cultural representation. Imagology looks to understand discourses, and refers to 'research in the field of our mental images of the Other and of ourselves' (Beller and Leerssen 2007a, xiii). In *Imagology*, Beller and Leerssen divide stereotypes into two categories: standardised images of others are called 'heterostereotypes' and self-images are called 'autostereotypes' (Beller 2007, 429). These notions of self-images and images-created-by-others prove useful analytical tools when examining the discourses and stereotypes of the Scandinavian nations. The simplified dichotomy of these national representations has also been described in terms of, for example, domestic 'imaginings' and external 'imagings' (Clerc and Glover 2015, 6). Kazimierz Musiał (2002; 2009) refers to the 'interaction between foreign images of Scandinavia, i.e. its xenostereotypes, and the images conceived among the inhabitants of the region, i.e. the autostereotypes' (Musiał 2002, 20–1), and Jonas Harvard and Peter Stadius explain that '[i]mages of regions are produced both within the areas themselves (auto-stereotypes) and on the outside (xeno-stereotypes)' (2013a, 14). The terms 'autostereotypes' and 'xenostereotypes' have most commonly been used by Scandinavian Studies scholars.

Autostereotypes in this context encompass how Scandinavians see themselves and also 'brand' themselves, for instance via state tourism agencies and cultural initiatives such as the aforementioned *NordLit*. Xenostereotypes are the images those outside Scandinavia have of its people, culture and places. The two categories of stereotypes are labelled distinctly for the purposes of analysis, but in practice they are interdependent and closely feed into one another. For instance, Denmark's agricultural co-operative movement has been a long-standing autostereotype associated with Danishness by Danes and utilised as part of nation-building efforts in the early-to-mid twentieth century. Yet, in Britain especially, stronger xenostereotypes endure relating to the products themselves (butter, beer and bacon) than their production methods, reinforced by advertising campaigns for Danish Bacon, Lurpak and Carlsberg.

Place Branding

'Brand Scandinavia' is a shorthand for the imagery and stereotypes of the Scandinavian countries as a unified region. The concept of place branding refers to a region's attempts to promote a particular image via national cultural bodies or tourism agencies, but can also be used to describe the image-making of a particular place by external observers. The Nation Brands Index (NBI), founded by private consultancy the Anholt Institute in 2005, was embraced in the early twenty-first century by many western nations looking to improve and cultivate a positive global image for their region, thereby approaching soft power and cultural diplomacy in a similar manner to corporate marketing.

However, a Scandinavian incident with international impact led NBI founder Simon Anholt to concede that place branding in fact could not be approached like corporate commercial branding (Mordhorst 2015, 249). In 2005, Danish national newspaper *Jyllands-Posten* published twelve satirical cartoons of the prophet Mohammed in an attempt to prove a point about freedom of speech (or *ytringsfrihed* in Danish). As a direct result of circulation of these cartoons outside Denmark alongside more inflammatory illustrations not published in the newspaper, violent protests took place on the streets near Danish Embassies in some Middle-Eastern countries in early 2006. Denmark's positive brand ranking in the NBI immediately collapsed in predominantly Muslim countries between the last quarter of 2005 and the first quarter of 2006: 'the most striking result was in Egypt, where Denmark's overall ranking [in the NBI] fell from 15th place to 35th, at the bottom of the list' (Anholt 2006a, 269). Denmark's so-called Cartoon Crisis (or *Muhammed-krisen* in Danish, referring to the prophet depicted in the cartoons) has been described as 'the most heated international political conflict Denmark had been involved in since the Second World War' (Mordhorst 2015, 244). Fallout from the Cartoon Crisis had an impact on other Scandinavian countries too, demonstrating the indistinctness of the Nordic region in many xenostereotypes. When consumers in the Middle East attempted to boycott Danish products, exported products from other northern European countries including Norway 'suffered because they happen to lie in the same geographical region and have some brand values in common' (Anholt 2006b, 182).

Yet Denmark's ranking in the NBI very quickly recovered, despite a concerted lack of engagement by Denmark's politicians in denouncing *Jyllands-Posten* (Mordhorst 2015, 250; Anholt 2006b, 182). The mere short-term blip in the NBI suggests that attempting to influence xenostereotypes might prove futile: positive xenostereotypes of Brand Scandinavia prevailed regardless of this controversial, internationally-renowned incident, demonstrating a remarkably stable brand image for the region.

Utopia from Abroad

Positive xenostereotypes of Scandinavia have a long history, often based in a sense of 'othering' which valorises the region for the observers' own purposes. This is a type of exoticism, which from an imagological perspective is 'ethnocentrism's friendly face' (Leerssen 2007, 325), where another culture is appreciated for its supposed strangeness. A North-South opposition played a formative role in European cultural nation building (Arndt 2007, 388), for instance the positive exoticised xenostereotyping of Scandinavia during the Viking revival in Victorian Britain. In nineteenth-century Britain, a romanticised perceived shared heritage with Danish and Norwegian 'Vikings' 'gave historical and ethnic coherence to the British state' (Newby 2013, 155). Literary cultural artefacts from the Nordic countries, particularly the Old Norse sagas, fuelled this Victorian-era emphasis on a shared northern heritage. Xenostereotypes therefore have a function for their observers, revealing more about the stereotyper than the stereotyped. This has also been apparent in the utopian xenostereotyping of Scandinavia (Sweden in particular) in the twentieth century.

Imagery and stereotypes of Sweden in particular dominate Brand Scandinavia (Harvard and Stadius 2013a, 3). Sweden has the largest population of the three Scandinavian nations, and a commanding position in nation branding and soft power abroad via its state institutions, especially the Swedish Institute, which has no comparable organisations in Denmark or Norway. Significantly, the dominance of Sweden in international perceptions of Scandinavia stems from constructions that first originated in the USA in the early twentieth century, where social scientists and politicians looking abroad for inspiration after the Great Depression admired Sweden as a 'middle way' between potential extremes in the process of state modernisation (Marklund 2009, 264). American author and journalist Marquis Childs' bestseller *Sweden: The Middle Way* (1936) described Sweden as a progressive modern welfare state, inspiring US President Roosevelt who had commissioned a study into European cooperative societal systems. This American socio-political commentary fixed the international image of Sweden as a socially progressive system that was successfully following what Childs had identified as a pragmatic capitalism: 'small, happy, and capitalist' (Marklund 2009, 271). The positive reception in anglophone contexts of the Swedish Model was in turn utilised as a positive autostereotype to strengthen part of Sweden's own identity and assist with its early twentieth-century nation building (cf. Andersson and Hilson 2009, 221–2). In the twenty-first century, the Nordic Model (*Den Nordiska Modellen*) has even been granted protected copyright status as a brand by the Swedish Patent and Registration Office (Harvard and Stadius 2013b, 326). The 'middle way' of the Nordic Model is still referred to today both within and outside Scandinavia, as discussed in more depth in chapter 5 in this volume.

The tendency of the Nordic welfare model to narrow the gap between rich and poor citizens in Scandinavian nations is still regularly remarked upon positively in foreign media. The positive xenostereotypes focus on Scandinavia's societal equality, good work/life balance, strong support of family life and protection of the rights of women. These xenostereotypes are often presented in aspirational, exotic, utopian terms. Yet, as British researcher and journalist Dominic Hinde puts it in the introduction to *A Utopia Like Any Other: Inside the Swedish Model*: 'Often when we talk about Sweden abroad we are not interested in the country at all, but in the apparent deficiencies of ourselves and where we happen to live' (Hinde 2016, 10). Scandinavia (Sweden especially) has regularly been stereotyped from abroad as a social utopia in order to push an agenda of what is 'wrong' with an author's own nation. This is still illustrated regularly in popular journalism, with rose-tinted examples such as Adrian Mackinder's article 'Priced out of London, we moved to Denmark', in which he argues that while the cost of living is the same in Copenhagen and London, the quality of life would be far superior in Denmark owing primarily to cheaper childcare and better-quality accommodation (2015). This *Guardian* article describes how the commute from Copenhagen to London by air is much more cost-effective than public transport from Brighton to London (without mention of the practicalities, the time differential or the impact on the environment), and Denmark's strict and often-criticised immigration policy that denies young people nationalisation via marriage is glibly dismissed: 'Clearly the Danes are aware they've got it good and don't want to share'. The xenostereotype of Scandinavia as a social utopia is here in clear evidence.

Ethnic Stereotypes, Racism and Dystopia

With the rise of far-right politics worldwide, from extreme neo-Nazism to populist governments, various discussions have played on internationally-recognised stereotypes of Scandinavia's perceived historic ethnic homogeneity. A stereotype of white, blonde Scandinavians has been politicised by particular white extremist groups from the late twentieth century onwards; the ethnic Scandinavian stereotype is perceived as positive, desirable and utopian by white supremacists who view the Nordic nations as an idealised homeland. As a result, Scandinavian imagery is often present in neo-Nazi rallies in the USA, ranging from Viking symbolism such as runes to the present-day flags of the Scandinavian countries themselves (SPLC). The pervasive (auto- and xeno-) stereotypes of Scandinavia as naturally white have come to influence attitudes towards immigrants and immigration in Scandinavia within and outside its nations.

Scandinavia has never, of course, been fully ethnically or culturally homogeneous. Increasingly, evidence suggests immigration from the Middle East and perhaps further afield has been present since the Viking era, and in the latter half of the twentieth century Scandinavia was particularly open to receiving refugees affected by civil wars in south-eastern Europe, the Middle East and Africa. In fact, Scandinavia's openness to accepting refugees and asylum seekers since the 1980s and 1990s bolstered its autostereotypes of being a compassionate, civilised region. Swedish politicians and press have been particularly vocal against Denmark's recent anti-immigration policies, and outsiders note that twenty-first-century 'Danish hostility to refugees is particularly startling in Scandinavia, where there is a pronounced tradition of humanitarianism' (Eakin 2016). Denmark's attitude to immigrants has shifted international perceptions of the nation, too. *Monocle Magazine* dropped Denmark's position in its global Soft-Power ranking of 2016/17 to ten from nine, explaining that the 'home of *hygge*' lost its former higher ranking owing to 'a rise of illiberal attitudes' (Serventi 2016). In mid-2018, the Danish government's new regulations for welfare recipients in so-called ghettos (populated primarily by non-European immigrants), including compulsory attendance at state-run childcare for pre-schoolers in order to receive family welfare benefits, mainly attracted negative international press coverage (for instance, in *The Guardian* and *The New York Times*).

This shift from positive to negative xenostereotype in certain international spheres demonstrates how stereotypes of Scandinavia are used to illustrate a particular narrative. Denmark is facing a challenge to its liberal utopian xenostereotype. Sweden stereotypically represents a successful society based on progressive and liberal principles, too, but this image can easily be subverted in representations of the repercussions of change:

When the march of progressivism seemed inexorable, Sweden was happy to play poster child and humbly let uninformed outsiders label the place a social paradise. Now that the spread of progressive values around the world is facing its stiffest test in decades, Sweden finds itself on the front line.

(Rapacioli 2018)

One of US President Donald Trump's rally speeches in 2017 was particularly mocked internationally because no terrorist or immigrant-related incident had occurred 'last night in Sweden', despite his claims to the contrary (Chan 2017), and Malmö is not the 'rape capital' of the world (or even Sweden), despite far-right commentator Nigel Farage's shock-jock assertions (Rapacioli 2018). Even Scandinavia's long-standing xenostereotype of purportedly high suicide rates stems from US President Eisenhower's anti-socialist rhetoric in 1960, from a speech in which he also proposed that Sweden's socio-political approach had increased its citizens' drunkenness and lack of ambition (Marklund 2009, 276). Negative xenostereotypes of Sweden as a land of 'manipulative social engineering and patronizing social control' (ibid.) also emerged in the USA, functioning to counter contemporary utopian stereotypes in the mid-twentieth century that had themselves been fixed in the USA thirty years earlier. Scandinavia's shift to the dystopia described above as a result of immigration is, of course, exaggerated, and such rhetoric has a longstanding precedent in which external commentary plays on existing strong xenostereotypes of the region as a utopia.

Sexy Scandinavians

Another enduring xenostereotype of Scandinavia involves sex and sexuality. Conservatism prevailed in some Nordic contexts, such as Norway's high-profile post-war literary obscenity trials including the prosecution of Agnar Mykle for the novel *The Song of the Red Ruby* (1956). Yet a xenostereotype developed in the mid-to-late twentieth century of a sexually liberated Scandinavia. This was inspired by the cessation of the regulation of pornography (Denmark was the first country in the world to legalise pornography, in 1969), a relaxed societal attitude to nudity in public settings such as beaches, and risqué imagery in visual media stemming from both uncensored nudity and sex in mainstream cinema, as well as a burgeoning Swedish pornographic film industry. In this exotic xenostereotypical view of Scandinavia, persistent risqué 1970s porn stereotypes have tended to be viewed with a mix of admiration and titil-lation, rather than negatively. For instance, reviews in the British press of Norwegian author Mykle's *Lasso Round the Moon* (1960) received its sex-ualised themes as a positive depiction of love, even in religious publica-tions such as *The British Weekly* (Routley 1960), despite its erotic content. Scandinavian sexuality as a positively-received xenostereotype is also illustrated by contemporary book covers for translated fiction by Swed-ish authors Maj Sjöwall and Per Wahlöö in France in the mid-twentieth century. Erotic images of a nude woman on 1970s book covers served to emphasise the xenostereotyped setting: 'The exotic representation of this land of the North cultivates a view of Sweden as a pornographic paradise, where sexual liberation is in full swing' (Grydehøj 2017).

This xenostereotype for many years functioned as a shorthand for erotic material, illustrated for instance by 'the German expression *Schwedenfilm* which stood for any blue movie, not necessarily one from Sweden' (Larsson 2015, 218).

The 'sexy Scandinavia' stereotype endures, though attempts at utilising it in marketing have sometimes misfired, as chronicled in crit-icism of the retrograde posters on the London Underground advertising currency exchange *WeSwap* in 2015. In the posters, a full-length photo of a tall blonde woman in a dress standing in a clichéd coquettish pose features beside the slogan: 'We can't swap your missus for a Swedish supermodel, but we can swap your money for her krona' (Lynch 2015). Criticism of the advertisement suggested that its 1970s sexist tone was outmoded, although even in its negative reception on social media and resulting press, the inference was that the 'sexy Scandinavian' stereotype itself was not in question.

Scandinavians, too, are apparently unsure how to handle this xenos-tereotype. A controversial stealth marketing attempt revealed to be from state tourism agency VisitDenmark in 2009 demonstrates an awkward mismatch between autostereotypes and xenostereotypes. The ostensibly amateur 'Danish Mother Seeking' YouTube video went viral, with over a million views within days of its release. A young blonde woman holding a baby films herself describing (in English) a past encounter with a stranger, stating she simply wishes him to know of the existence of the child. The video reinforces popular xenostereotypes of attractive, sexually-liberated Danish women, imagery which overwhelmed VisitDenmark's stated aim of promoting a rather more innocent message of a happy woman able to live in a free society accepting her circumstances. The ad was pulled after four days once it had been revealed as stemming from the state tourism agency, following a negative reaction from the Danish public and press to the reinforcement of the stereotype of sexually permissive Danes. However, the video had already gained international media coverage, and the controversial incident appears to have had no negative impact on Denmark's brand image: 'If the aim of the ad was to attract international attention to Denmark by exploiting familiar and therefore believable national stereotypes, it was certainly a success' (Allen 2016, 225). In this example, existing international xenostereotypes of Denmark were most pervasive and influential in shaping the video's reception, overriding the purported intention of its creators.

Yet 'sexy Scandinavia' has generally continued in the twenty-first century as a positive stereotype rather than a salacious one, bolstering other cool imagery and aspirational exports. Over the last ten to fifteen years in particular, popular Scandinavian cultural artefacts which have transferred across to the British market include literature (especially crime fiction), films, television, fashion, food and home furnishings. Norway's *Skam* (English: 'Shame', though usually reviewed and promoted using its original Norwegian title in anglophone media) is a popular internet-based television series whose positive reception abroad is likely to be influenced by xenostereotypes. *Skam* has been likened repeatedly in reviews to the British Channel 4 television show *Skins*, broadcast around a decade earlier: 'There are the wild parties, the drinking and smoking, the good-looking guys and girls falling in and out of love, but Skam is different for a number of reasons' (Hughes 2016). The main reason dwells in the aspirational xenostereotyped exoticism, which makes Scandinavian teenage escapades cool and sexy, with *Skam* described as a 'gritty representation of teen life without cliches or the sort of amped up controversy than [sic] came with shows such as Skins' (Zemler 2017). The exotic settings and aesthetic reinforced xenostereotypical conceptions of Scandinavia in which, among other things, the sex was seen as realistic and not clichéd, contributing to the positive reception of this show with international audiences.

Selling Danish Stereotypes

The twenty-first-century popularity in Britain of translated Scandinavian crime fiction and related cultural exports, often described as Nordic Noir, draws heavily on xenostereotypes of Scandinavia. Even the umbrella term Nordic Noir itself brings to mind typical cold, dark imagery. Drawing on positive imagery of woollen Nordic jumpers and dark winter nights as part of these stereotypes, in the early twenty-first century the

Danish concept of *hygge* was expanded from being an everyday national concept within Denmark to an international marketing phenomenon. While *hygge* contributes somewhat to the overall perception of Brand Scandinavia, as a xenostereotype in Britain it has most closely been associated with Denmark. *Hygge* fully grabbed international attention in late 2016, when a glut of lifestyle books on the concept was published in the UK, inspired by fascination with international well-being indexes, which ranked Denmark (and other Scandinavian nations) as the happiest nations in the world. The most commercially successful *hygge* book in the UK was Penguin's *The Little Book of Hygge* (Wiking 2016), which sold around 150,000 copies from its launch in Autumn 2016 up to Christmas (according to Nielsen BookScan data), and the word entered the Oxford English Dictionary as a noun and adjective in June 2017 (OED 2019a). What had suddenly become a popular xenostereotype of Denmark was adopted by VisitDenmark in its campaigns in 2017 in an example of state-mediated nation branding (for example, a quiz called 'How Hygge Are You?' prescribing a trip to Copenhagen).

Commercial companies marketing in Britain also embraced *hygge*. In 2017, Carlsberg launched a markedly Danish campaign featuring internationally-known actor Mads Mikkelsen riding a bicycle through Danish scenery, including Copenhagen and a forest, asking whether *hygge* (among other things) is the secret to finding happiness. As demonstrated by the marketing campaign's title #TheDanishWay, the stereotypes presented in the adverts were projected as being understood as typically Danish by the audience and, importantly for a commercial brand, desirable and positive. Mikkelsen's monologue is repeated on the website (with an ungrammatical yet deliberately identifiable Scandinavian diacritic in the final word, matching new packaging for Carlsberg Expørt [*sic*]):

> Many say that we Danes are the happiest nation in the world – but what's our secret? Living life the Danish way, of course. That means enjoying a work-life balance, nature and craft, spending time together feeling *hygge*. That's the Danish way. Is that what makes us such a happy nation? Perhaps. Or, could it be that we brew the best beer in the world? Prøbably.
>
> (Carlsberg UK)

Carlsberg has traditionally taken the route of using its 'Probably the Best Beer in the World' slogan as part of its light-hearted marketing communications, along with a focus on a typical beer drinking market: football fans. (Carlsberg has famously sponsored Liverpool Football Club since

1992: LFC 2016.) Since 2017, Carlsberg UK states, 'We've gone back to our roots to celebrate what it means to be Danish' (Carlsberg The Danish Way). Vice president of marketing at Carlsberg UK explains that, in the British context, 'Our Danish provenance may be a bit more interesting than four or five years ago, as there's been this explosion of Scandi-cool' (Roderick 2017). This illustrates how this commercial brand now embraces and monetises well-received popular British xenostereotypes about Denmark.

Contemporaneously with its 'The Danish Way' campaign in Britain, Carlsberg's marketing took a different approach in other non-European territories; for example 'The Art of Making Beer', in Canada, focuses on the brand's ingredients and heritage, and 'Probably the Smoothest Beer in the World', in Hong Kong, focuses on the product's taste (carlsberg. ca and carlsberg.com.hk). Xenostereotypes of Scandinavia are therefore culturally bound: Carlsberg is riding the *hygge* publishing boom in its marketing in Britain, but not in other foreign markets where this marketing trend has not been apparent. Marketing copy on the Danish Carlsberg website between 2017 and September 2018, however, imitated the message of Carlsberg UK's campaign:

> Hvad gør Carlsberg til måske verdens bedste øl, og hvad gør Danmark til et af verdens lykkeligste lande? Er det vores smag for naturen? At vi er gode til at hygge os sammen? Eller er det fordi vi har en lang tradition for at gøre os umage og skabe smukke ting? Probably. (Carlsberg Danmark)
> [What makes Carlsberg probably the best beer in the world, and what makes Denmark one of the happiest countries? Is it our taste for nature? That we are good at *hygge*? Or is it because we have a long tradition of taking the trouble to create beautiful things? Probably. (my translation)]

Carlsberg has therefore integrated xenostereotypes of Denmark from its UK marketing campaign into its advertising in Denmark, thereby contributing to Danish autostereotypes. A bid to UNESCO in 2018, backed by Meik Wiking's Happiness Research Institute, to protect *hygge* as an item of 'Intangible Cultural Heritage' (VisitDenmark 2018) further propelled the marketing phenomenon into an enduring Danish stereotype. *Hygge* is a twenty-first-century example of how a positively received xenostereotype has been adopted as a stronger autostereotype domestically to shore up national identity more effectively than might have been possible without external impetus.

Conclusion

This chapter has discussed some fixed images of Scandinavia and how these can be analysed via notions of autostereotypes (self-images) and xenostereotypes (images-created-by-others). These internal and external images often feed into each other, as described in relation to the Swedish Model in the twentieth century, where its positive reception in the USA impacted on nation building in Sweden, and the use of *hygge* in marketing in twenty-first-century Britain and then Denmark. The positive xenostereotype of Scandinavia as a utopia prevails, enabling some commentators to respond by suggesting that demographic changes in the region have led it to becoming a dystopia. Stereotypes can therefore be used for rhetorically disparate purposes by the agents involved in sustaining this imagery, from US Presidents, and international corporations like Carlsberg and Penguin, to state tourism agencies.

As nations seek to differentiate themselves in an increasingly globalised world, cultural diplomacy and soft power approaches, including place branding, have taken precedence. Regional image-making and identity formations have been analysed across academic disciplines, from the comparative literature approach of imagology to interpretations of nation branding within the social sciences, international relations and marketing. Analysing stereotypes in and of Scandinavia illustrates the complexities of projecting and perceiving images of a region and its inhabitants.

Further Reading

Further perspectives on the imagery and image-making of Scandinavia can be found in *Communicating the North* (Harvard and Stadius 2013c), *Histories of Public Diplomacy and Nation-Branding in the Nordic and Baltic Countries* (Clerc, Glover, and Jordan 2015), *Roots of the Scandinavian Model: Images of Progress in the Era of Modernisation* (Musiał 2002), and the special issue of *Scandinavian Journal of History* (34/3) entitled 'Images of Sweden and the Nordic Countries' (cf. Andersson and Hilson 2009).

References

Allen, Julie K. 2016. 'Sexy Danes, Tipsy Germans: The Use of Positive Cultural Stereotypes in Nation Branding Efforts', *Linguistik Online* 79 (5): 215–30.

Andersson, Jenny and Mary Hilson. 2009. 'Images of Sweden and the Nordic Countries', *Scandinavian Journal of History* 34 (3): 219–28.

Anholt, Simon. 2006a. 'The Anholt Nation Brands Index: Special Report on Europe's International Image, Q2 2006, plus an Update on the Status of "Brand Denmark"', *Place Branding* 2 (3): 263–70.

Anholt, Simon. 2006b. 'Editorial', *Place Branding* 2 (3): 179–82.

Arndt, Astrid. 'North/South'. In *Imagology: The Cultural Construction and Literary Representation of National Characters: A Critical Survey*, edited by Manfred Beller and Joep Leerssen, 387–9. Amsterdam: Rodopi.

Beller, Manfred. 2007. 'Stereotype'. In *Imagology: The Cultural Construction and Literary Representation of National Characters: A Critical Survey*, edited by Manfred Beller and Joep Leerssen, 429–34. Amsterdam: Rodopi.

Beller, Manfred and Joep Leerssen. 2007a. 'Foreword'. In *Imagology: The Cultural Construction and Literary Representation of National Characters: A Critical Survey*, edited by Manfred Beller and Joep Leerssen, xiii–xvi. Amsterdam: Rodopi.

Beller, Manfred and Joep Leerssen, eds. 2007b. *Imagology: The Cultural Construction and Literary Representation of National Characters: A Critical Survey*. Amsterdam: Rodopi.

Carlsberg.ca. Accessed 4 September 2018. http://www.carlsberg.ca.

Carlsberg.com.hk. Accessed 4 September 2018. http://www.carlsberg.com.hk.

Carlsberg Danmark. Accessed 4 September 2018. http://www.carlsberg.dk/#!carlsberg-pilsner/8919-the-danish-way.

Carlsberg The Danish Way. Accessed 4 September 2018. http://www.carlsberg.co.uk/#!the-danish-way/8457-watch-the-ads.

Carlsberg UK. Accessed 4 September 2018. http://www.carlsberg.co.uk/#!home.

Chan, Sewell. 2017. '"Last Night in Sweden"? Trump's Remark Baffles a Nation', *New York Times*, 19 February. Accessed 4 September 2018. https://www.nytimes.com/2017/02/19/world/europe/last-night-in-sweden-trumps-remark-baffles-a-nation.html.

Childs, Marquis W. 1936. *Sweden: The Middle Way*. London: Faber and Faber.

Clerc, Louis and Nikolas Glover. 2015. 'Introduction: Representing the Small States of Northern Europe: Between Imagined and Imaged Communities'. In *Histories of Public Diplomacy and Nation Branding in the Nordic and Baltic Countries: Representing the Periphery*, edited by Louis Clerc, Nikolas Glover and Paul Jordan, 3–20. Leiden: Brill Nijhoff.

Clerc, Louis, Nikolas Glover and Paul Jordan, eds. 2015. *Histories of Public Diplomacy and Nation Branding in the Nordic and Baltic Countries: Representing the Periphery*. Leiden: Brill Nijhoff.

Eakin, Hugh. 2016. 'Liberal, Harsh Denmark', *New York Review of Books*, 10 March. Accessed 4 September 2018. http://www.nybooks.com/articles/2016/03/10/liberal-harsh-denmark.

Grydehøj, Anne. 2017. 'Manufactured Exoticism and Retelling *The Story of a Crime*: The Case of Sjöwall and Wahlöö's Reception in France', *Australian Journal of Crime Fiction* 1 (1). Accessed 6 October 2019. http://www.australiancrimefiction.com/grydehoj.

Harvard, Jonas and Peter Stadius. 2013a. 'A Communicative Perspective on the Formation of the North: Contexts, Channels and Concepts'. In *Communicating the North: Media Structures and Images in the Making of the Nordic Region*, edited by Jonas Harvard and Peter Stadius, 1–24. Farnham: Ashgate.

Harvard, Jonas and Peter Stadius. 2013b. 'Conclusion: Mediating the Nordic Brand – History Recycled'. In *Communicating the North: Media Structures and Images in the Making of the Nordic Region*, edited by Jonas Harvard and Peter Stadius, 319–32. Farnham: Ashgate.

Harvard, Jonas and Peter Stadius, eds. 2013c. *Communicating the North: Media Structures and Images in the Making of the Nordic Region*. Farnham: Ashgate.

Hinde, Dominic. 2016. *A Utopia Like Any Other: Inside the Swedish Model*. Edinburgh: Luath Press.

Hughes, Sarah. 2016. 'Shame: A Scandi TV Sensation for the Social Media Generation', *The Observer*, 4 December. Accessed 4 September 2018. https://www.theguardian.com/tv-and-radio/2016/dec/04/shame-skam-norway-teen-tv-drama-social-media-sensation.

Larsson, Mariah. 2015. 'A National/Transnational Genre: Pornography in Transition'. In *Nordic Genre Film: Small Nation Film Cultures in the Global Marketplace*, edited by Tommy Gustafsson and Pietari Kääpä, 217–29. Edinburgh: Edinburgh University Press.

Leerssen, Joep. 2007. 'Exoticism'. In *Imagology: The Cultural Construction and Literary Representation of National Characters: A Critical Survey*, edited by Manfred Beller and Joep Leerssen, 325–6. Amsterdam: Rodopi.

LFC (Liverpool Football Club). 2016. 'LFC and Carlsberg Extend Long-Standing Partnership', *Liverpool Football Club News*, 23 March. Accessed 4 September 2018. https://www.liverpoolfc.com/news/announcements/212901-lfc-and-carlsberg-extend-long-standing-partnership.

Lynch, Alison. 2015. 'WeSwap is the Latest Tube Ad to Infuriate Londoners with Its "Grossly Sexist" Message', *Metro*, 12 June. Accessed 4 September 2018. https://metro.co.uk/2015/06/12/weswap-is-the-latest-tube-ad-to-infuriate-londoners-with-its-grossly-sexist-message-5242140/.

Mackinder, Adrian. 2015. 'Priced Out of London, We Moved to Denmark', *The Guardian*, 11 November. Accessed 7 September 2018. https://www.theguardian.com/money/2015/nov/11/priced-out-of-london-moved-to-denmark.

Marklund, Carl. 2009. 'The Social Laboratory, the Middle Way and the Swedish Model: Three Frames for the Image of Sweden', *Scandinavian Journal of History* 34 (3): 264–85.

Mordhorst, Mads. 2015. 'Public Diplomacy vs Nation Branding: The Case of Denmark after the Cartoon Crisis'. In *Histories of Public Diplomacy and Nation Branding in the Nordic and Baltic Countries: Representing the Periphery*, edited by Louis Clerc, Nikolas Glover and Paul Jordan, 237–56. Leiden: Brill Nijhoff.

Musiał, Kazimierz. 2002. *Roots of the Scandinavian Model: Images of Progress in the Era of Modernisation*. Baden-Baden: Nomos Verlagsgesellschaft.

Musiał, Kazimierz. 2009. 'Reconstructing Nordic Significance in Europe on the Threshold of the 21st Century', *Scandinavian Journal of History* 34 (3): 286–306.

Mykle, Agnar. 1960. *Lasso Round the Moon*, translated by Maurice Michael. London: Barrie and Rockliff.

Mykle, Agnar. 1956. *Sangen om den røde rubin*. Oslo: Gyldendal.

Newby, Andrew. 2013. '"One Valhalla of the Free": Scandinavia, Britain and Northern Identity in the Mid-Nineteenth Century'. In *Communicating the North: Media Structures and Images in the Making of the Nordic Region*, edited by Jonas Harvard and Peter Stadius, 147–69. Farnham: Ashgate.

OED (Oxford English Dictionary). 2019a. 'hygge, n. and adj.', *OED Online*. Accessed 7 October 2019. https://www.oed.com/view/Entry/58767802.

OED (Oxford English Dictionary). 2019b. 'stereotype, n. and adj.', *OED Online*. Accessed 7 October 2019. https://www.oed.com/view/Entry/189956.

Oxford Dictionaries. 2017. 'What Are the Origins of "Stereotype" and "Cliché"?', *OxfordWords* blog, 11 October. Accessed 5 December 2018. https://blog.oxforddictionaries.com/2017/10/11/origin-stereotype-cliche/.

Rapacioli, Paul. 2018. 'How Sweden Became a Symbol', *New York Review of Books*, 8 February. Accessed 4 September 2018. http://www.nybooks.com/daily/2018/02/08/how-sweden-became-a-symbol/.

Roderick, Leonie. 2017. 'Carlsberg Focuses on Its Danish Roots as New Campaign Taps into 'Hygge' Trend', *Marketing Week*, 20 April. Accessed 4 September 2018. https://www.marketingweek.com/2017/04/20/carlsberg-revitalise-brand/.

Routley, Erik. 1960. 'G.W. Target Again', *The British Weekly* 144 (3823).

Serventi, Cesare, ed. 2016. 'Soft Power Survey 2016/17', *Monocle*, 18 November. Video. Accessed 7 October 2019. https://monocle.com/film/affairs/soft-power-survey-2016-17/.

SPLC (Southern Poverty Law Center). n.d. 'Neo-Volkisch'. Accessed 4 September 2018. https://www.splcenter.org/fighting-hate/extremist-files/ideology/neo-volkisch.

VisitDenmark. 2018. 'Danes Launch Bid for Hygge to Receive UNESCO Status', *VisitDenmark*, 12 April. Accessed 4 September 2018. https://www.visitdenmark.com/denmark/danes-launch-bid-hygge-receive-unesco-status.

Wiking, Meik. 2016. *The Little Book of Hygge*. London: Penguin Life.

Zemler, Emily. 2017. 'Small Screen Queens: How Teen Angst Took Over the TV Scene', *The Guardian*, 9 February. Accessed 4 September 2018. https://www.theguardian.com/tv-and-radio/2017/feb/09/teen-tv-shows-riverdale-vampire-diaries-pretty-little-liars.

Index

Page numbers in italics are figures

CPSIA information can be obtained
at www.ICGtesting.com
Printed in the USA
LVHW061317251020
669765LV00003B/160